Legal Rights

Legal Rights

The Guide for Deaf and Hard of Hearing People

Fourth Edition

National Center for Law and Deafness

Gallaudet University Press
Washington, D.C.

Legal
Rights

The Guide for Deaf and Hard of Hearing People

Fourth Edition

National Center for Law and Deafness

Gallaudet University Press
Washington, D.C.

Fourth Edition 1992, Fourth Printing 1998
Published by Gallaudet University Press
Washington, DC 20002

Fourth Edition, Published 1992. Fourth Printing 1998
Printed in the United States of America

Library of Congress Cataloguing in Publication Date

DuBow, Sy.
    Legal rights: the guide for deaf and hard of hearing people: featuring the Americans
with Disabilities Act/National Center for Law and Deafness.—4th ed., updated and rev.
        p. cm.
    Authors, Sy DuBow, Sarah Geer, Karen Peltz Strauss.
    Rev. ed. of: Legal rights of hearing-impaired people/National Center for Law and the
Deaf. 3rd. ed. 1986.
    Includes bibliographical references and index.
    ISBN 1-56368-000-9
    1. Deaf—Legal status, laws, etc.—United States.   2. Hearing
impaired—Legal status, laws, etc.—United States.   I. Geer, Sarah.
II. Strauss, Karen Peltz.   III. National Center for Law and Deafness
(U.S.) IV. Legal rights of hearing-impaired people.   V. Title.
KF480.5D4L43   1992
346.7301'3—dc20   91-44372
347.30613]   CIP

The National Center for Law and Deafness was a public service of Gallaudet University from
1975 until 1996. Deaf people in need of legal advice or information can now contact the
National Association of the Deaf Law Center at 814 Thayer Avenue, Silver Spring, MD 20910,
(301) 587-1788 (Voice/TTY).

FOURTH EDITION

Sy DuBow
  Legal Director
  **National Center for Law
  and Deafness (NCLD)**
  J.D., George Washington
  University

Sarah Geer
  Staff Attorney, NCLD
  J.D., University of North
  Carolina

Karen Peltz Strauss
  Staff Attorney, NCLD
  J.D., University of
  Pennsylvania

PREVIOUS EDITIONS

Sy DuBow
  Legal Director
  **National Center for Law
  and the Deaf (NCLD)**
  J.D., George Washington
  University

Larry Goldberg
  **U.S. Department of Health
  and Human Services**
  **Associate Legal Director,
  NCLD, 1976–83**
  J.D., George Washington
  University

Sarah Geer
  Staff Attorney, NCLD
  J.D., University of North
  Carolina

Elaine Gardner
  **Associate Legal Director,
  NCLD**
  J.D., Georgetown University

Andrew Penn
  Attorney
  **Maryland Advocacy Unit
  for the Developmentally
  Disabled**
  **Staff Attorney, NCLD,
  1978–81**
  J.D., University of California,
  Berkeley

Sheila Conlon Mentkowski
  **NorCal Center on
  Deafness**
  **Staff Attorney, NCLD,
  1981–88**
  J.D., Georgetown University

Marc Charmatz
  Litigation Attorney
  **National Association of
  the Deaf Legal Defense
  Fund**
  J.D., Northwestern
  University

In memory of Fred Schreiber, the happy warrior for deaf people's rights

Contents

Preface   x

Acknowledgments   xi

ONE
Communicating with Deaf and
Hard of Hearing People   1

TWO
The Americans with
Disabilities Act   15

THREE
The Rehabilitation Act of 1973   47

FOUR
Public School Education   67

FIVE
Postsecondary Education   87

SIX
Health Care and Social
Services   101

SEVEN
Mental Health   121

EIGHT
Employment   141

NINE
Architectural Barriers   167

TEN
The Legal System   173

ELEVEN
Television   191

TWELVE
Telephone Service   203

THIRTEEN
State Legislatures and
Commissions   217

APPENDIX A
Reference Publications on
Deafness and PL 94-142   232

APPENDIX B
Appropriate Public Education:
Sample Letters of Request   235

APPENDIX C
Providing Interpreter Service:
One Agency Example   239

APPENDIX D
A Model Act to Provide for the
Appointment of Interpreters for
Hearing-Impaired Individuals
for Administrative, Legislative,
and Judicial Proceedings   245

APPENDIX E
State Commissions and
Councils for Deaf People   251

APPENDIX F
Enabling Legislation for a
State Commission: The
Example of Virginia   256

Index   261

Preface

Deaf and hard of hearing people are confronted with barriers to communication throughout and in all aspects of their lives.

State and federal laws have begun to break down these barriers. This book explains how these laws can help people in areas where their needs have been ignored or inadequately addressed.

We have tried to provide one comprehensive and current resource on legal rights and remedies for deaf and hard of hearing citizens. We also describe flexible ways to ensure effective communication and better understanding through technological advances, interpreting alternatives, and deaf awareness.

This fourth edition of *Legal Rights* includes vital information on the Americans with Disabilities Act (ADA), landmark legislation for all disabled people. The ADA's requirements for removing communication barriers for deaf and hard of hearing people in employment, state and local government services, public accommodations, and telecommunications are discussed in depth. This new edition also discusses recent legislative advances, such as the Television Decoder Circuitry Act and the Hearing Aid Compatibility Act, that will provide equal access to television programming and telephone service.

Our democratic society has a responsibility to ensure that all its citizens, including those with disabilities, are given an equal opportunity to lead productive lives. This book discusses the legal tools now available to all citizens concerned with securing this fundamental equality.

NATIONAL CENTER FOR LAW AND DEAFNESS   SY DUBOW
GALLAUDET UNIVERSITY
WASHINGTON, DC 20002

Acknowledgments

The authors thank Cynthia Compton for the section on assistive listening systems in chapter one, and Heidi Norton for editorial assistance.

Permission to use copyrighted material was kindly granted by

Houghton Mifflin Company, for a quotation in chapter four;

Legal Services Corporation, for parts of chapters four, five, six, eight, and ten;

Grune & Stratton Incorporated, for the substance of chapter seven;

Temple Law Review, for part of chapter eleven;

The Deaf American, for a section of chapter thirteen;

University of Richmond Law Review, for Appendix B.

Text illustrations are by Laura Warren Stutzman. The staff of Gallaudet University's Art and Photography Services produced many of the photographs. Other photographs were provided courtesy of the

National Captioning Institute, Inc. (page 194);

Washington Post (page 220);

The White House (page 16).

Parts of several chapters originally appeared in NCLD newsletters and special reports and were adapted for inclusion here.

CHAPTER ONE

Communicating with Deaf and Hard of Hearing People

More than merely a barrier to sound perception, hearing loss is a barrier to communication and understanding. It is a major, chronic disability that affects one out of every sixteen Americans. One in every 100 Americans is profoundly deaf—unable to hear speech well enough to understand it.[1] The wide range of impairment, the variety of methods of communication, and differences in the age of onset of disability make it difficult to generalize about deaf and hard of hearing people. But certain facts are apparent.

Deaf and hard of hearing people rely on information they can see. Some means of making communication visible is necessary to ensure that they are able to explain their needs effectively and understand what is expected of them. With some auxiliary aid or accommodation and some sensitivity to their condition by those around, deaf and hard of hearing people can communicate and participate fully and easily in most settings.

Deaf and hard of hearing people have not received fair treatment from professional, social, and government service providers or from the courts and police. Some accommodation to the condition of hearing loss can make a critical difference in whether deaf and hard of hearing people receive services they need and to which they are entitled and whether they can participate satisfactorily in society. The material cost of such accommodation is modest in comparison with the gain realized.

As we review the various methods that deaf and hard of hearing people use to communicate, one general rule to bear in mind is that each person has a preferred method, because he or she has spent a lifetime negotiating the problems that hearing loss imposes. Whatever method is natural for that person is the method that should always be used, preferably from the first moment of contact.

SIGN LANGUAGE AND INTERPRETERS

American Sign Language (ASL) is a visible language that is linguistically independent of English. Its signals are handshapes and movements that represent words, concepts, or letters of the English alphabet. Many deaf people use sign language rather than English as their primary mode of communication. For many deaf people it is a native language with rich cultural associations.

An interpreter is a skilled professional who can translate the meaning of spoken words into sign language as the words are spoken and translate sign language messages into correct English as they are signed. Interpretation of written or spoken English into ASL requires a high degree of skill. It takes as much time and effort to learn sign language as any other language.

At times a specialized interpreter must be used. For example, a person who is both deaf and visually impaired may need a specially trained deaf-blind interpreter. Some deaf people do not use sign language but require an "oral" interpreter who silently mouths the speaker's words to them. The oral interpreter is usually a person whom the deaf person finds easy to lipread and who knows how to substitute synonyms for words that are difficult to lipread. Another unusual situation occurs when the deaf person has rudimentary language skills or does not use conventional sign language. In this situation, another deaf person may have to provide interpretation into conventional sign language, which can then be interpreted into English by the regular interpreter.

Qualified interpreters can be found through local and state chapters of the Registry of Interpreters for the Deaf

(RID), a national professional organization that certifies interpreters in various skill specialties, including legal interpreting.[2] Interpreters can also be located through local organizations of deaf people, the state association of the deaf, a state commission or agency for hearing-impaired people, or schools for deaf children. In addition, deaf people may themselves suggest local interpreters. Professional offices and service agencies should develop their own lists of interpreters whom they know to be reliable and competent.

Using the same interpreter regularly can enhance the quality of the communication, since an interpreter who is familiar with a speaker's vocal style and customary phrases will be able to interpret more effectively. The interpreter also can provide valuable assistance to service providers by advising them about effective use of an interpreter and about other means of communicating with deaf people.

While professional certification may be useful in evaluating the skills of an interpreter, the ultimate authority on an interpreter's qualifications should be the deaf person. An interpreter who cannot provide effective communication to a deaf person in a particular situation cannot be considered qualified despite professional certification.

Interpreter Guidelines

A professional interpreter should uphold the National Registry of Interpreters for the Deaf Code of Ethics, which carefully defines the role of an interpreter. This code prohibits an interpreter from continuing in any assignment if attempts to communicate are unsuccessful for either party.

The following are guidelines for use of interpreters:

- When talking, look at the deaf person, not the interpreter; speak directly to the person as if the interpreter were not present. For example, say, "The hearing will be on Tuesday," rather than, "Tell him that the hearing will be on Tuesday." The interpreter will sign exactly what is said.
- Some deaf people will speak for themselves. Others will not speak, so the interpreter will say in English what the person signs. In both cases, respond by talking to the deaf person, not the interpreter.
- The interpreter should be directly beside the speaker so that he or she is easily visible to the deaf person.
- The interpreter should not be placed in shadows or in front of any source of bright light, such as a window.
- No private conversation should occur with the interpreter or with anyone else in the deaf person's presence. The interpreter must interpret everything that is said in front of the deaf person. Any discussion of the deaf person's language or communication level should take place privately with the interpreter. Ask the deaf person, not the interpreter, if he or she understands what is being said.
- Speak naturally and not too fast. Remember that names and some other words must be fingerspelled and that this takes more time than signing. The interpreter will indicate whether it is necessary to slow down. Avoid jargon or other technical words with which the deaf person may be unfamiliar. If possible, meet with the interpreter before the interview to discuss the best way to interpret certain technical concepts into sign language without losing any of the meaning.
- Make sure that the interpreter understands the need for complete confidentiality. Do not allow the interpreter to discuss the deaf person's problems with the person or to give any advice about the problem. The interpreter's only role is to facilitate communication with the deaf person.

Relying on amateurs who may know some sign language is a frequent error. The ability to make or read a few signs or to fingerspell is no substitute for proficiency. A well-meaning, beginning signer will usually not know sign language well enough to interpret or to communicate effectively with most deaf people.

Many inexperienced interpreters do not sign in ASL but use signs borrowed from ASL in an English word order. They may frequently impose a completely incorrect English meaning on a sign, such as using the sign for the adjective *fine,* meaning "good," to connote the noun *fine,* meaning "penalty." An unqualified interpreter might fingerspell words when he or she does not know a sign; but directly translated English idioms are rendered meaningless in ASL. For example, a direct translation of the English idiom *have to* would mean "possess" in ASL.

COMMUNICATION BARRIERS

Problems of Notewriting

Many deaf people rely on written notes to communicate with hearing people or to supplement other modes of communication. However, writing is not always effective or appropriate. A written conversation is tedious, cumbersome, and time-consuming. Written messages are frequently condensed. The writer omits much of the information that would otherwise be exchanged, so the deaf person does not get the same amount of detail that a hearing person would.

Some deaf people are highly educated. Others are not. A common misconception is that deaf people compensate for their inability to hear by reading and writing. Many deaf people, especially those who lost their hearing before they learned to talk, have difficulty with written as well as spoken English. Data from a 1971 national survey of hearing-impaired students showed that reading comprehension is the hearing-impaired person's most difficult academic area. It is the area most severely affected by deafness.[3]

Most people learn their native language by hearing it spoken around them from infancy. But a person who is born deaf or who loses the ability to hear when very young cannot learn English in this way. Therefore, despite normal intelligence, a deaf person may have limited competence in English. For such people, English is virtually a second language. They may have a limited English vocabulary and grammar, a condition that can lead to numerous misunderstandings.

The extensive use of idioms in English also poses significant reading problems for deaf people. For example, the expression *under arrest* in the *Miranda* warnings (discussed in chapter ten) would be puzzling to many deaf people because *under* to them means only "beneath."[4] For these reasons, written notes or materials will often be inadequate to achieve effective communication with a deaf person. The limitations of notewriting as a communication method should be observed carefully to avoid miscommunication.

Lipreading Comprehension

A common misconception about deaf people is that they all read lips. Very few people can read lips well enough to understand speech, even under optimum conditions. Information collected during the 1972 National Census of the Deaf Population indicated that 21.4 percent of deaf adults who completed one or more years of senior high school considered their lipreading ability to be poor to nonexistent.[5] "In fact, even the best speechreaders in a one-to-one situation were found to understand only 26 percent of what was said [and m]any bright deaf individuals grasp less than 5 percent."[6]

This low level of comprehension occurs because many English speech sounds are not visible on the mouth or lips. Certain spoken words or sounds create similar lip movements. The ambiguity of lipreading is demonstrated by the fact that the sounds of T, D, Z, S, and N all look identical on the lips. The words *right, ride,* and *rise* would be indistinguishable to a deaf person, as would the sentences, "Do you have the time?" and "Do you have the dime?" The meaning of entire sentences can be lost because a key word is missed or misunderstood. When a deaf person does not understand a sentence, the speaker should repeat the thought using different words. The speaker should use gestures freely, for example, pointing to a wristwatch to indicate time.

Many factors hinder one's ability to lipread. Lipreading is difficult when

- the speaker is in motion or not directly facing the lipreader;
- the lips are obscured by hands, beards, or mustaches;
- the speaker does not articulate carefully or has distorted speech;
- the speaker has a regional or foreign accent;
- the speaker is using technical or unfamiliar words;
- the lipreader is not familiar with the language structures and vocabulary of spoken English;
- the speaker is not well-lighted;
- the lipreader must look into a glare or light;
- the lipreader has poor vision.

Lipreading often supplements other modes of communication, but it is seldom sufficient in itself to ensure effective communication. Unless the deaf person indicates a preference for using only lipreading, it should not be relied upon extensively.

Environmental Interferences

Environmental factors often interfere with communication with a deaf person. The room should be adequately lighted, without glare. While profoundly deaf people will not be affected by background noises, they will be distracted by a great deal of background movement or changes in lighting. A person who uses a hearing aid or who has residual hearing may be seriously distracted by background noises. One should try to talk in a quiet place, away from the noises of machinery, other conversations, and distractions.

When talking to a hearing-impaired person, one should speak directly to the person without moving around, turning away, or looking down at papers or books. Speak naturally, without shouting or distorting normal mouth movements.

Some deaf people have normal and intelligible speech. Others do not speak at all. Early deafness interferes with language and speech acquisition. Many deaf people who can speak exhibit unusual tones, inflections, or modulations. Whether or not a deaf person uses speech is a matter of individual preference. Difficulty in understanding a deaf person's voice can be relieved by listening without interruption for a while until the person's particular voice patterns become familiar.

The phrases "deaf-mute" and "deaf and dumb" are considered by most deaf people to be insults and should not be used.

COMMUNICATION DEVICES

One frustration of deafness is the inability to use a conventional telephone. Hearing people rely heavily on the telephone and take it for granted in communicating with businesses, friends, government agencies, and emergency services. With new devices for deaf people coming into more frequent use, the telephone has become a means rather than a barrier to communication.

A TDD (Telecommunication Device for the Deaf), or text telephone, is a machine with a typewriter keyboard connected by an acoustic coupler to a regular telephone. Two people with compatible equipment can have a typed conversation over the telephone, enabling hearing- and speech-impaired people to have the same functional telephone service as other people. The devices are relatively inexpensive and easy to use.

If a professional, agency, or business office does not have a TDD, deaf people will not be able to get information, make appointments, or transact business by telephone. The office will be unable to contact deaf clients except by mail, resulting in frustrating delays, inefficient service, and lost business. The office should publicize the fact that its telephone is TDD-equipped and should indicate this fact in all telephone directory listings and on all announcements, brochures, and letterheads. The TDD capability is indicated by placing the letters "(TDD)" after the phone number or by "(Voice or TDD)" if both options are available.

Other devices are available that adapt telephones to the

individual needs of hearing-impaired people. Amplifier switches can be added to telephone receivers. Telephones and other auditory systems—alarms, doorbells, or inhome buzzers—can be connected to a blinking light that alerts a hearing-impaired person. Many hearing aids are equipped with inductive coil "telephone switches." These hearing aids use electromagnetic leakage from compatible telephone receivers to transmit the message. If, in a job situation, a person using this kind of hearing aid is assigned to an incompatible telephone, a compatible model can be acquired at reasonable cost.

Assistive Listening Systems

Background noise and reverberation degrade intelligibility much faster for individuals who are deaf or hard of hearing, whether they wear hearing aids or not. Thus, deaf and hard of hearing people are prevented from participating on equal terms with normal hearing people in larger assembly areas that are not equipped with an assistive listening system. Even the best in sound systems technology combined with the best in hearing aid technology cannot solve the intelligibility problems faced by people who are deaf or hard of hearing. In recognition of this, requirements for installation of assistive listening devices in places of public accommodation were included in the Americans with Disabilities Act (ADA), which was signed into law in July of 1990.

The purpose of an assistive listening system is to transmit the sound as directly as possible to the deaf or hard of hearing person's ear. Such systems should not be confused with audio systems (e.g., PA systems) generally designed to enhance the sound quality for people without hearing aids. There are three basic wireless technologies available today that provide different methods of meeting the requirements: induction loop technology, FM broadcast technology, and infrared light technology. No single technology is best for all applications. All three types of assistive listening systems can be easily and successfully installed in new and old facilities alike, as long as their individual limitations are kept in mind.

Induction Loop Technology

Induction loop technology is based on electromagnetic transmission and has a unique advantage in that the signal is received directly by the user's hearing aid when it is equipped with a telecoil circuit or "T" switch. There is no need for an additional receiver, as is required by all other technologies. However, if the listener does not have a hearing aid equipped with a telecoil, or has no hearing aid at all, then induction receivers must be used. There are three types—a wand-like device, a pocket-sized device with headphones, and a telecoil installed inside a plastic shell that looks like, but is not, a hearing aid. The first two are most common.

FM Broadcast Technology

FM systems operate at FCC designated frequencies. Since each system may use its own broadcast frequency, several systems may operate simultaneously at one location without interfering with one another. However, unlike the loop system, the FM system requires a special receiver for each person, whether she or he has a hearing aid or not. Several options for coupling a hearing aid to an FM system are available. The most convenient for public places consists of either a neckloop or a silhouette inductor(s) that is used with the hearing aid's telecoil circuit.

Infrared Light Technology

From a practical point of view, the infrared receiver system is in many ways similar in operation to the FM system. However, receivers must be in the line-of-sight of the emitter (transmitter); the signal can only be received inside the covered room. As with FM technology, each person, hearing aid wearer or not, must use a receiver. The options for coupling the infrared receiver to the hearing aid are the same as for FM systems.

The communication methods and the assistive listening systems described above are the means of crossing and thus eliminating the communications barriers that separate deaf, hard of hearing, and hearing people from one another.

NOTES

1. J. Schein and M. Delk, *The Deaf Population of the United States* (Silver Spring, Md.: National Association of the Deaf, 1974), p. 15.
2. The national office of the Registry of Interpreters for the Deaf is located at 8719 Colesville Road, Suite 310, Silver Spring, MD 20910. Telephone (301) 608-0050 (V/TDD).
3. Gallaudet College, *Academic Achievement Test Results of a National Testing Program for Hearing-Impaired Students in the United States,* Spring 1971 monograph.
4. Mary Furey, personal communication, June 1976.
5. Schein and Delk, *Deaf Population,* p. 63.
6. M. Vernon and E. Mindel, *They Grow in Silence: The Deaf Child and His Family* (Silver Spring, Md.: National Association of the Deaf, 1971), p. 96.

CHAPTER TWO

The Americans with Disabilities Act

The Americans with Disabilities Act (ADA) is landmark civil rights legislation for all citizens with disabilities.[1] The ADA prohibits discrimination in almost every aspect of society. This legislation provides legal protections in employment (Title I), access to state and local government and public transportation (Title II), public accommodations (Title III), and telecommunications (Title IV). The ADA will be of tremendous benefit to deaf and hard of hearing people in their efforts to gain equal access to society. The ADA and its regulations provide legal requirements to remove communication barriers.

TITLE I: EMPLOYMENT

Title I of the ADA and its Equal Employment Opportunity Commission (EEOC) regulations[2] prohibit an employer from discriminating against a "qualified individual with a disability" in the following areas: (1) job application procedures; (2) hiring; (3) discharge; (4) compensation; (5) advancement; and (6) any other terms, conditions, and privileges of employment.

Employers Covered Under the ADA

Beginning in July 1992, the ADA will cover employers with 25 or more employees. After July 26, 1994, the ADA will expand its coverage to all employers with 15 or more employees. Title I also covers employment agencies, unions, and joint labor/management committees. Exempted from the ADA's requirements are the United States government, Indian tribes, and tax-exempt private membership clubs.[3]

A "Qualified" Individual

The Title I protections apply only to a "qualified" individual with a disability.[4] Under the ADA, a "qualified" individual is one who, with or without "reasonable accommodation, is able to perform the essential functions of the employment position held or desired." "Essential functions" are those job tasks that are fundamental, not marginal. Tasks that can be easily transferred to another employee without hurting the employer's business are marginal. All too often employers have broadly excluded deaf and hard of hearing people from jobs by stating that ability to answer the telephone is necessary. The ADA focuses on job performance and not marginal duties (such as answering the telephone) in determining what is an essential function of the job.

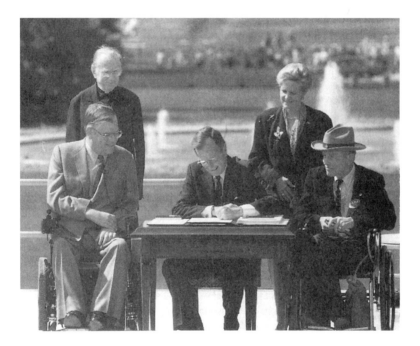

In an Illinois case, a federal court held that answering the telephone was not an essential function of a time-and-attendance clerk position at the post office, despite the fact that a job posting said it was. The standard job description for the position and testimony on actual performance showed that the clerk was responsible for tallying, documenting, and analyzing the hours that postal service employees worked. The court held that these were the essential functions of the job, and that a deaf person can perform these functions. (*Davis v. Frank*, 711 F. Supp. 447 [N.D. Ill. 1989]).

In determining whether or not a particular function is essential, both the ADA statute and the EEOC regulations emphasize that a factual determination must be made on a case-by-case basis. Evidence of whether a particular function is essential can include (1) the employer's judgment as to which functions are essential, (2) written job descriptions prepared before advertising or interviewing applicants for the job, (3) the amount of time spent on the job performing the function, (4) the terms of a collective bargaining agreement, and (5) the work experience of past or present workers in the job or similar jobs. These factors are not conclusive and can be rebutted, as was done in the *Davis* case cited earlier, based on testimony of actual performance or past performance.

Reasonable Accommodation

Reasonable accommodation means modifications or adjustments to the job application process and the workplace to allow a disabled person to perform the essential functions of the job.[5] It also means providing a disabled employee equal access to the benefits and privileges of employment. Both the ADA and its regulations list the most common types of reasonable accommodation. However, this list is not intended to be exhaustive. Reasonable accommodation may include (1) making existing work facilities readily accessible and usable to individuals with disabilities; and (2) job restructuring; part-time or modified work schedules;

reassignment to a vacant position; acquisition or modifications of equipment or devices; appropriate adjustment or modifications of examinations, training materials, or policies; the provision of qualified interpreters or readers.

For deaf and hard of hearing people, these accommodations may mean the following:

1. *Job restructuring*—may include an employer transferring nonessential marginal job functions. For example, where telephone answering is a marginal part of the job, the employer can reallocate that task to hearing coworkers.
2. *Reassignment*—can include moving a hard of hearing worker in a noise-intensive working environment to another position that is less noise intensive. Reassignment can be especially effective in large companies that have many similar positions.
3. *Acquisition of equipment*—can include a telecommunications device for the deaf (TDD) or assistive listening devices.
4. *Modification of equipment*—can include a phone amplifier or telephones compatible with hearing aids for hard of hearing employees.

In addition, employers can make appropriate adjustment or modification of examinations, training materials, or policies by captioning training films, providing a qualified interpreter for training sessions, and modifying written tests that measure a deaf person's language skills instead of his or her ability to do the specific job.

Discrimination Prohibited

The ADA and the EEOC regulations make it unlawful for an employer to discriminate on the basis of disability against a qualified individual in the following areas:[6]

1. Recruitment, advertising, and job application procedures;
2. Hiring, upgrading, promotion, award of tenure, demo-

tion, transfer, layoff, termination, right of return from layoff, and rehiring;

3. Rates of pay;
4. Job assignments, job classifications, position descriptions, and seniority lists;
5. Leaves of absence, sick leave, or any other leave;
6. Fringe benefits;
7. Selection and financial support for training;
8. Activities sponsored by the employer including social and recreational programs; and
9. Any other term, condition, or privilege of employment.

Some examples of prohibited discrimination against a deaf or hard of hearing person include being denied a qualified interpreter for a job interview, not being hired or promoted because the employer says communication is required and does not consider any reasonable accommodation, being hired at a lower rate of pay for doing the same job as hearing workers, and being denied an opportunity to participate in training because the employer refuses to pay for a qualified interpreter.

Qualification Standards, Tests, and Other Selection Criteria

It is unlawful under the ADA for an employer to use qualification standards, employment tests, or other selection criteria that screen out or tend to screen out individuals with disabilities.[7] Tests may be given if they are job-related and required by business necessity. It would be discriminatory, for example, for an employer to require every applicant to pass a written test that measures language skills when the essential functions of the job in question do not require those skills. Too often such tests have excluded deaf persons from being hired or promoted. In some situations, parts of written tests may be waived as an appropriate accommodation for a deaf person.

Under the ADA, an employer must select and administer tests to a person with a sensory, manual, or speech impairment that accurately reflect the skills or aptitude of the test taker rather than his or her impairment. For example, it would be illegal to require an oral test for a person that does not have the ability to speak without substituting a written test.

Medical Examinations

Prior to a job offer, an employer cannot conduct medical examinations or ask about an applicant's disability.[8] However, an employer can ask about the person's ability to perform job-related duties. An employer can also require a medical examination after an offer of employment has been made and before the start of employment. The employer may make the offer of employment contingent on the results of the examination if all entering employees take the examination, not only the person with a disability, and the information obtained during the examination is kept separately as a confidential medical record. However, supervisors and managers may be informed regarding necessary restrictions or accommodations to the work of the employee, and first aid and safety personnel may be informed if the disability might require emergency treatment. Government officials investigating compliance with the ADA may also be informed of the examination results. Finally, the employer cannot discriminate against the disabled person on the basis of the examination. Repeatedly, deaf and hard of hearing applicants have been excluded from consideration for jobs on the basis of medical examinations before jobs have been offered. This section of ADA will prohibit such practices.

Employer Defenses

Direct Threat

An employer can sometimes defend against a charge of discrimination by requiring that individuals cannot pose a direct threat to their own health or safety or to that of others in the workplace.[9] However, the ADA has a strict definition of "direct threat," which states that such a determination be based on an individualized assessment of the person's present ability to safely perform the essential functions of the job. If a person poses a direct threat, the employer must see if a reasonable accommodation would either eliminate or reduce the risk to an acceptable level.

In determining a direct threat, decisions must be made on a case-by-case basis based on objective, factual evidence rather than on fears or stereotypes. The ADA legislative history and the EEOC refer to a federal case involving a hard of hearing person, *Strathie v. Department of Transportation*, 716 F2d 227(3d Cir. 1983), as an example of the requirement that decisions on safety be based on actual facts of risk. In the *Strathie* case, the state of Pennsylvania had a rule prohibiting hard-of-hearing hearing aid users from obtaining licenses to drive school buses. A district court had supported the ban on issuing such licenses to hearing aid users on the basis of general safety concerns. The federal appeals court reversed the lower court, finding evidence in the record rebutting the state's safety concerns and showing that an appropriate hearing aid would enable a hard of hearing person to drive a school bus without appreciable risk to passenger safety. This evidence had to be considered in determining whether a driver wearing a hearing aid actually would present an appreciable risk to the safety of school bus passengers.

Undue Hardship

Another defense an employer can use when charged with not making a reasonable accommodation is that the requested accommodation would be an "undue hardship" on the operation of the business. Undue hardship means significant difficulty or expense for the business. In deciding whether an accommodation would be an undue hardship to the business, the following conditions should be considered:

1. The nature and net cost of the accommodation needed, taking into consideration the availability of tax credits and deductions, and/or outside funding;
2. The overall financial resources of the business site providing the accommodation, the number of employees, and the effect on resources;
3. The overall financial resources of the business, including its size in terms of number of employees and number and type of business sites;
4. The type of operation of the business and the relationship of the facility to the overall business.

The Analysis to the EEOC regulations gives the following example involving a deaf applicant. The analysis explains how to weigh some of the factors just listed—An independently owned fast-food franchise receives no money from the parent company that gives out the franchises. The franchise refuses to hire a deaf person because it says it would be an undue hardship to provide an interpreter for monthly staff meetings. Since the financial relationship between the local franchise and the parent company is only a franchise fee, only the financial resources of the local franchise would be considered in deciding whether providing the accommodation would be an undue hardship. However, if a factual determination shows that there is a financial or administrative relationship between the parent company and the local site providing the accommodation, then the parent company's resources should be considered in determining whether the hardship is undue.

Enforcement Provisions

Individuals with disabilities will have the same remedies available to all other minorities under Title VII of the Civil Rights Act of 1964, as amended by the Civil Rights Act of 1991. An employer found in violation of the employment section of the ADA may be ordered to discontinue discriminatory practices, to correct policies and practices, to hire a qualified individual with a disability, or to rehire the person with back pay and provide the person with a reasonable accommodation. In addition, the Civil Rights Act of 1991 amends Title VII to include compensatory and punitive damages for intentional discrimination. Individuals with disabilities are protected by the Civil Rights Act of 1991 remedies under both Section 501 of the Rehabilitation Act of 1973, which covers federal employees, and the ADA. Damages may not be awarded where the employer demonstrates "good faith efforts" to identify and make reasonable accommodations. Employers who lose a specific case will be required to pay the disabled person's attorney's fees and costs.

TITLE II: STATE AND LOCAL GOVERNMENTS

Title II of the ADA requires all state and local government agencies to make all of their services accessible to individuals with disabilities. It also requires public transportation agencies to be accessible.

This is important to deaf and hard of hearing people because it extends protection to many agencies that were not covered by Section 504 of the Rehabilitation Act of 1973 (see chap. three) because they did not receive any federal funding. For example, many courts and police or sheriff's offices do not receive federal financial assistance.

Deaf people could not use Section 504 to complain about discrimination when these courts or police departments did not provide interpreter services. Now they can rely on the ADA to insist on equal access.

The goal of Title II is to make sure that all services, programs, and activities of state and local governments can be used by people with disabilities. The law applies to anything a government agency does. Any person with a disability who meets the essential eligibility requirements for getting services or participating in a government program is protected by the ADA.

Title II became effective on January 26, 1992. Regulations implementing and explaining the requirements of Title II were adopted by the U.S. Department of Justice. They can be found in Title 28, Part 35 of the Code of Federal Regulations.

Agencies That Must Be Accessible

Title II of the ADA applies to all state and local "public entities," as well as to AMTRAK and commuter transportation agencies. Public agencies include school systems; motor vehicle departments; police and fire departments; parks and recreation programs; jails and prisons; libraries; food stamp offices; welfare and social service agencies; and public hospitals, clinics, and counseling centers. This part of the law also applies to state and local courts and city, county, and state legislatures.

The ADA also applies to government activities that are actually carried out by private contractors. For example, the concession activities in state parks are often operated by private contractors, and shelters and halfway houses may be operated by private nonprofit agencies but receive state and local government contracts.

Title II of the ADA does not apply to federal government agencies. Federal buildings and federal executive agencies must be accessible, too, but they are covered by the Rehabilitation Act and the Architectural Barriers Act, not by the Americans with Disabilities Act.

Defining Discrimination

If a person with a disability meets the "essential eligibility requirements" for a government service, the ADA says that the government agency cannot (1) exclude the person from participating in the service; (2) deny the benefits or services, programs or activities of the agency; or (3) subject the person to discrimination, by reason of the disability. In addition, government agencies must comply with the following guidelines:

1. A government agency cannot exclude people or refuse to serve them because of a disability. For example, city recreation programs may not turn away people who are deaf or impose additional requirements on them. A counseling service may not refuse to accept a deaf client because of difficulty in communication.

2. A government agency must make reasonable modifications to rules, policies, and practices that are unfair to persons with disabilities. For example, an agency that requires a driver's license as the only acceptable means of identification, must change its policy because blind individuals or individuals with other disabilities may not be able to get driver's licenses. If the agency imposes safety requirements that are necessary for the safe operation of the program (such as a requirement to have a valid driver's license), the requirement must be based on actual risk and not on mere speculation, stereotype, or generalizations about individuals with disabilities.

   A public park cannot ask a deaf individual to pay a higher deposit or take out additional insurance to rent equipment. There is no valid evidence that deafness is more likely to cause the person to have an accident or damage equipment. If a licensing agency requires applicants to take an oral test, it must either provide an interpreter for the test or allow a deaf applicant to take a written test, unless the agency is actually testing the applicant's ability to hear for a reason related to getting the license.

3. A government agency must remove architectural, communication, or transportation barriers. The agency does not have to remove physical barriers in every part of every public building, as long as the programs it offers can be made available to people who cannot use the facility. For example, the agency could serve a person with a disability in an accessible location, or provide an aide, an assistant, or a device that will enable the person with a disability to use the service. Not all pay telephones in public buildings have to be equipped with TDDs, but a certain percentage should be usable by deaf people.
4. Most important to deaf individuals, a government agency must also provide the "auxiliary aids and services" the person needs in order to communicate.

What Are Auxiliary Aids and Services?

State and local governments must ensure effective communication with individuals with disabilities.[10] In order to make sure that communication for a person with a hearing, vision, or speech impairment is as effective as communication with others, the public entity must provide appropriate auxiliary aids.

Auxiliary aids include qualified interpreters, assistive listening systems (loop, FM, and infrared systems), television captioning and decoders, TDDs, videotext displays, transcriptions, readers, taped texts, brailled materials, and large print materials.[11] Any similar device or service that is needed to make spoken or aural information accessible is also considered an auxiliary aid.

The government agency may have to provide special equipment, or modify its existing equipment, to make sure deaf people can communicate effectively. For example, an entry system that requires a person to open a door in response to a signal from a buzzer or an intercom should be modified. A government agency may have to hire interpreters, transcribers, or other personnel to provide necessary communication services.

The agency should establish and publicize procedures for notifying the public about how to request these special services.

Which Auxiliary Aids Should Be Provided?

The government agency must provide auxiliary aids that are necessary to give the deaf person an equal opportunity to participate in and enjoy the government services, programs, or activities.[12] The appropriate auxiliary aid will depend on the type of activity and the needs of the person. A deaf person who uses sign language may need an interpreter to understand a PTA meeting or to talk to a county social worker or police officer. But a deaf or hard of hearing person who does not use sign language may need a transcription or amplification system or another method of making communication understandable. A televised or videotaped program should be captioned and shown on a machine with a decoder, if an interpreter is not provided.

The Justice Department defines a qualified interpreter as one who can "interpret effectively, accurately, and impartially both receptively and expressively, using any necessary specialized vocabulary."[13] An interpreter who is qualified enough for one type of interpreting assignment may not have sufficient skills for interpreting in another situation.

In determining whether or not an interpreter is needed, and the necessary skill level, the government agency should consider the context in which the communication is taking place, the number of people involved, the importance of the communication, and whether the information being communicated is complex or lengthy. In certain circumstances, a family member or friend may not be qualified to interpret because of factors such as emotional or personal involvement or considerations of confidentiality that may adversely affect the ability to interpret "effectively, accurately, and impartially."

Although the public agency has the final decision about the type of auxiliary aid that will be provided, the deaf individual is in the best position to evaluate his or her own needs and the effectiveness of the service. The Justice Department rule states that in determining what type of auxiliary aid or service is necessary, the government agency must give "primary consideration" to the requests of the individual with disabilities.[14] The Justice Department analysis to its ADA rule states:

> The public entity must provide an opportunity for individuals with disabilities to request the auxiliary aids and services of their choice. This expressed choice shall be given primary consideration by the public entity. The public entity shall honor the choice unless it can demonstrate that another effective means of communication exists or that use of the means chosen would not be required under [the regulation].[15]

Deaf individuals should notify government agencies if interpreters are not sufficiently skilled or if an auxiliary aid is not effective to give them equal access to a program.

Who Pays for the Interpreters and Other Auxiliary Aids?

The government may not charge a person with a disability any extra fee for providing an interpreter or other auxiliary aid.[16] For example, courts may not include an interpreter fee as "court costs" when a deaf person is involved in a trial and is ordered to pay the "costs" of the trial.[17]

The ADA does not require an agency to provide an auxiliary aid if it would result in an undue burden or if it would make a fundamental alteration in the nature of the services the agency provides. Interpreters would seldom be considered an undue burden on an agency since the cost is compared to the overall budget of the state or local government that is available to support a government program.

Even if a particular auxiliary aid is considered to be too expensive or burdensome, the agency must still furnish another auxiliary aid, if available, that does not cause a fundamental alteration or undue burden on the agency.

What TDD Services Are Required?

Where a government agency communicates by telephone with individuals with disabilities, TDDs or equally effective telecommunication systems are required to communicate with persons with impaired hearing or speech.[18] Title IV of the ADA establishes a nationwide relay system that may be adequate to give TDD users access to many government services. But public agencies must still provide TDDs and direct access to incoming TDD calls if the relay service will not give them equal access to services offered by telephone.

Telephone emergency services, including 911 services, must provide direct access to individuals with speech or hearing impairments.[19] Local governments that provide 911-type services must make sure that a TDD user can call directly, without going through a relay system or a separate telephone number. Emergency-service operators must be trained to recognize and respond to TDD emergency calls.

When a public agency offers use of a telephone as part of its services, it must be able to offer TDDs and hearing-aid-compatible telephones to individuals with hearing impairments. For example, patients in community hospitals or other residential facilities need equal access to telephones. Agencies that provide pay telephones for public use must make sure that some of their telephones are equipped with a TDD. New public buildings must meet a high standard of accessibility, including requirements for visual flashing alarms, TDD equipment, and intercom accessibility.

When a relay system is not adequate to give access to a telephone service, the government office should have its own TDD for incoming calls. For example, offices with frequent contacts with the public or with clients who use TDDs should have on-site TDDs to provide for direct communication between the government agency and the individual.

Filing a Complaint

A person who believes that he or she is a victim of discrimination by a state or local government may enforce the ADA by a lawsuit or by filing an administrative complaint. The same remedies are available as those provided under Section 504 of the Rehabilitation Act of 1973, including a reasonable attorney's fee to the prevailing party (see chap. three).

Administrative complaints may be filed with any agency that provides financial assistance to the program, or with the U.S. Department of Justice, or with one of eight federal agencies that have been assigned enforcement authority over specific subject areas.

- *Department of Agriculture*: Farming and raising of livestock, including extension services.
- *Department of Education*: Education systems and institutions (other than health-related education) and libraries.
- *Department of Health and Human Services*: Schools of medicine, dentistry, nursing, and other health-related schools, health care and social service providers and institutions, and preschool and day-care programs.

- *Department of Housing and Urban Development*: State and local public housing, and housing assistance and referral.
- *Department of Interior*: Lands and natural resources, including parks and recreation, water and waste management, environmental protection, energy, historic and cultural preservation, and museums.
- *Department of Justice*: Public safety, law enforcement, and the administration of justice, including courts and correctional institutions; commerce and industry, including banking and finance, consumer protection, and insurance; planning, development, and regulation; state and local government support services; and all other government functions not assigned to other designated agencies.
- *Department of Labor*: Labor and work force.
- *Department of Transportation*: Transportation, including highways, public transportation, traffic management (non-law enforcement), automobile licensing and inspection, and driver licensing.

Complaints should be made in writing, signed by the complainant or an authorized representative. The complaint must contain the complainant's name and address and a description of the discrimination by the public entity. For more information, or to file a complaint, contact:

Coordination and Review Section
Civil Rights Division
U.S. Department of Justice
P.O. Box 66118
Washington, DC 20035–6118

TITLE III: PUBLIC ACCOMMODATION

Title III of the ADA provides disabled people with the rights to equal access to public accommodations. For deaf and hard of hearing people, Title III and its regulations will be of tremendous help in removing communication barriers.[20] Title III covers a wide range of places, such as hotels, theaters, restaurants, doctors' and lawyers' offices, retail stores, banks, museums, parks, libraries, day-care centers, and private schools. All of these public accommodations are required to provide auxiliary aids and services to ensure effective communication with deaf and hard of hearing people as well as individuals with vision impairments.

Auxiliary Aids

The Department of Justice regulations to implement Title III provide a comprehensive list of auxiliary aids and services required by the ADA.[21] Qualified interpreters are included in this list of auxiliary aids. The regulation defines "qualifed interpreter" to mean "an interpreter who is able to interpret effectively, accurately, and impartially both receptively and expressively, using any necessary specialized vocabulary." This definition focuses on the interpreter's actual ability to make communication effective in a particular interpreting situation. In certain circumstances, a family member or friend may not be qualified to interpret because of factors such as emotional or personal involvement or considerations of confidentiality that may adversely affect the ability to interpret "effectively, accurately, and impartially."

Other examples of auxiliary aids listed in the regulations are notetakers, computer-aided transcription services, written materials, telephone handset amplifiers, assistive listening devices, assistive listening systems, telephones compatible with hearing aids, closed caption decoders, open and closed captioning, telecommunication devices for deaf persons (TDDs), videotext displays, or other effective methods of making aurally delivered materials available to individuals with hearing impairments.

Auxiliary aids also include the acquisition or modification of equipment. The ADA analysis gives the example that a hotel conference center may need to provide permanent or portable assistive listening systems for people with hearing impairments.

The list is not intended to be all-inclusive or exhaustive. The Justice Department noted such an attempt would omit new devices that will become available as technology advances.

Defense to the Requirements

The ADA does make allowances for the provision of auxiliary aids in specific situations. For example, the ADA does not require the provision of any auxiliary aid that would result in an "undue burden" or in a fundamental alteration in the nature of the goods and services provided by a public accommodation. An undue burden is defined as significant difficulty or expense to the public accommodation. However, the public accommodation is not relieved from the duty to furnish an alternative auxiliary aid, if available, that would not result in an undue burden. The costs of compliance with the auxiliary aids requirements may not be financed by surcharges on deaf persons.

Effective Communication

A public accommodation must provide an auxiliary aid or service where necessary to ensure effective communication with individuals with disabilities. The Justice Department strongly encourages that a public accommodation consult with an individual before providing him or her with a particular auxiliary aid or service. In certain cases, the Department analysis to the regulation points out, an interpreter may be necessary to ensure effective communication. According to the analysis, there is a wide range of communication situations, including areas such as health, legal matters, and finances, that would be sufficiently lengthy or complex to require an interpreter for effective communication.

TDD Requirements

Title III also requires public accommodations to provide TDDs upon request when such facilities offer a customer, client, patient, or participant the opportunity to make outgoing telephone calls on more than an incidental convenience basis. Where entry to a place of public accommodation requires use of a security entrance telephone, a TDD or other effective means of communication must be provided for use by an individual with impaired hearing or speech. Hotels should also provide a TDD at the front desk in order to take calls from guests who use TDDs in their rooms.

Decoders and Captioning

Hospitals that provide televisions for patient use and places of lodging that provide televisions in five or more guest rooms must provide, upon request, a means for decoding captions. While movie theaters are not required to present open-captioned films, other public accommodations that impart verbal information through soundtracks on films, videotapes, or slide shows are required to make such information accessible to deaf and hard of hearing participants through such means as captioning.

Conferences and Performances

Trade associations or performing artists that lease space for a conference or performance at a hotel, convention center, or stadium become a public accommodation that must comply with the ADA. The analysis to the regulation states that the trade association or performing artist should be responsible for providing auxiliary aids and services, which could include interpreters, for the participants in its conference or performance. The determination of who actually provides auxiliary aids (the landlord or the renters) can be decided during the lease negotiations. For example, if a theater rents out to a performing artist, the question of who provides for a requested interpreter will be decided by their contract. Both the landlord and tenant are subject to the requirements of the ADA.

Use of Service Animals

The Title III regulation also provides broad protections for the use of service animals.[22] Public accommodations have to modify their policies and practices to allow the use of service animals. Service animals are broadly defined to include any guide or signal dog or other animal individually trained to provide assistance to a person with a disability.

Examinations and Courses

The ADA requires private organizations that offer examinations or courses for licensing, certification, or credentials to provide appropriate auxiliary aids such as interpreters.[23] This applies to high school or college education and to professional and trade training. The private organization would not be required to provide an auxiliary aid if it could show the provision of the auxiliary aid would fundamentally alter the skills or knowledge the examination intends to test or the course offered. Examinations must be used that best reflect an individual's aptitude or achievement level rather than reflecting the person's impaired sensory, manual, or speaking skills. The only exception is where those skills are what the examination seeks to measure.

Existing Facilities

The ADA requires that structural communication barriers be removed from existing facilities.[24] Some examples of how this can be accomplished are installing flashing alarm systems, permanent signage, and adequate sound buffers.

New Construction and Alterations

The U. S. Architectural and Transportation Barriers Compliance Board has developed ADA Accessibility Guidelines.[25] According to these guidelines, all new construction and building alterations must be accessible to disabled people. The requirements for TDDs, public telephones, assistive listening systems, and visual alarms are as follows:

1. One TDD must be provided inside any building that has four or more public pay telephones, including both interior and exterior phones. In addition, one TDD must be provided whenever there is an interior public pay phone in a stadium or arena; a convention center; a hotel with a convention center; a covered shopping mall; or a hospital emergency, recovery, or waiting room.
2. One accessible public pay phone must be provided for each level of a public accommodation. If a level has two or more banks of phones, there must be one accessible phone for each bank.
3. Fixed-seating assembly areas that accommodate 50 or more people or that have audio-amplification systems must have a permanently installed assistive listening system.

4. Hotels must make four percent of the first 100 rooms and approximately two percent of the remaining rooms accessible to people with a hearing loss. These rooms must contain visual alarms, notification devices, volume-control telephones, and an accessible electrical outlet for a TDD.

Enforcement

The public accommodations requirements became effective, in most situations, on January 26, 1992. Individuals with disabilities can bring lawsuits for court orders to stop discrimination, but they cannot collect damages. If the individuals win in their court case, they can recover attorney's fees and costs. Individuals with disabilities can also file complaints with the Attorney General, who has the power to initiate lawsuits in cases of public importance or where a "pattern or practice" of discrimination is alleged. In such cases, the Attorney General may seek money damages and civil penalties.[26]

TITLE IV: TELECOMMUNICATIONS

Title IV of the ADA requires telephone companies to provide both local and long distance telecommunications relay services across the nation by July 26, 1993. These relay services will enable individuals who use TDDs, also now known as text telephones, to have telephone conversations with individuals who use conventional voice telephones anytime, any place, and for any reason whatsoever.

Relay Services Required Under the ADA

To use a relay service, a TDD user places a call to a third party, known as a relay operator or a communications assistant (CA). The TDD user tells the CA the name and number of the individual he or she wishes to call. The CA then places the call to the party requested. When the connection is made, the CA reads to the called party what the TDD user types and types to the TDD caller everything that the called party says. The same process can be performed in reverse when the call is initiated by a hearing person to a TDD user.

Prior to the introduction of the ADA, fewer than one-half of the states had state-mandated relay programs. Even those programs that had already existed tended to impose many restrictions on the number, length, and type of calls that could be made through their relay services. The ADA changed all that by requiring that relay services provided after July 26, 1993, offer telephone communication for persons with hearing and speech disabilities that is "functionally equivalent" to the telephone services available to individuals who do not have these impairments.

Functionally Equivalent Relay Services

On July 26, 1991, the Federal Communications Commission (FCC) adopted regulations to implement Title IV.[27] In those regulations, the FCC explained that the ADA's requirement for "functionally equivalent" relay services is intended to fulfill the telephone companies' general obligation to provide universal telephone service to all individuals who rely on TDDs for telephone communications. The FCC regulations outline functional equivalence as follows:

1. Relay services must be provided 24 hours a day/7 days a week for all local and long distance calls.
2. Relay systems must accept calls in both the Baudot and ASCII computer formats. The Baudot and ASCII codes are two formats for sending typed transmissions across the telephone wires. The Baudot format, which was developed more than 50 years ago, is now highly criticized for being an ineffective format for TDD use. In contrast, the ASCII format has become the nationwide standard for computer transmissions.[28] ASCII is faster and allows the transmission of many more characters than does Baudot. Unlike the Baudot format, it also allows conversations to take place in

two directions at the same time. Many predict that the advantages of the ASCII format will likely result in the elimination of Baudot within the next few years. For now, however, the great majority of individuals who use TDDs still rely on the Baudot format. For this reason, the FCC regulation requires that relay services be accessible to both of these codes.

3. Relay calls must be relayed verbatim, unless one of the relay parties requests that the messages be summarized.

4. Individuals using relay services may not be charged any more for their calls than voice telephone users are charged for calls with the same points of origination and destination.

5. No restrictions may be placed on the type, length, or number of calls made by any relay user. This means that relay systems must be capable of handling coinsent, third-party number, calling card, collect, and all other calls normally handled by telephone companies. The burden of proving that relaying a particular kind of call is not technologically possible rests on the telephone companies.

This requirement also allows relay callers to request CAs to make several calls for them each time they call into a relay center. For example, an individual who wishes to call five different appliance shops to find out the cost of purchasing a particular dishwasher may call into the relay center one time and request the same CA to make all five calls. This is a significant change from the former practice of many relay centers, which required callers to call the relay center each time they wanted to place a new call.

6. CAs may not consider the content of a particular call in determining whether to relay that call. In other words, under the FCC's regulation, CAs cannot decide that they do not want to relay a call because they do not like the legal, moral, or ethical nature of the call. For example, while a particular CA may not personally approve of certain explicit music videos, she

would nevertheless be required to complete a conversation on this topic between two teenagers.

Moreover, CAs cannot be held criminally liable for relaying unlawful conversations unless they are knowingly involved in the illegal transactions or have actual notice of the illegality of the telephone transmissions. The FCC regulation makes clear that, in the normal performance of their responsibilities, CAs will not be deemed to have a high level of involvement in any criminal activity that might be taking place in a relayed conversation. One example might be a drug transaction that takes place in a relay conversation. Unless the CA has active knowledge of the transaction taking place and is involved in the transaction in some way, he will not be held criminally liable for relaying the conversation.

The FCC's prohibition against refusing calls based on their content is critical to the proper and effective operation of relay services. Without such a prohibition, practices regarding call content would vary from state to state, or CA to CA, resulting in inconsistent practices throughout the nation. What one operator might consider light-hearted humor, another might find extremely offensive. What one operator might consider a harmless phrase, another operator might mistake for clues concerning illegal behavior. Never knowing when their calls could be terminated or refused, both deaf and hearing people would quickly lose all trust in the relay system if this requirement were not in place. The FCC's regulation to require the relay of all calls, regardless of their content, ensures that this will not happen.

7. CAs are also prohibited from keeping records of relayed conversations beyond the length of the telephone call. They are required to keep the content of all *intrastate* relayed calls confidential so that relay users have confidence in the privacy of their conversations. CAs are also prohibited from disclosing *interstate and*

foreign relayed conversations with two exceptions. Specifically, under Section 705(a) of the Communications Act of 1934, CAs may be required to disclose interstate or foreign conversations when directed to do so by a court-issued subpoena or upon the demand of some other lawful authority.

8. A functionally equivalent relay service also means that CAs must maintain certain skills and qualifications to properly perform their relay duties. Specifically, CAs must be trained to meet the communication needs of relay users who are deaf, hard of hearing, speech impaired, or otherwise disabled. They must be sufficiently acquainted with American Sign Language and with the cultures of the various communities that their relay systems are intended to serve. Additionally, they must have competent skills in grammar, typing, spelling, and relay etiquette.

9. Relay systems must have very low "blockage" rates. In the past, relay users were often confronted with busy signals and long delays when trying to obtain access to relay systems. The high demand for relay services, coupled with the threadbare budgets of most of these systems, greatly frustrated the individuals who depended daily on these systems. The FCC regulation resolves this problem. Essentially, it requires that relay users receive busy signals from relay systems at approximately the same rate that voice telephone users receive busy signals over the voice telephone network. In addition, the regulation requires that relay systems be capable of answering 85 percent of all incoming calls within 10 seconds. After receiving dialing information from the caller, CAs then have 30 seconds to dial the requested number.

10. Relay users must be given their choice of long-distance telephone companies.

11. Relay users must have the same access to all telephone operator services available to voice telephone users.

Relay Services Providers

Under the ADA, telephone companies are responsible for providing relay services in the geographic areas in which they provide conventional telephone service. In addition, individual states can receive certification from the FCC to operate and enforce their own state relay programs. Both telephone companies and states are permitted to provide relay services individually, through a competitively selected vendor, or together with other telephone companies or states. The statewide relay programs already in existence demonstrate the various options for establishing relay systems. For example, in Utah, a single nonprofit organization, the Utah Association of the Deaf, has a contract with the state to provide relay services. In contrast, in New York, 41 local telephone companies joined efforts under their umbrella organization, the New York Telephone Association, to contract with AT&T for the provision of relay services. The telephone companies of New York have also agreed to join efforts with the state of Maine in a regional relay center. This allows both states to reduce the overall costs of relay staff, administration, and equipment.

A state that wishes to receive certification to operate its own relay system must submit documentation to the FCC that proves that its program will (1) meet or exceed all of the operational, technical, and functional minimum standards contained in the FCC's regulation; (2) provide adequate procedures and remedies to enforce the state program; and (3) not conflict with federal law where its program exceeds the minimum standards contained in the FCC regulation.

Many of the relay programs now in existence will need to revise their practices in order to meet the FCC requirements for certification. For example, many states still do not relay interstate calls. Other states place restrictions on the hours each day that calls may be relayed. These and other limitations on relay service must be eliminated if these states wish to receive certification.

When a state requests certification, the FCC must give the public notice and an opportunity to comment on that request. Once it is granted, certification remains in effect for a five-year period. A state can apply to the FCC for recertification one year before its certification expires. Alternatively, the FCC may revoke or suspend a state's certification if that state's practices do not follow the FCC's minimum guidelines.

Notice to the Public

The goal of relay systems is to integrate TDD users into the general public telecommunications network. In order for this goal to be achieved, potential users must learn about the benefits and functions of relay systems. Toward this end, the FCC regulation specifically requires telephone companies to publish information about their relay systems, including the phone numbers of their relay centers, in telephone directories and billing inserts. Additionally, these companies must ensure that information about relay services is available through directory assistance services.

Enforcement

Consumers who are not satisfied with a relay service may file a complaint either with the state agency responsible for implementing the local program or with the FCC. When an individual files a complaint with the FCC against a relay program in a certified state, the FCC will refer that complaint back to the certified state. Both the states and the FCC are responsible for resolving complaints within 180 days.

A telephone company that violates the ADA's relay provisions may be ordered to begin compliance immediately and may have to pay damages to the complaining party. Willful violations of the relay section may be subject to criminal penalties, including fines of up to $10,000.

Captioning of Public Service Announcements

Title IV of the ADA also requires all television public service announcements that are produced or funded by the federal government to include closed captioning. Occasionally, federal agencies have taken part in the development of television announcements on AIDS, aging, and other general health and consumer issues. In the future, the vital information in these and other federally assisted announcements will finally reach individuals who rely on closed captions to receive the verbal content of television.

Notes

1. Public Law 101-336, 42 *United States Code* (U.S.C.) 12101 *et. seq.*
2. 29 *Code of Federal Regulations* (C.F.R.), Part 1630
3. 29 C.F.R. §1630.2
4. Id.
5. Id.
6. 29 C.F.R. §1630.4
7. 29 C.F.R. §1630.10
8. 29 C.F.R. §1630.14
9. 29 C.F.R. §1630.15
10. 28 C.F.R. §35.160
11. 28 C.F.R. §35.104
12. 28 C.F.R. §35.160(b)
13. 28 C.F.R. §35.104
14. 28 C.F.R. §35.160(b)(2)
15. 56 Fed. Reg. 35711-12 (July 26, 1991)
16. 28 C.F.R. §35.130(f)
17. The Analysis to the Justice Department ADA regulation states that "the costs of interpreter services may not be assessed as an element of 'court costs.' The [Justice]Department has already recognized that imposition of the cost of courtroom interpreter services is impermissible under section 504 . . . Accordingly, recouping the costs of interpreter services by assessing them as part of court costs would also be prohibited." 56 Fed. Reg. 35706 (July 26, 1991)
18. 28 C.F.R. §35.161
19. 28 C.F.R. §35.162
20. 28 C.F.R. Part 36
21. 28 C.F.R. §36.303
22. 28 C.F.R. §36.302
23. 28 C.F.R. §36.309
24. 28 C.F.R. §36.304

25. 28 C.F.R. §36.401
26. 28 C.F.R. §501–505
27. A summary of these regulations can be found at 56 Fed. Reg. 36729 (August 1, 1991). The complete Report and Order, CC Docket No. 90-571, may be obtained directly from the FCC at 1919 M Street, NW, Washington, DC 20036.
28. ASCII is an acronym for American Standard Code for Information Interchange.

CHAPTER THREE

The Rehabilitation Act of 1973

Historically, disabled people have been unemployed and underemployed. In 1920 Congress passed the first federal laws to help disabled people get job training and find employment. But these laws were clearly inadequate; even qualified disabled people could not find good jobs because of widespread discrimination against them by private employers and by federal, state, and local governments. Congress addressed the problem by enacting the Rehabilitation Act of 1973, Title V of which has been hailed as a "bill of rights" for disabled people.

The purpose of Title V is to make sure that programs receiving federal money can be used by all disabled people. The four major sections of Title V prohibit discrimination and require accessibility in employment, education, and health, welfare, and social services.

Section 501 applies to federal government employment practices.[1] It requires of each executive department and agency, including the U.S. Postal Service, an affirmative action plan for the hiring, placement, and advancement of qualified handicapped people. (For more information, see chapter eight, Employment.)

Section 502 creates the Architectural and Transportation Barriers Compliance Board.[2] The board's primary functions are to ensure compliance with a 1968 federal law prohibiting architectural barriers in federally funded buildings and to eliminate barriers from public transportation systems. (For more information, see chapter nine: Architectural Barriers.)

Section 503 requires affirmative action in the hiring, placement, and promotion of qualified handicapped people by employers who have contracts or subcontracts with the federal government of more than $2,500 a year.[3] Contractors with fifty or more employees or contracts for more than $50,000 are also required to have written affirmative action plans. (See chapter eight: Employment.)

Section 504 prohibits discrimination against qualified handicapped people in any federally supported program or activity.[4] Recipients of federal financial assistance include most public and some private institutions, from schools and nursing homes to museums and airports. This chapter will be devoted to the implementation, regulation, and application of Section 504.

SECTION 504

As amended in 1978, Section 504 of the Rehabilitation Act reads:

> No otherwise qualified handicapped individual in the United States . . . shall, solely by reason of his handicap, be excluded from participation in, be denied the benefits of, or be subjected to discrimination under any program or activity receiving federal financial assistance or under any program or activity conducted by any Executive Agency or by the United States Postal Service.[5]

The statute is implemented by detailed regulations that every federal agency giving financial assistance must promulgate, spelling out the Section 504 obligations of its recipients.[6] In 1977 the U.S. Department of Health, Education, and Welfare (HEW)* became the first agency to publish its regulation and detailed analysis.[7] The department also issued a set of standards for other agencies to use in developing their own Section 504 regulations.

---

*HEW was divided into two cabinet-level departments—the Departments of Education (ED) and of Health and Human Services (HHS)—effective May 4, 1980. Hereafter, references to HEW will be restricted to actions taken before that date. Unless noted otherwise, HEW policies remain in effect at ED and HHS.

Primary authority to monitor the regulations of the agencies was given to the Department of Justice in 1980.

Who Must Obey Section 504?

The federal government assists many programs and activities around the country. The HHS regulation defines "federal financial assistance" as "any grant, loan, contract (other than a procurement contract or a contract of insurance or guaranty), or any other arrangement by which the Department provides or otherwise makes available assistance in the form of funds or services of federal personnel or property."[8] The exclusion of procurement contracts means that private businesses that manufacture items purchased by the government do not have to obey Section 504. However, they are subject to Section 503, which prohibits employment discrimination. Some organizations have both procurement contracts with and financial assistance from the federal government. They have to obey both Sections 503 and 504 of the law.

Because the definition of federal financial assistance is so broad, many private as well as public institutions must obey Section 504. The types of institutions usually receiving some form of federal financial assistance include elementary and secondary schools, colleges and universities, hospitals, nursing homes, vocational rehabilitation agencies, public welfare offices, state and local governments, police and fire departments, correction and probation departments, libraries, museums, theater programs, parks, recreational facilities, mass transit systems, airports and harbors, subsidized housing programs, legal services programs, and most parts of the judicial system.

Section 504 is applicable whether the federal assistance is received directly or indirectly, for example, through a state or local government. A "recipient" is defined as any institution that receives federal assistance or that indirectly benefits from such assistance.

Sometimes it is difficult to determine whether and from what agency an institution gets federal financial assistance. If the institution is public, citizens usually can examine its financial records and reports to see if it receives federal assistance. Many federal agencies keep public lists of the programs and activities they fund. If the agency does not have such a list, or if the particular institution is not listed, a request can be filed under the Freedom of Information Act (FOIA) with each federal agency thought to be the funding source.[9]

The FOIA request should identify the possible recipient, state that the information is being sought under the Freedom of Information Act, and ask if the particular institution receives federal financial assistance and, if so, for what purpose. It is important to identify the institution fully and correctly and to give the name and address of any parent organization(s) to which it belongs. For example, a local branch library may not be listed as a direct recipient of federal assistance. Instead, the state, regional, or county association may be the formal recipient. The federal agency is supposed to respond to an FOIA request within ten days.

A complaint against an institution for violation of Section 504 can be filed with a federal agency even if it is not clear whether that institution gets financial assistance from that agency. If the agency does not financially support that institution, the agency will simply refuse to accept the complaint.

If an institution receives any federal financial assistance for one part of its activities, then it must obey Section 504 in all of its activities which "receive or benefit from" the financial assistance, even if those other activities do not receive any direct aid.[10] Section 504 was amended in 1987 to make it clear that the law applies to "all of the operations" of an agency, department, college, hospital, or other organization that receives any federal financial assistance.[11]

Since 1978, Section 504 has applied to federal executive agencies and the U.S. Postal Service as well as to recipients of federal financial assistance. Because the original 1973 law did not apply to federal agencies, the current Section 504 regulations are all written to apply only to recipients of assistance from the agency and not to the agency itself. Since the 1978 amendments, however, the agencies themselves must obey Section 504, whether or not they have adopted specific regulations that apply to their own activities.

Section 504 Protections

Section 504 protects people with many different kinds of physical and mental disabilities. The definition of "handicapped" adopted by HEW is very broad. It includes any person who (1) has a physical or mental impairment that substantially limits one or more major life activity, (2) has a record of such an impairment, or (3) is regarded as having such an impairment.[12]

Major life activities are defined as "taking care of oneself," walking, hearing, doing manual tasks, seeing, speaking, breathing, learning, and working. Section 504 therefore protects almost anyone with a disabling condition, whether due to a congenital handicap, disease, accident, or any other reason.

For example, Section 504 protects deaf, hard of hearing, and blind people; people in wheelchairs; people with cerebral palsy, diabetes, epilepsy, cancer, speech defects, or emotional disturbance; recovering alcoholics and other drug abusers; and mentally retarded people. A person who is not actually disabled but who is considered handicapped in some way is still protected by Section 504. For example, people who experienced mental illness in the past may encounter employers unwilling to hire them because of their history of illness. Such persons are protected by Section 504 even though they are not ill at the present time. The law also protects people who were misdiagnosed or misclassified as handicapped.

Section 504 does not guarantee handicapped people jobs or services merely because they are handicapped. To be protected by Section 504, a handicapped person must also be "qualified" for the job or service in question. The HEW regulation defines a "qualified handicapped person" as:

• With respect to employment, a handicapped person who with reasonable accommodation, can perform the essential functions of the job in question.

- With respect to public preschool, elementary, secondary, or adult education, a handicapped person (i) of an age during which nonhandicapped persons are provided such services, (ii) of any age during which it is mandatory under state law to provide such services to handicapped persons, or (iii) to whom a state is required to provide a free appropriate public education under §612 of the Education for All Handicapped Children Act; and
- With respect to postsecondary and vocational education services, a handicapped person who meets the academic and technical standards requisite to admission or participation in the recipient's education program or activity; and
- With respect to other services, a handicapped person who meets the essential eligibility requirements for the receipt of such services.[13]

A handicapped person must fall under the applicable definition in order to be protected by the nondiscrimination provisions of Section 504.

GENERAL NONDISCRIMINATION PROVISIONS

The HEW Section 504 regulation lists general categories of discriminatory behavior against handicapped people that are prohibited. It also establishes broad policy guidelines to determine whether a particular discriminatory act is prohibited by Section 504.

Equal Opportunity

The most significant principle is that no recipient or federal agency may deny, on the basis of handicap, a qualified person an opportunity to participate in or benefit from its programs or services.[14] A federally funded program cannot refuse to serve a handicapped person merely because of that handicap. A deaf person cannot be denied admission to a mental health counseling program merely because he or she is deaf. If a counseling program is available only to people who live in a certain county, however, and the deaf person does not live in that county, he or she can be denied admission to the program for that particular reason.

A handicapped person must be given an opportunity to participate in or benefit from a program in a manner that is equal to and as effective as the opportunity provided to nonhandicapped people.[15] To be equally effective, a program does not have to produce the identical result or level of achievement for handicapped and nonhandicapped participants; the requirement is only that handicapped people be provided an equal opportunity to obtain the same result, to gain the same benefit, or to reach the same level of achievement as nonhandicapped people.[16] For example, the administrator of an adult education program might tell a deaf person simply to read the written materials for a class, without attending lectures and discussions. This would be unfair. Because the lectures and discussions help to explain and amplify the written material, the deaf person would not have an equal opportunity to benefit from the class.

Different or Special Treatment

Sometimes handicapped people will need different or special treatment in order to give them genuine equal opportunity. In the area of race or sex discrimination, equal opportunity usually means treating people in exactly the same way. But a handicapped person may need some special assistance or accommodation in order to get benefits or services equivalent to those of a nonhandicapped person. Failure to provide that special assistance or accommodation would constitute discrimination. As explained in the analysis accompanying the HEW Section 504 regulation,

> Different or special treatment of handicapped persons because of their handicaps, may be necessary in a number of contexts in order to assure equal opportunity. Thus, for example, it is meaningless to "admit" a handicapped person in a wheelchair to a program if

the program is offered only on the third floor of a walk-up building. Nor is one providing equal educational opportunity to a deaf child by admitting him or her to a classroom but providing no means for the child to understand the teacher or receive instruction.[17]

At the same time, Section 504 also prohibits unnecessary special or different treatment if it would tend to stigmatize handicapped people or set them apart from nonhandicapped people. Different or separate aids, benefits, or services to handicapped people are prohibited unless the separation is necessary to provide them with services that are as effective as those provided to others.[18] A legal services organization, for example, may designate a special office to serve handicapped clients, if the office is physically accessible and has lawyers trained in handicap law. But it would be unfair to require all handicapped clients, regardless of their legal problems or handicaps, to use only that special office.

Communication Barriers

The general nondiscrimination provisions in the Section 504 regulation apply to the communication barriers faced by deaf people as well as to physical barriers to people in wheelchairs. A deaf woman may be able to walk up a flight of stairs to a job counseling center without difficulty. But if she cannot understand the intake worker's explanations about filling out the forms, she will not be able to do it correctly. She will not know what services are available or how to get them. A deaf man may be able to walk into a hospital or mental health center; but if he cannot communicate with the doctor or counselor, he does not have meaningful, equivalent access to the program and its facilities.

The analysis of the regulation gives an example of a welfare office that has a telephone.[19] Clients can call the office for information or to reach caseworkers. Staff can call clients to schedule appointments. But this office must also provide an alternative means to communicate with its deaf clients. The best example of such an alternative would be a TDD-equipped telephone.

Communication problems are specifically addressed in the Section 504 regulation of the U.S. Department of Justice, which requires recipients to ensure that communications are effectively conveyed to persons with impaired vision or hearing.[20] The regulation requires recipients to provide appropriate auxiliary aids, including qualified sign language interpreters and telephone equipment, to deaf persons in order to give equal access to programs and services.[21]

When the Justice Department implemented the Americans with Disabilities Act, it clarified Section 504 by defining auxiliary aids and services to also include amplifiers, assistive listening devices and systems, hearing aid-compatible telephones, television decoders, captioning, TDDs, videotext displays, or other effective methods of making aurally delivered materials available to individuals with hearing impairments. The Justice Department also defined a qualified interpreter as one who is able to interpret effectively, accurately, and impartially both

receptively and expressively, using any necessary specialized vocabulary.[22]

Program Accessibility

The regulation requires that programs be operated so that
handicapped people can use them easily and have equal
opportunity to benefit from them.[23] This is called "program
accessibility." For people in wheelchairs, this means
removing architectural and physical barriers. For deaf
people, it means removing communication barriers. Deaf
people do not have equal access to—they cannot fully
utilize—programs and facilities in which they cannot
communicate effectively with the people operating them.
Programs and facilities must be "usable" by handicapped
people. This requirement of the Rehabilitation Act suggests much more than physical accessibility to a site or
building. In effect, the act requires that handicapped
people have functionally equivalent services and programs. As a policy concept, "program accessibility" should
be invoked aggressively to help deaf people overcome
their isolation and exclusion from many programs and
services.

The government regulation lists methods to make
programs accessible.[24] While the list does not provide
much guidance for making specific programs accessible to
deaf people, the phrase "re-design of equipment" encom-
passes modifications to telephones and auditory alarm
systems; captions for films and videotapes; and stage,
podium, and audiovisual system designs that include
facilities and lighting for interpreters. The phrase "assignment of aides" can be interpreted to mean the provision of
appropriate interpreters, notetakers, or other aides needed
by deaf people. Because the list of methods in the regulation is not inclusive, deaf and handicapped people should
feel free to request any other method that makes programs
and activities accessible.

Accessible Meetings

An example of program accessibility is a new HHS regulation for accessible meetings.[25] This regulation establishes

not only physical accessibility standards for meetings, seminars, conferences, and other events sponsored by HHS but also necessary service requirements to ensure that sensory-impaired people can participate fully. The regulation specifically lists notetakers, trained interpreters (with adequate lighting to enable them to be seen), and volume-controlled and TDD-equipped telephones.

Interpreters should be available for any meeting, class, or other group activity held by an agency that receives federal financial assistance. Section 504 requires interpreters for cultural events, city government meetings, adult education classes, park programs, or any other event that deaf people may wish to attend. Publicity for meetings should announce the availability of special services and interpreters and should describe the procedures for requesting them.

The needs of deaf people are specifically addressed by one HHS regulation that requires funding recipients to ensure that people with impaired vision or hearing can obtain information about the various services that are accessible to them.[26] For example, incoming telephone lines for inquiries must be TDD-equipped and be indentified as such in the recipient's directory listing, letterhead, and anywhere else that the recipient's telephone number is given. Televised public service announcements should be signed or captioned. If programs or services are announced by radio, a recipient might ensure that hearing-impaired people receive the same information by direct mail or by announcements inserted in local newsletters or newspapers distributed by clubs or associations of hearing-impaired people.

ENFORCEMENT OF SECTION 504

A handicapped person who believes that a recipient of federal financial assistance has discriminated against him or her on the basis of the handicap has several alternative procedures for seeking redress.

Administrative Enforcement

There is no central enforcement mechanism for Section 504. Although the Department of Justice has overall supervision, every agency that provides federal financial assistance is required to adopt its own enforcement procedures as well as its own substantive regulation. Each agency must make its recipients sign assurances of compliance with Section 504 and use the same enforcement procedures as those established to enforce Title VI of the Civil Rights Act of 1964.[27] Within this framework, the procedures used by the various agencies can differ substantially. However, most of the agencies have adopted procedures that are modeled on those developed by HEW and now used by the Departments of Education and of Health and Human Services.

Self-Evaluation

All recipients must conduct a self-evaluation of their Section 504 compliance, assisted by interested people including handicapped people or organizations representing them.[28] Recipients of HEW funding were given until June 3, 1978, to complete their self-evaluations, modify any policies or practices that were not in compliance with Section 504, and take appropriate remedial steps to eliminate the effects of any discrimination that resulted from past policies and practices.[29] If a recipient has not yet conducted a self-evaluation or made appropriate modifications, a person bringing a complaint against it can use this mechanism to focus attention on discriminatory practices. If a recipient refuses to conduct a self-evaluation, any interested person can file a complaint asking the appropriate federal agency to compel compliance.

Internal Grievance Procedure

The Departments of Education and of Health and Human Services require recipients with fifteen or more employees to adopt grievance procedures for complaints alleging discrimination under Section 504. Such recipients must also designate at least one person to coordinate Section 504 compliance. The grievance procedure must incorporate appropriate due process standards and provide for "prompt and equitable" resolution of complaints.[30] Complaint procedures need not be established for applicants seeking employment or admission to postsecondary institutions.

A grievance procedure can be a useful, inexpensive mechanism to resolve simple complaints, especially those stemming from ignorance or misunderstandings about handicaps and Section 504 obligations. Correspondence, memoranda, and other documents generated in grievance proceedings can be used later as evidence of the recipient's discriminatory attitudes or policies. Because the grievance procedure is set up and operated by the recipient itself, though, it will usually be ineffective to resolve major or contested complaints.

Complaint to the Federal Agency

A handicapped person, or other interested person who believes that a recipient of federal financial assistance has violated Section 504, can file a complaint with the federal agency that provided the financial assistance. Complaints against recipients of funding from agencies of the Departments of Education or of Health and Human Services should be filed with that agency's regional Office for Civil Rights. The appropriate regional office is that region in which the recipient is located.

Filing Complaints

Complaints must be filed within 180 days of the alleged discriminatory act. For example, if a deaf person went to a hospital on February 1st, and did not get an interpreter, the person must send a complaint to HHS by August 1st. If he or she waits longer than that, the department will not be required to do anything about the complaint. However, the time for filing can be extended at the discretion of the department. Many discriminatory acts are continuous;

they represent a general policy or course of conduct. When this is the case, the 180-day limit is not a problem. If there is any doubt whether the time period has elapsed, the complainant should try to use the program or service again—re-apply for benefits or employment, or renew the request for auxiliary aids—so there will be no question that the discriminatory act took place within the time limits.

The complaint can be a simple letter that merely notifies the federal agency of an alleged discriminatory act. However, it will have more impact if it sets out all of the important facts of the discrimination and fully identifies the parts of the Section 504 regulation that have been violated.

The complaint should include the following information:

1. The name, address, and telephone number of the person lodging the complaint ("complainant"), and any special instructions for telephoning a deaf complainant;
2. The name, address, and telephone number of complainant's attorney or other representative, if any;
3. A statement that the complainant is a "qualified handicapped person" under Section 504;
4. The name, address, and telephone number of the program or facility that discriminated and a statement that this program receives financial assistance from the federal agency;
5. A complete description of the discriminatory acts, in chronological order; (The complaint should be as specific as possible about the dates, places, names, and titles of the people involved. The complainant should also explain why the conduct was discriminatory and how the complainant was qualified for the job, benefit, service, or program.)
6. A description of any attempts to complain about the discrimination and the organization's response;
7. Any other information or documents that help explain the discrimination and describe what happened;
8. A list of witnesses, including names, addresses, titles, and telephone numbers; and

9. If possible, an analysis of the parts of the Section 504 regulation that have been violated.

Any relevant documents should be photocopied and attached to the complaint. Do not send original documents. Any attached documents should be numbered and clearly identified by number in the text of the complaint.

Agency Investigation

The federal agency will then investigate to determine whether there has been a violation of Section 504. Agency investigators should interview the complainant, representatives of the program, and other relevant witnesses. The complainant is not a formal "party" to the investigation. The complainant should try to be actively involved in the investigation, however, to make sure that the federal investigator has contacted important witnesses and is familiar with the issues raised by the complaint. This is particularly important in Section 504 complaints involving deafness. Because few investigators are knowledgeable about deafness and the types of auxiliary aids or reasonable accommodations that may be necessary to overcome communication barriers, the investigator may need to meet with experts or other people who can provide relevant information.

If the federal agency finds that a recipient has violated Section 504, it will notify the complainant and the recipient in writing. It will then try to negotiate with the recipient to provide the appropriate relief. The agency can require the recipient to take necessary remedial action to overcome effects of the discrimination.[31] Remedial action can include reinstatement of employees. The agency can also require a remedial action plan that shows what steps the recipient will take within a specific time period to come into compliance. The plan requires the recipient to document its efforts. If the recipient fails to take the required corrective steps, or if negotiations do not result in a satisfactory resolution, the federal agency will then institute enforcement proceedings to terminate federal financial assistance to the recipient.

Judicial Enforcement

A person has the right to bypass Section 504 agency complaint procedures by bringing a lawsuit in federal court. Investigations by federal agencies can take a long time; by the time they are finished, it may be too late to help the handicapped person. A lawsuit in federal court can often provide a quicker and more effective remedy; and, if the person wins, attorney's fees and other court costs can be awarded. A deaf woman who was about to have a baby found out that her hospital would not allow an interpreter in the delivery room. She could not wait for HEW to investigate her complaint, so she filed a lawsuit in federal court and got immediate help. Federal injunctions have also been upheld in cases involving college students needing classroom interpreters on short notice.

Each of these methods to enforce Section 504 should be reviewed carefully to determine which will be most effective in a particular case.

NOTES

1. 29 *United States Code* §791
2. 29 U.S.C. §792
3. 29 U.S.C. §793
4. 29 U.S.C. §794
5. Id.
6. Executive Order No. 11,914 (1976), printed in 41 *Federal Register* 17,871, April 28, 1976.
7. 45 *Code of Federal Regulations* §84
8. 45 C.F.R. §84.3(h)
9. 5 U.S.C. §552
10. 45 C.F.R. §84.2
11. Civil Rights Restoration Act of 1987, P.L. 100-259, 29 U.S.C. 794(b)
12. 45 C.F.R. §84.3(j)
13. 45 C.F.R. §84.3(k)
14. 45 C.F.R. §84.4(b)(1)(i)
15. 45 C.F.R. §84.4(b)(1)(ii and iii)

16. 45 C.F.R. §84.4(b)(2)
17. 42 Fed. Reg. 22,676 (1977)
18. 45 C.F.R. §84.4(b)(3)
19. 42 Fed. Reg. 22,687 (1977)
20. 28 C.F.R. §42.503(e)
21. 28 C.F.R. §42.503(f)
22. 28 C.F.R. §35.104
23. 45 C.F.R. §84.22(a)
24. 45 C.F.R. §84.22(b)
25. 45 Fed. Reg. 25,394 (1980)
26. 45 C.F.R. §84.22(f)
27. 28 C.F.R. §41.5
28. 28 C.F.R. §41.5(b)(2)
29. 45 C.F.R. §84.6(c)
30. 45 C.F.R. §84.7
31. 45 C.F.R. §84.6(a)(1)

Public School Education

In these days, it is doubtful that any child may reasonably be expected to succeed in life if he is denied the opportunity of an education. Such an opportunity, where the state has undertaken to provide it, is a right which must be made available to all on equal terms.

Brown v. Board of Education[1]

The *Brown* case was decided in 1954, but many handicapped children are still denied their right to equal educational opportunity. In 1975 Congress found that more than half of this nation's eight million handicapped children were not receiving appropriate educational services, and one million were excluded from the public school system entirely.[2] Congress has enacted several laws, discussed in this chapter, that guarantee handicapped children the right to qualified teachers, accessible classrooms, and appropriate materials and programs.

Section 504 of the Rehabilitation Act of 1973 applies, among other things, to school systems and educational agencies that receive federal financial assistance. Like all other institutions that receive federal money, schools are prohibited from discriminating against handicapped people. Their programs must be accessible to and usable by handicapped people. In the Department of Education's Section 504 regulation, public elementary and secondary

---

Parts of this chapter and chapters five, six, eight, and ten are adapted from S. DuBow and S. Geer, "Communications Barriers." In P. Hearne, ed., *Legal Advocacy for the Handicapped: A Legal Services Practical Manual* (Washington, D.C.: Legal Services Corp., 1981), chapter 3. Used by permission of the publisher.

---

schools are required to provide a "free, appropriate public education" to qualified handicapped children, regardless of the nature of their handicap.[3]

This means that, if the local school system does not have appropriate teachers or programs to educate a child, it must send the child to another school that does, paying the child's tuition if the school is private. The school system cannot make the child's parents pay for any of the special services the child needs. If the school system refuses to provide an appropriate education to a handicapped child, ED can cut off federal funds.

PUBLIC LAW 94-142

Congress passed another law in 1975 that is more specific about the education of handicapped children. This law is Public Law 94-142, the Education for All Handicapped Children Act; in 1990, this act was renamed the Individuals with Disabilities Education Act.[4] It is similar to Section 504 in that it requires public school systems to give handicapped children a free, appropriate public education. But this law is more comprehensive than the education provisions of Section 504. It provides the states with money for special education and imposes clear procedural and substantive requirements on how that special education should be provided. Regulations implementing PL 94-142 were adopted in 1977.

The law and its regulations are intended to fulfill four major purposes:

1. to ensure that all handicapped children have available to them a free, appropriate public education which emphasizes special education and related services designed to meet their unique needs;
2. to ensure that the rights of handicapped children and their parents or guardians are protected;
3. to help states and localities pay for the education of all handicapped children;

4. to ensure and assess the effectiveness of the educational programs.[5]

The rest of this chapter will discuss the specific requirements of PL 94-142 as they relate to the education of deaf children and to some of the parallel requirements of Section 504. In addition to these two federal laws, most states have adopted their own laws or regulations to go along with the PL 94-142 requirements. They usually give handicapped children similar educational rights under state law and establish procedures for getting special education services that meet the standards of PL 94-142.

The handicapped children protected by PL 94-142 are defined in very specific terms. The law covers children who need special education and related services because of their handicaps. The list includes children who are mentally retarded, hard of hearing, deaf, speech-impaired, visually handicapped, seriously emotionally disturbed, orthopedically impaired, deaf-blind, multihandicapped, or who have other health impairments and specific learning disabilities.

Under PL 94-142

- "Deaf" means a hearing impairment that is so severe that the child is impaired in processing linguistic information through hearing, with or without amplification, which adversely affects educational performance.
- "Deaf-blind" means concomitant hearing and visual impairments, the combination of which causes such severe communication and other developmental and educational problems that they cannot be accommodated in special education programs solely for deaf or blind children.
- "Hard of hearing" means a hearing impairment, permanent or fluctuating, which adversely affects a child's educational performance but which is not included under the definition of "deaf" in this section.[6]

Appropriate Education

The heart of the law is the guaranteed right of every child to a free, appropriate education. Under PL 94-142 and Section 504, every handicapped child has a right to (1) specially designed instruction to meet his or her unique needs and (2) related services that may be necessary to help the child benefit from the special program. Moreover, this education must take place in the least restrictive environment. Public Law 94-142 requires states to ensure that, to the maximum extent possible, handicapped children are educated with children who are not handicapped. Special classes and separate school placements are appropriate only when the handicap is of such a nature or severity that placement in regular classes with the use of supplementary aids and services will not meet the educational needs of that child satisfactorily. The physical integration of handicapped and nonhandicapped children in school classrooms is called "mainstreaming."*

Mainstreaming can reduce the stigma and isolation for many handicapped children, but it is not always appropriate for deaf children. Without substantial support systems and services, the assignment into a classroom of hearing children constitutes a more socially and educationally restrictive environment than a setting in which the students and teachers have a shared language. The individual child's specific needs must govern any decision about his or her program.

THE INDIVIDUALIZED EDUCATION PROGRAM

Under PL 94-142 a school system must devise an appropriate Individualized Education Program (IEP) for each handicapped child. The IEP is a written report that identifies and assesses the child's disability, establishes long- and short-term learning goals, and states which services

---

*See Appendix A for a reference list of publications on deafness and PL 94-142, including a special section on publications that deal with mainstreaming.

the school must provide to help the child achieve them. Special education and related services are then provided in accordance with the terms of the IEP.

A school violates PL 94-142 if it draws up an IEP and merely presents it to parents for their consent. Parents work with school officials to develop it. The meetings where this work is done can also include the child's current teacher, a representative of the school system who is qualified to provide or supervise the special services, the child (where appropriate) and other people at the discretion of the parents or the school.[7] Parents may ask professional and legal experts to attend the meeting. If the parents are deaf, the law specifically requires that the school system provide an interpreter so they can participate fully in the meeting. Before the IEP meeting, the parents should exercise their right to review, without cost to them, their child's school records to make sure that the information is accurate and complete.

Public Law 94-142 says that parents must be involved in the identification, evaluation, and placement decisions involving handicapped children and that no child can be placed in a special education program without parental consent. The law requires that parents be fully informed about placement and educational decisions affecting a child and consent to the initial programs and later changes in placement.[8]

The IEP must include:

1. A statement of the child's present levels of educational performance.
2. A statement of annual goals, including short-term instructional objectives.
3. A statement of the specific special education and related services to be provided to the child, and the extent to which the child will be able to participate in regular educational programs.
4. The projected dates for initiation of services and anticipated duration of the services.
5. Appropriate objective criteria and evaluation procedures and schedules for determining, on at least an annual basis, whether the short-term instructional objectives are being achieved.[9]

The goals and objectives that are written into the IEP are not limited to academic performance. The goals should relate to social, psychomotor, communication, and emotional needs as well as to conventional academic curriculum goals.

The IEP is the critical mechanism whereby parents may make certain that their child receives an appropriate education. The school is legally required to provide the services that are written into the IEP. Parents should be certain that it includes every special service that the child needs. They should not sign an IEP that does not specify in great detail the services they believe the child needs in order to benefit from a special education. Parents who disagree with the proposed service plan, have any complaints, or are unconvinced that the school has the necessary resources should not sign the IEP. They instead should initiate due process procedures (discussed later).

Parents should ask for and keep a copy of their child's IEP so they can remember what was agreed upon and hold the school to its promises. If they later have to go to court to obtain the services, the IEP will be the primary item of evidence.

The IEP must be worded to ensure the deaf child's access to communication in the classroom. Some hearing-impaired children benefit from having supplementary hearing devices that range from conventional hearing aids to specialized auditory training devices and amplification equipment. Besides these, a child may need special services to increase use of residual hearing. These services should be specified in the IEP and provided as part of the child's program.

For example, control of background noise may be essential if a child is to receive the full benefit of a hearing aid. If so, this need should be identified so the school can take appropriate steps to improve acoustics. Improved lighting may be necessary to ensure that information presented visually is clear and understandable. Speech therapy, auditory training, and media support services (such as captioned TV and films) are other related services that a deaf child might need; if so, these services should be written into the IEP.

Public Law 94-142 specifically mentions these related services: transportation, speech pathology, audiology, psychological services, physical and occupational therapy, recreation, counseling services, and medical services for diagnostic or evaluation purposes.

Supreme Court Decisions

In June 1982 the U.S. Supreme Court decided its first case involving PL 94-142. The case was *Hendrick Hudson School District v. Rowley*.[10] Lower courts had ruled that Amy Rowley, a mainstreamed elementary school student, required a sign language interpreter to make classroom instruction fully accessible. The Supreme Court affirmed the right of all handicapped children to receive personalized instruction and the support services they need to benefit from their educational program. In Rowley's particular case, however, the Court found that she did not need an interpreter because she was doing well in school without one. She was receiving sufficient other support services, said the Court, to enable her to benefit from her education (e.g., a phonic ear listening device and a personal tutor).

This does not mean that other deaf children will be unable to get interpreter services or total communication programs. It merely means they must show that they cannot benefit from their education without such a service. Amy's lipreading skills, residual hearing, and high intelligence made her a special case.

A majority of the Court found that Congress did not intend to give handicapped children a right to "strict equality of opportunity or services" because that would require impossible measurements and comparisons. But PL 94-142 does require access to a free, appropriate public education for handicapped children that is "meaningful." The Court held that a state ". . . satisfies this requirement by providing personalized instruction with sufficient supportive services to permit the child to benefit educationally from that instruction."

The Court upheld the major purposes of PL 94-142 as outlined on pages 68–69. The IEP and the due process hearing for parents were not changed. They remain at the heart of the law and continue to give parents the opportunity to prove that their child needs a particular service or program.

Another Supreme Court decision in 1984 supported a child's right to related services necessary for her "meaningful access" to education. In *Irving Independent School District v. Tatro*, 104 S.Ct. 3371 (1984), the Court held that a school district must provide a child who has spina bifida with catheterization so that she can remain at school during the day.

In 1985, the Court held that public schools must reimburse parents for the costs of a private school tuition when a court finally decides that their child should have been placed in that private school. *Town of Burlington v. Massachusetts Department of Education*, 105 S.Ct. 1996 (1985). These unanimous Supreme Court decisions will also help hearing-impaired children and their parents. They show the Court's intention to uphold the Individuals with Disabilities Education Act and to require necessary services for handicapped students.

Writing the IEP

In the case of deaf children, the statutory mandate of a free and appropriate public education poses unusual and controversial problems that affect the writing of the IEP. An emotional and sometimes bitter historical debate exists concerning the best methods for teaching deaf children. Many professionals are firm proponents of one method or another, which complicates the task of a parent or attorney seeking expert guidance in formulating a child's IEP.

In addition to the four primary methods of instruction (see box), "total communication" has received wide atten-

Methods of Instruction

Four primary methods of instruction currently used in the United States are described by D. F. Moores:

1. **Oral method.** In this system, also called the oral-aural method, children receive input through speechreading (lipreading) and amplification of sound, and they express themselves through speech. Gestures and signs are prohibited.

2. **Auditory method.** This approach, as opposed to the oral, is basically unsensory. It concentrates on developing listening skills in children, who are expected to rely primarily on hearing. Early reading and writing are discouraged, as is a dependence on speechreading or signs. Although this method was developed for children with moderate hearing losses, some attempts have been made to use it with profoundly impaired children.

3. **Rochester method.** This is a combination of the oral method plus fingerspelling. Children receive information through speechreading, amplification, and fingerspelling, and they express themselves through speech and fingerspelling. Reading and writing usually receive great emphasis. The proficient teacher spells every letter of every word in coordination with speech and can present at the rate of approximately one hundred words per minute. The system of neo-oralism developed in the Soviet Union also utilizes speech and fingerspelling.

4. **Simultaneous method.** This is a combination of the oral method plus signs and fingerspelling. The children receive input through speechreading, amplification, signs, and fingerspelling. They express themselves in speech, signs, and fingerspelling. Signs are differentiated from fingerspelling in that they may represent complete ideas or words rather than standing for individual letters of the English alphabet.[11]

tion in recent years. Perhaps the best definition of the term comes from the Conference of Executives of American Schools for the Deaf: "Total communication is a philosophy incorporating appropriate aural, manual, and oral modes of communication in order to ensure effective communication with and among hearing-impaired persons."[12]

Appropriate Language Medium

Any consideration of educational methods using manual components is complicated by the existence of sign language dialects and by the number of different possible systems for using manual language with children in a learning setting. "Sign language" is a continuum of language systems that can be differentiated by the types of visual components (signs, fingerspelling, body movement, and facial expression) used and by the degree to which a particular system parallels formal English syntax and vocabulary.

American Sign Language (ASL) is linguistically independent of English. However, a number of other systems used in schools are closely related to English. They have been devised to "make English visible" by providing word-by-word translation of English through use of signs and fingerspelling, with additional signs to represent word endings and other grammatical forms. Cued speech is another method that has been introduced in some school systems in recent years. The method is not a language but a system of specific handshapes placed at specific locations around the head; the combination of handshapes and locations represent the phonemes of English. The child lipreads while simultaneously reading the manual cues.

In determining the proper educational program for a hearing-impaired child and in writing the IEP, the critical first step is to identify the language medium that is appropriate for that child. What is best varies from child to child, depending on his or her native language, the amount and type of residual hearing (if any), the level of the child's communication skills, his or her exposure to manual communication methods, age of onset of deafness, and other conditions. What is found to be appropriate should be spelled out in the IEP.

Selecting the proper communication medium is important because it makes instruction possible and meaningful. All educators of deaf children are concerned with maximizing the child's speaking and understanding of the English language. A related but more immediate goal is to make what happens in the classroom accessible to that child. With some children, this might mean providing only a hearing aid; other children will require both an aid and a sign language interpreter; and still others will need a special teacher and a range of support services. The IEP should spell out the individual's requirements.

Experienced Professionals

Childhood deafness is a low-incidence disability. Most school systems have relatively few deaf children in each age group, a factor that increases the difficulty of providing properly trained teachers and highly specialized, related services to ensure an appropriate education in mainstream classes.

A 1976 position paper of the International Association of Parents of the Deaf (now the American Society for Deaf Children) noted:

> Currently, many local and public schools lack qualified diagnostic staff for making the placement, lack supportive services, lack trained personnel, lack necessary amplification equipment and a desirable visual environment, lack an understanding of total communication which may be essential for communication with students, and in many cases, lack financial resources required for the education of deaf children and lack commitment.[13]

School systems are required by law to evaluate children for hearing loss, to create special programs to prevent hearing loss, and to provide counseling and guidance to students, parents, and teachers. They are responsible for

determining a child's need for amplification, for selecting
and fitting an appropriate aid, and for evaluating the
effectiveness of the amplification.[14] These responsibilities
can overwhelm teachers and administrators who lack
special training. Opportunities for such training must be
made available to school staff so they may become more
knowledgeable about deafness and other disabilities, the
range of possible solutions and accommodations, and how
they may best meet their responsibilities under the law.
In-service training, special certification, and sign language training may be appropriate.

PROCEDURAL SAFEGUARDS

Both Section 504 and PL 94-142 provide procedural safeguards by which parents can be assured of both their own

participation in the decision-making process and an appropriate education for their child.

A school system must give written notice to parents when it wishes to initiate or change the identification, evaluation, or placement of a handicapped child.[15] The notice must describe procedural protections, the action that the school system proposes or refuses to take, and its reasons. The notice must also describe any options the school system considered and explain why those options were rejected. Each evaluation procedure, test, record, report, or other relevant factor the school system used as a basis for the proposal or refusal must be described in the notice.

The notice must be written in language understandable to the general public and provided in the native language of the parent or any other possible form of communication used by the parent. If the native language or form of communication is not a written language, the school system has to translate the notice and ensure that the parent understands it.[16] The notice must be translated and explained to deaf parents by a qualified sign language interpreter.

If the parents do not accept the school system's evaluation and proposed placement or program, or if they are not confident that the school system has the resources to provide an appropriate education, they can request a due process hearing.* They simply notify the school officials that they are dissatisfied, state their reasons, and ask for a hearing. The notification should but does not have to be in writing. The hearing and a final decision must be completed within forty-five days of the request.

The due process hearing is intended to be an informal dispute–resolution process during which both the parents and the school can present their grievances to a neutral hearing officer. Either the parents or the school can request a hearing. A neutral hearing officer is appointed

---

*See Appendix B for sample letters requesting any of the following: an evaluation of a child's education program, a child's school records, a due process hearing, or a state review.

according to procedures established by the state. The hearing officer may not be an employee of the agency or unit involved in the education or care of the child and cannot have any personal or professional interest that would impair his or her objectivity in the hearing. Public agencies must keep a list of hearing officers and their qualifications.

Preparation for the Hearing

There are several steps to be taken in preparation for the hearing. One essential step is to find experts in education who can testify in support of the parents' position that the placement is inappropriate. The expert should visit the proposed and current placements before the hearing in order to testify whether the proposed placement can meet the specific needs of that individual child. The parents themselves should visit the proposed placement and see how the IEP could be implemented with the school's resources.

The parents also should examine all school records relevant to their child's placement. Under PL 94-142, the school system must comply with any reasonable request by the parents to inspect and receive an explanation of their child's records before any hearing. If the parents believe that information in the file is incorrect, they can request amendment of the record. If the parents disagree with the educational evaluation of their child, they have the right to an independent evaluation; the school system is required to take this evaluation into account in deciding the child's placement. Well before the hearing date, the parents should request a list of witnesses who will be testifying for the school.

Parents have the right to request attendance of their child's proposed classroom teacher, and they should exercise that right. It is essential that the hearing officer be made aware of the teacher's qualifications and that the parents have an opportunity to question how the teacher hopes to implement the individual educational plan for

their child. The parents should also request the attendance of teachers from any alternative placement the
parents may wish to propose; these teachers can testify as
to how they would meet the individual needs of the child.

The key issue at the hearing is whether the proposed
placement is appropriate to meet the individual needs of
that disabled child. At the hearing, the parents can have a
lawyer and can call witnesses who are experts in educating disabled children. They also have the right to present
evidence and to confront and cross-examine any of the
witnesses.

Parents can obtain a written or electronic verbatim
record of the hearing, which is important in an appeal.
The hearing officer must provide written findings of fact
for his/her decision. Until a decision is rendered, the child
must remain in the present educational placement unless
the school and the parents agree otherwise. If, however,
the complaint involves application for initial admission to
public school, the child must be placed in the public school
program until completion of all proceedings.

Decisions and Appeals

The hearing officer has the authority to determine the
appropriate placement for the child and is not restricted to
merely accepting or rejecting the school's program. The
hearing officer can order services that are necessary to
provide a free, appropriate education for the child. The
decision of the hearing officer is final and must be obeyed
by the school system, unless it is appealed to the state
department of education or the courts.

If an appeal is made to the state education agency, the
agency must conduct an impartial review of the decision.
The official who conducts the review must examine the
entire hearing record, ensure that the procedures at the
hearing were consistent with the due process requirements
of the law, seek additional evidence if necessary, afford the
parties an opportunity for oral or written argument or
both, make an independent decision on completion of the

review, and give a copy of written findings and the decision to the parties.

The parents may file a civil lawsuit in state or federal court to challenge the decision of the state agency. Complaints to the federal Department of Education's Office for Civil Rights or the Bureau for Education of the Handicapped may be appropriate if there are systematic violations of Section 504 or PL 94-142 by a school system. If the school system fails to comply with the laws, the federal agency can order the termination of federal funds for the entire system.

School Activities

Public Law 94-142 applies only to deaf and handicapped school children, but some school activities are open to adults as well as to children. Because most school systems receive federal financial assistance, they must obey Section 504 in all their programs. Deaf people must be able to use the programs of the school, even if the deaf person is not a student at that school. For example, many school systems offer continuing education classes for adults or hobby classes that take place in the schools during evenings and weekends. If these programs receive or benefit from federal financial assistance, they must be open and

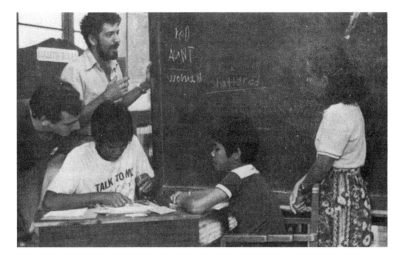

accessible to deaf people, and the school should provide interpreters for the deaf students to enable them to participate in the classes.

Schools also should provide interpreters for deaf parents who need them in order to participate in parent-teacher conferences and other school activities involving parents. The provision should be made regardless of whether the child of the deaf parents is also deaf.

NOTES

1. 375 U.S. 438 at 493 (1954)
2. 20 *United States Code* §1401
3. 45 *Code of Federal Regulations* §84.33(a)
4. 20 U.S.C. §1401 *et seq.*
5. 34 C.F.R. §300.1
6. 34 C.F.R. §300.5(b)
7. 34 C.F.R. §300.343, 300.344(a)
8. 34 C.F.R. §300.345
9. 34 C.F.R. §300.346
10. 102 S. Ct. 3034 (1982)
11. D. F. Moores, *Educating the Deaf: Psychology, Principles, and Practices,* 2d ed. (Boston: Houghton Mifflin, 1982), p. 9. Used by permission of the publisher.
12. Quoted in Mervin D. Garretson, "Total Communication," in Robert D. Frisina, ed., *A Bicentennial Monograph on Hearing-Impairment: Trends in the U.S.A.* (Washington, D.C.: Alexander Graham Bell Association for the Deaf, 1976), p. 91.
13. International Association of Parents of the Deaf, October 1976 position statement.
14. 34 C.F.R. §300.303
15. 45 C.F.R. §84.36
16. 34 C.F.R. §300.505(b)(1)

Postsecondary Education

The Department of Education's regulations for Section 504 help make postsecondary education accessible to disabled people. Basically, the regulation prohibits those institutions which receive federal money, including vocational and commercial schools, from discriminating against disabled people in recruitment, admissions, and programs. To accommodate a disabled person, the institution is not obligated to change substantially the requirements of its academic program; it must, however, afford equal opportunity for the person to benefit from the program, without segregation from the other students or limits on participation. Auxiliary aids are mandated by the regulations, and methods of evaluation are required to measure the student's actual achievement and not his or her ability to take tests.

RECRUITMENT AND ADMISSIONS

Educational institutions may neither refuse to admit disabled applicants because of their handicap nor subject them to any form of discrimination in admission or recruitment procedures.[1] If the college requires pre-admission interviews of its applicants, deaf applicants must be interviewed too, with interpreters provided. If the college has tours or orientation meetings, the deaf applicant must be able to participate with an interpreter present. If a college sends promotional information or makes recruitment visits to area high schools, then it must do the

---

same for area deaf schools. The institution cannot place a limit or quota on the number or proportion of disabled students who may be admitted.

In addition, the ED regulation prohibits colleges and universities from making pre-admission inquiries about handicaps, except in two situations: (a) when the school is taking remedial action to overcome the effects of past discrimination, or (b) when it is taking voluntary action to overcome the effects of conditions that limited the participation of disabled persons in the school's programs in the past. In either of these circumstances, the school must clearly state that the information sought is intended for use only in connection with remedial or voluntary action. After the student is admitted, the school can make confidential inquiries about handicaps that may require some accommodation.

The Supreme Court has decided a case concerning pre-admission inquiries about a person's handicap. In *Southeastern Community College v. Davis* (discussed later in more detail), the Court held that a nursing school could require "reasonable physical qualifications for admission to a clinical training program" and reject a student whose handicap would require substantial modifications of a program.[2] For other kinds of academic programs, however, the section of the Department of Education regulation concerning pre-admission inquiries was left intact. Except for professional clinical programs, such as the nursing program in the *Davis* case, educational institutions are still prohibited from asking about or considering physical handicap in the admission process.

Educational institutions must ensure that admissions tests are selected and administered so that the test results accurately reflect the applicant's actual aptitude or achievement level and not the effects of his or her hearing impairment.[3] For example, oral instructions should be translated into sign language or put into writing. Oral examinations should be conducted with a qualified sign language interpreter or other appropriate aid. If a test is designed to measure aptitude for or achievement in some area other than English language skills, then the test should be modified for the deaf applicant

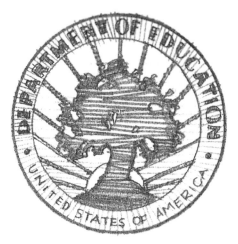

who does not have standard English skills. More time might be provided or another test, less reliant on English competence, might be used.

TREATMENT OF STUDENTS

Disabled students at federally funded colleges must be treated equally with nondisabled students. Programs must be conducted in an integrated setting. Separate facilities for disabled students are not permitted.[4] Recipient institutions must also ensure that other programs in which its disabled students participate do not discriminate. Examples of other programs are internships, clinical placement programs, student teaching assignments, or coursework at other schools in a consortium. The recipient institution may not continue its relationships with any program that in any way discriminates against its disabled students.[5]

Colleges and universities must make adjustments to those requirements that discriminate against a disabled student.[6] For example, a deaf student should be allowed to substitute a music history or art appreciation course for a required course in music appreciation. A college might permit a qualified deaf student seeking teacher certification to do an internship teaching a class of deaf students in order to meet degree requirements. The individual capabilities and needs of each student must be considered and academic adjustments made as appropriate. Since the *Davis* decision, however, a college is not required to make substantial modifications in its program in order to accommodate handicapped students. Nor is a college required to change those academic requirements that the college can prove are essential either to the program of instruction or for a particular degree.[7]

AUXILIARY AIDS

Postsecondary institutions must ensure that a handicapped student has any auxiliary aids that are necessary for him or her to fully participate in the educational program.[8] Examples of auxiliary aids in the ED regulation are taped texts, interpreters, readers in libraries, and classroom equipment adapted for use by students with manual impairments. For hearing-impaired students, auxiliary aids include any effective means of making orally-delivered material available to them. In addition to qualified interpreters, these aids might include notetakers or funds for copying the notes of a classmate, since the deaf student must constantly watch the interpreter and instructor and cannot write at the same time. Auxiliary aids might also include transcripts or interpretations of tape-recorded or filmed information and interpretation or captioning of films and videotapes.

A postsecondary educational institution can refer a student to another source for provision of auxiliary aids or try to obtain the necessary auxiliary aids from such outside sources as the local vocational rehabilitation office or charitable groups. However, the school remains responsible for seeing that the aids are received and that they in fact enable the deaf student to participate in the education program. The school has ultimate responsibility to find and pay for interpreters and other auxiliary aids.

Two federal district courts have decided since *Davis* that, for deaf college students who are vocational rehabilitation (VR) clients, the VR agency must pay for their

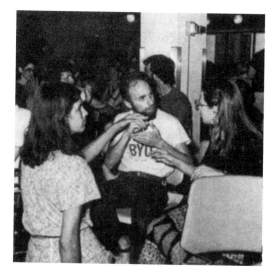

interpreters. A New Jersey district judge found that it is a
VR agency's legal duty to pay for interpreters based on
Title I of the Rehabilitation Act. An Illinois district court
judge held that when a student is a VR client, the state
VR agency has primary responsibility under Section 504
to pay for interpreter services for the student's classes.

THE TWO CASES

Ruth Ann Schornstein is a deaf VR client who attends
Kean College in New Jersey. Her plan is to earn a college
degree in social work/psychology. The New Jersey Division
of Vocational Rehabilitation Services accepted Ms. Schornstein as an eligible VR client and developed an individual
rehabilitation plan to meet her vocational goal. Although
the state agency provided tuition and books, they refused
to provide interpreter services. All groups involved agreed
she needs an interpreter to participate effectively in her
classes. The court later found that without the interpreter
these other benefits will be useless.

The National Association of the Deaf Legal Defense
Fund (NADLDF) filed a lawsuit against both the state
agency and Kean College. The federal court held that the

state agency's policy denying interpreter services to every deaf college student violates Title I of the Rehabilitation Act. Title I requires state VR agencies to provide certain rehabilitation services, including interpreters, to accepted VR clients. The federal court ruled that the state agency policy "completely contradicts the Act's requirements which ensure individualization of programs for handicapped individuals." The district court opinion was affirmed by an appellate court.[9]

The state agency argued that it could decide what services to provide. The court was not persuaded. It found that the Rehabilitation Act specifically requires VR agencies to (1) serve severely handicapped individuals, including deaf people, first; and (2) provide those services listed in the Rehabilitation Act which are necessary to assist the handicapped person to achieve his or her vocational goal.

Because the state agency accepted Schornstein as a client and also agreed that she requires interpreter services to meet her vocational goals, the court concluded that the agency is legally obligated to provide those services. Since the court decided the case solely on the basis of Title I, it did not find it necessary to rule on the obligation to provide interpreters under either Section 504 or the U.S. Constitution.

The case helps clarify the responsibility of VR agencies to provide interpreters to deaf VR clients who are attending college.

In the Illinois case, a deaf student majoring in mechanical engineering at the Illinois Institute of Technology (IIT) in Chicago, Illinois, needed an interpreter in order to understand and participate in his classes, which began in August 1979. Although he was an eligible VR client—receiving tuition, room and board, and books from the Illinois Department of Rehabilitation Services—the VR agency refused to provide him with interpreters. He was also refused these interpreter services by the college.

The court stated that when a student is a VR client, the state VR agency has primary responsibility under Section 504 to pay for interpreter services for the student's classes.

The court went on to say that if the student is not a VR client, and no other sources are available, then the college has the ultimate responsibility to pay for interpreter services.

The Illinois VR agency tried unsuccessfully to persuade the court that it was prohibited from providing interpreters to the student under Title I, if other "similar benefit" programs or community resources were available to pay for these services. The VR agency claimed that the college had a legal obligation under Section 504 to provide interpreters to deaf students. As a "similar benefit" program or community resource, the college, said the VR agency, should have to pay for interpreters. The court found that only other rehabilitation services were intended by Congress to be "similar benefit" programs. A federal appeals court affirmed the district court decision.[10]

OTHER LEGAL PRECEDENTS

The Department of Education and, before it, the Department of Health, Education, and Welfare have issued findings of violation against several colleges and universities for not providing interpreter services for deaf students.[11]

Courts have also found illegal the refusal of colleges and universities to provide interpreters.[12] In a case brought by the United States Department of Justice against the University of Alabama, the Eleventh Circuit Court of Appeals held that the university must provide qualified interpreters for deaf students, even if the students do not have financial need, and even if the students are in part-time or other special noncredit categories.[13] The court held that Congress intended colleges and universities to provide free auxiliary aids for students because without this assistance, a deaf student is denied meaningful access to an opportunity to learn.

In *Camenisch v. University of Texas,* the Fifth Circuit Court of Appeals upheld a district court's preliminary injunction requiring the University of Texas to provide an interpreter to a deaf graduate student.[14] The court also ruled that disabled people have a right to sue in federal court to enforce their Section 504 rights. Furthermore, said the court, a disabled person did not first have to exhaust administrative remedies before bringing a lawsuit.

The university appealed to the Supreme Court. After accepting the case, the Court refused to decide the Section 504 issues raised by the university.[15] Instead, it sent the case back to the district court to decide whether the university or Camenisch had to pay for the interpreter. The Court held that the university had only appealed a preliminary injunction order and had not waited for a trial on the merits. The Court found the case moot, because the terms of the preliminary injunction had been fulfilled with Camenisch being provided an interpreter and having already graduated.

The Supreme Court's first ruling on the merits of a case brought under Section 504 was the *Davis* case. The issue was whether Section 504 "forbids professional schools from imposing physical qualifications for admission to their clinical training programs."[16] In its decision, the court also sought to clarify the meaning of "qualified handicapped individual" in postsecondary education and the extent of affirmative relief required by Section 504.

Frances Davis, a licensed practical nurse with a hearing impairment, sought to enroll in a nursing school program to become a registered nurse. Despite evidence that she could perform well in this program, Southeastern Community College rejected Davis's application because of her hearing loss.

The district court upheld the college's decision, noting that in settings such as an operating room, intensive care unit, or postnatal care unit, the wearing of surgical masks would prevent Davis from reading lips to understand what was happening. The district court concluded that Davis's "handicap actually prevents her from safely performing in both her training program and her proposed profession."[17]

The Court of Appeals for the Fourth Circuit reversed the decision. In light of the HEW Section 504 regulation (issued after the district court's decision), the appeals court ruled that the college had to reconsider Davis's application without regard to her hearing disability.[18] The appeals court concluded that the district court erred in considering the nature of Davis's disability to determine whether she was "otherwise qualified" for the program rather than limiting its inquiry to her "academic and technical qualifications," which is the requirement of the regulation. Because the college said that it was not prepared to modify its nursing program to accommodate Davis's hearing disability, the appeals court sent the case back to the district court for it to consider what modifications required by the HEW regulation might accommodate Davis.

Supreme Court Decision

The Supreme Court agreed to review the case and found unanimously that the college had not violated Section 504. The Court held that:

> Nothing in the language or history of §504 reflects the intention to limit the freedom of an educational institution to require reasonable physical qualifications for admission to a clinical training program. Nor has there been any showing in this case that any action short of a substantial change in Southeastern's program would render unreasonable the qualifications it imposed.[19]

Writing for the Court, Justice Lewis Powell found that Section 504 does not compel schools to disregard an applicant's disabilities "or to make *substantial* modifications in their programs to allow disabled persons to participate" (our emphasis).[20] Instead, the Court interpreted Section 504 to mean that mere possession of a handicap is not a permissible ground for assuming an inability to function in a particular context.[21]

The Court also found that, under Section 504, an "otherwise handicapped person" is "one who is able to meet all of a program's requirements in spite of his handicap."[22] Davis was considered unable to meet those requirements since "the ability to understand speech without reliance on lipreading is necessary for patient safety during the clinical phase of the program.[23] The Court stated that, on the basis of meager evidence contained in the trial record, it was unlikely that Davis could successfully participate in the clinical program with any of the accommodations the regulation requires. The Court concluded that either close individual supervision or changing the curriculum to limit her participation to academic classes exceeded the "modification" required by the regulation.

The Court noted, however, that continuing some requirements may wrongly exclude qualified disabled people from participating in programs:

> Thus situations may arise where a refusal to modify an existing program might become unreasonable and discriminatory. Identification of these instances where a refusal to accommodate the needs of a disabled person amounts to discrimination against the handicapped continues to be an important responsibility of HEW.[24]

Section 504 Upheld

A significant step forward is the Supreme Court's 1985 opinion in *Alexander v. Choate*.[25] This case makes clear that Section 504 is a major civil rights statute with teeth and not a hollow promise.

In *Choate*, the Supreme Court decided that Section 504 requires recipients of federal funding to make reasonable accommodation "to assure meaningful access" to their programs. Support for its view was found in the federal regulations requiring reasonable accommodation in employment, buildings, and colleges and universities.

Significantly, the Court also ruled that federal recipients may be guilty of discrimination when their actions have a discriminatory effect, even if there is no proof they actually intended to discriminate. Justice Marshall, writing for the Court, stated that Congress often saw discrimination against handicapped people as a result of "thoughtlessness and indifference." The Court pointed out that it would be difficult, if not impossible, to stop discrimination if disabled persons had to prove that someone actually intended to discriminate against them.

The Court's ruling that Section 504 does not require substantial program modification has led some states and schools to oppose any modifications on grounds of undue costs. The Court's decision was limited to professional clinical programs, but some recipient institutions are using it as an excuse not to provide interpreters in purely academic programs.

The ruling also poses a danger that schools will set physical qualifications allowing only able-bodied students, or disabled students not in need of any accommodation, to be admitted; schools might argue that these are legitimate "technical" requirements for admission. Future Department of Education and court decisions will address issues of whether proposed modifications are "substantial" and whether physical qualifications are "reasonable" and "necessary."

NOTES

1. 45 *Code of Federal Regulations* §84.42
2. Southeastern Community College v. Davis, 442 U.S. 397 at 414 (1979)
3. 45 C.F.R. §84.42(b)(3)
4. 45 C.F.R. §84.43(d)
5. 45 C.F.R. §84.43(b)
6. 45 C.F.R. §84.44(a)
7. 42 *Federal Register* 22,692 (1977)
8. 45 C.F.R. §84.44(d)
9. Schornstein v. The New Jersey Division of Vocational Rehabilitation Services, 519 *Federal Supplement* 773 (D.N.J. 1981), affirmed 688 F.2d 824 (3d Cir. 1982) (mem.)
10. Jones v. Illinois Department of Rehabilitation Services, 504 F. Supp. 1244 (N.D. Ill. 1981), affirmed 689 F.2d 724 (7th Cir. 1982)
11. Manley v. Patterson College, Docket No. 79-0001 NE (Region II); Warso v. Southern Florida University, Docket No. 0419780109 (Region IV); and Arnold v. University of Alabama at Birmingham, Docket No. 04107902090 (Region IV)
12. Crawford v. University of North Carolina, 440 F. Supp. 1047 (M.D.N.C. 1977); Herbold v. Trustees of the California State Universities and Colleges, C-78-1358-RHS (N.D. Cal. 1978); and Barnes v. Converse College, 436 F. Supp. 635 (D.S.C. 1977)
13. United States v. Board of Trustees for the University of Alabama, 908 F.2d 740 (11th Cir. 1990)
14. 616 F.2d 127 (5th Cir. 1980)
15. Camenisch v. University of Texas, 451 U.S. 390 (1981)
16. Southeastern Community College v. Davis, 442 U.S. 397 at 400 (1979)
17. 424 F. Supp. 1341 at 1345
18. 574 F.2d 1158 (4th Cir., 1978)
19. 442 U.S. 397 at 414
20. 442 U.S. 397 at 405
21. Ibid.
22. 442 U.S. 397 at 406
23. 442 U.S. 397 at 407
24. 442 U.S. 397 at 412–413
25. 105 S.Ct. 712 (1985)

Health Care and
Social Services

Most communities have a complicated network of public and private agencies that provide important social and health services. Many of these agencies receive significant federal assistance and must therefore comply with Section 504 of the 1973 Rehabilitation Act. They are not allowed to discriminate against disabled people.

This does not mean that deaf people find it easy to get the services to which they are entitled. They are sometimes turned away from a program simply because no one on the staff can communicate with them or understand what they need. Deaf people often get little or no service in situations where hearing people receive good service. A hearing person may get answers to questions about food stamp eligibility, for example, or advice on how to complete an application or information on the details of a program. But the deaf person may be handed a standard written form with cursory explanations of office and program procedures. He or she may misunderstand the forms and lose benefits as a consequence. Straightening out the resulting red tape may be impossible for a deaf person. Few service agencies, health centers, hospitals, or public libraries have either TDDs or staff who know sign language, and very few employ qualified sign language interpreters.

APPLICATIONS OF SECTION 504

If a deaf person seeks service from any federally funded agency and is turned away or otherwise discouraged because of communication barriers, that agency has violated Section 504.[1] If a job training program takes a deaf person's application but, because of the deafness, does not actively seek to place that person, it has violated the law. If an agency provides information or services by telephone but does not have a TDD or access to a TDD relay service, it has violated Section 504.[2]

Health, welfare, and social service agencies with fifteen or more employees must provide appropriate "auxiliary aids" to people with impaired sensory, manual, or speaking skills when necessary to afford such people an equal opportunity to benefit from the service in question.[3] Auxiliary aids are specifically defined to include braille, taped material, interpreters, and other aids.[4] Smaller agencies may also be required to provide auxiliary aids when doing so would not impair the agency's ability to provide its normal benefits or services.[5] Interpreters can be hired for a reasonable hourly fee for occasional deaf clients. Many TDDs can be acquired for a one-time investment of a few hundred dollars. These expenses are not unduly burdensome for most agencies.

The section obligating social service agencies to ensure adequate communication with deaf people applies to many public and nonprofit agencies. For example, food stamp offices must provide an interpreter to assist in explaining the application procedure, eligibility criteria, and available benefits to deaf applicants. In addition, such offices must have a TDD so that deaf people can telephone for information, schedule appointments, or consult with caseworkers. New Jersey provided TDDs in all vocational rehabilitation offices that serve deaf clients.

While such an agency is not required to have an interpreter on staff at all times, deaf people should be able to request an interpreter if needed and to schedule an appointment when an interpreter is available. This appointment procedure is a reasonable method of providing equivalent services, even if applications are ordinarily handled on a first-come, first-served basis. The agency should also post a notice clearly explaining that interpreters are available and how to arrange an interpreted appointment.

Agency Responsibilities

Deaf people should be aware that many service agencies attempt to evade their legal responsibilities. Small agencies may try to do so by claiming that provision of auxiliary aids is beyond their financial means. They may, on the basis of their small size and budget, seek a waiver of the requirement that they provide aids. But some aids are critical for deaf people, and most of the essential aids are not excessive in cost. Deaf clients are entitled by law to aids they need. They should be provided free of charge to the deaf client. The cost is the responsibility of the agency receiving and making use of the federal money.

There are many ways an agency, health center, or hospital can make its services available and useful to deaf people. The Social Security Administration (SSA), for example, has announced a policy of providing interpreter services in all SSA proceedings and activities.* The SSA uses either an employee who is proficient in sign language or a professional sign language interpreter. No hearing-impaired person is required to use an interpreter with whom he or she is unable to communicate; the ultimate judge of an interpreter's competence is the deaf client.

The SSA has also installed a nationwide toll-free TDD. Operators at this number will relay calls to local SSA offices if necessary. The SSA also has installed TDD units in some local and regional offices. The decision to provide auxiliary aids shows wisdom and prudence. In the long run the aids will save money and staff time because communication will be effective and paperwork will be done correctly the first time.

Agency Rules and State Laws

In addition to the requirements of Section 504, most agencies have specific rules that prohibit discrimination against handicapped people in services they support.[6] Some states have adopted laws that prohibit discrimination against handicapped people by government and private social service agencies. Others have laws specifically requiring certain services for deaf people. A New Mexico law requires state health, welfare, and educational agencies to provide interpreters whenever a deaf person seeks services or needs to communicate with agency personnel. Virginia has established a special agency, the Virginia Council for the Deaf, to provide interpreters to state departments and agencies, local governments, and any other organization or individual needing them. The government agencies are required to pay for the interpreters. A few states have laws that require installation of TDDs in hospitals and public agencies such as police stations.[7]

Most states have civil rights laws prohibiting discrimination by facilities open to the public. Traditionally, these

---

*See Appendix C for a Social Security Administration memorandum outlining procedures to be used by SSA personnel in securing interpreter services.

laws have dealt only with racial or religious discrimination; more recently, some of them have been amended to prohibit discrimination based on handicap as well. In addition to commercial enterprises such as restaurants, hotels, and stores, these laws apply to service agencies that are open to the public.[8] A few states have adopted detailed laws mandating access and service for handicapped people. The Michigan Handicapper's Civil Rights Act, for example, guarantees a handicapped person full and equal utilization of public accommodations and services.

Hospital Communication Barriers

Before HEW's Section 504 regulations became effective in 1977, hearing-impaired people had virtually no right to effective communication in hospital care. When deaf people entered a hospital, they had to take what was offered them, sometimes settling for ineffective health care because they did not understand what was being said to them. Complicated medical terms were used with the hope that the deaf patient would understand them. Drugs were prescribed without any explanation of how to take them. Sometimes deaf people took these drugs with other medicines, not knowing the possible reactions. Hospital admissions procedures were rarely explained to them. If they wanted assistance from the nursing staff, they could not use the intercom to request specific kinds of services. If a pregnant woman went into the labor room, she could not bring an interpreter with her. She could not understand what her doctor wanted her to do, because the doctor's surgical mask made lipreading impossible.

A very important ingredient of health care is communication. Without communication, the patient cannot explain the symptoms of his or her illness to the medical staff. Without communication, the patient cannot comprehend the routines of preventive medicine. If all medical patients were treated like this, the general population would be outraged. Yet hearing-impaired people face these circumstances daily.

For the deaf person who has been deaf since birth (pre-lingually deaf), the English language is as comprehensible as a foreign language would be to an English-speaking person. The deaf person, having never heard English, has difficulty understanding.

The postlingually deaf person (deafened after the acquisition of language) has developed language, but he or she must compensate for that hearing loss by either matching words to lip movements or using sign language. Since lipreading is generally only 30 percent understandable, other means of communication must compensate for the remaining 70 percent. The postlingually deaf person usually can make use of signs, guesswork, or notes to grasp the remaining 70 percent.

Compounding the Stress

When a person is in a medical situation, he or she is sometimes apprehensive, nervous, confused, and in pain. When those feelings are compounded by the stress of trying to understand what a medical person is saying, the experience can be traumatic.

In the past, many hospitals have generally relied on the exchange of written notes, lipreading, or other less than satisfactory means to communicate with their deaf patients. For a deaf person with limited English skills, written English can be both ineffective and frustrating. Understanding is further hampered by unfamiliar medical terms and the need for fast, efficient communication during a medical emergency. Some hospitals attempt to get by with a staff member who has some knowledge of sign language, instead of bringing in a skilled interpreter from outside the hospital. This would be acceptable if the staff member were qualified, but this is rarely the case. More often the staff member's limited understanding of sign language creates serious misunderstandings, leading to ineffective treatment and even misdiagnosis.

Communication that is "effective" and aids that are "appropriate"—two terms used in federal regulations—are best determined by the deaf patient. A series of complaints filed with HHS, however, demonstrates how hospital personnel often assume that they are better able than the deaf patient to decide how to communicate. In one case a hospital insisted that, since they could understand the deaf patient's voice, the patient could therefore understand them, despite the patient's repeated requests for an interpreter. In another case, a hospital stated that communication by means of pen and paper was adequate and that the decision to utilize an interpreter was up to the doctor. In a third case, a hospital arbitrarily stated that it would use a typewriter instead of an interpreter to communicate with a patient. In another case involving medical care for fourteen elderly deaf patients, a hospital claimed to have an interpreter on its staff. In fact, the interpreter had studied sign language for only one semester and could not read many of the deaf patients' signs.

The importance of using a qualified sign language interpreter cannot be overemphasized. A qualified interpreter has both the expressive and receptive skills to communicate effectively with a deaf person.

Clarifying the Regulations

In 1979 the National Center for Law and the Deaf (NCLD) filed complaints with the Office for Civil Rights (OCR) in Chicago. The complaints concerned interpretation of Section 504 regulations then in effect at HEW (see box on p. 109). Investigations of eight major hospitals were conducted. The investigations pointed out the need for further clarification of the regulations. A policy on the provision of auxiliary aids for hearing-impaired patients in inpatient, outpatient, and emergency treatment settings was released by OCR to its regional offices in May 1980. The policy states:

> The Department's Section 504 Regulation requires that health care providers be prepared to offer a full variety of communication options (auxiliary aids) in order to make sure that hearing-impaired persons are provided effective health care services. Those communication options are required to have been selected with consultation by "handicapped persons or organizations representing handicapped persons" in a self-evaluation which is done by the health provider. This variety of options, which must be provided at no cost to the hearing-impaired patient, must include:
>
> - formal arrangements with interpreters who can accurately and fluently express and receive in sign language;
> - supplemental hearing devices such as amplified telephone and loop systems for meetings;
> - written communication;
> - flash cards and staff training in basic sign language expressions related to emergency treatment.
>
> The names, addresses, phone numbers, and hours of availability of interpreters must be available to the health provider's employees. Health care providers have a responsibility to make sure that hearing-impaired persons seeking treatment are given advance notice of the various communication options. Family members may be used only if they are specifi-

The HHS Section 504 regulations and guidelines seek to address the unique problems facing deaf health care patients. The regulations state:

A. General. In providing health, welfare, or other social services or benefits, a recipient may not, on the basis of handicap;

    1. Deny a qualified handicapped person these benefits or services;

    2. Afford a qualified handicapped person an opportunity to receive benefits or services that are not equal to that offered nonhandicapped persons;

    3. Provide a qualified handicapped person with benefits or services that are not as effective (as defined in § 84.4[b]) as those provided to others;

    4. Provide benefits or services in a manner that limits or has the effect of limiting the participation of qualified handicapped persons; or

    5. Provide different or separate benefits or services to handicapped persons except where necessary to provide qualified handicapped persons with benefits and services that are as effective as those provided to others.

B. Notice. A recipient that provides notice concerning benefits or services or written material concerning waivers of rights or consent to treatment shall take such steps as are necessary to ensure that qualified handicapped persons, including those with impaired sensory or speaking skills, are not denied effective notice.

C. Emergency treatment of the hearing-impaired. A recipient hospital that provides health services or benefits shall establish a procedure for effective communication with persons with impaired hearing for the purpose of providing emergency health care.

D. Auxiliary aids.

    1. A recipient to which this sub-part applies that employs fifteen or more persons shall provide appropriate auxiliary aids to persons with impaired sensory, manual, or speaking skills, where necessary to afford such persons an equal opportunity to benefit from the service in question.

    2. The Director may require recipients with fewer than fifteen employees to provide auxiliary aids where the provision of aids would not significantly impair the ability of the recipient to provide its benefits or services.

    3. For the purpose of this paragraph, auxiliary aids may include brailled and taped materials, interpreters, and other aids.[9]

cally requested by the hearing-impaired person. In addition, health care providers must have at least one teletypewriter (TDD/TTY) or an arrangement to share a TTY line with other health facilities.

In most circumstances, the deaf person is in the best position to judge which means of communication will give him/her equal opportunity in health service. The patient's judgment in choosing effective communication must be considered of utmost importance. If there is any disagreement between the health care provider and the hearing-impaired person regarding communication needs, the usual practice is to respect the hearing-impaired person's judgment. The risks are greater when there is inaccurate or incomplete communication than when the health care staff have little or no information on the patient's medical history or specific health care needs. Wrong diagnosis can be made, wrong medicine can be given, or an operation can be performed for the wrong reasons if inaccurate or incomplete information is given.

But, in emergency health care, it may not always be possible to provide a specific kind of communication for a hearing-impaired person. Health care facilities must, however, provide the most effective communication in view of the limits of time in the emergency situation.[10]

Emergency Care

The emergency health care regulations are especially important. Hospitals are required to establish a special emergency health care procedure for "effective communication" with deaf and hearing-impaired people in emergency rooms.[11] The hospitals should be able to locate qualified sign language interpreters on very short notice. They should also have TDD-equipped telephones, so that a deaf person can alert the hospital that a deaf patient is coming in and will need an interpreter or other special services. The TDD equipment also will permit the hospitalized deaf person to make calls to family or medical personnel. Emergency room staff can be trained to use and recognize basic sign language necessary for emergency care. In addition they should be trained to recognize quickly that a person is hearing impaired and to know how to find appropriate auxiliary aids.

Hospital Compliance

The following examples show how a hospital or health center may accommodate deaf patients and comply with other sections of the regulations. A hospital that ordinarily allows only one person to accompany a woman through natural childbirth may have to alter its delivery room rules to allow both the husband and an interpreter to be present during the delivery. A hospital that prohibits admission of deaf people to its psychiatric unit unless they read lips will have to change its policy to comply with Section 504 regulations. Services must be equivalent.

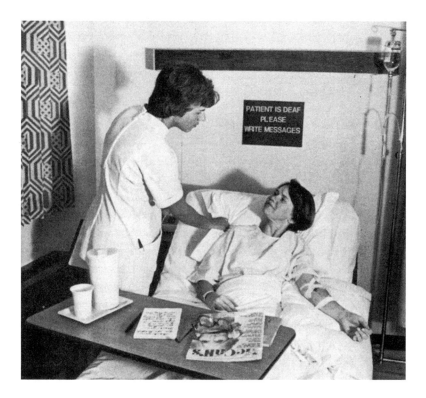

When a patient is in a hospital room, there are many devices that he or she can depend on to make the hospital stay easier. For the deaf patient, many of these devices are useless and might just as well not exist. For example, if a deaf patient presses the intercom button, the nurse at the station will answer—but they cannot communicate. After repeated attempts to contact each other, the nurse and the deaf patient may become exasperated with each other. The deaf patient assumes the nurse knows that he or she is deaf, not realizing that the nurse just came on duty and "forgot" there was a deaf patient in Room 121. The nurse may think that the patient is hitting the button by accident and decide to ignore the buzzing intercom. This typical problem can be prevented by "flagging" deaf patients' charts and intercom buttons so that all pertinent hospital personnel are aware of the special situation.

Hospitals must also provide ongoing staff training to sensitize personnel to other special needs of hearing-impaired people: adequate, glare-free lighting; control of background noise for all hearing-aid wearers; modifications to auditory fire alarm systems; changes in oral evaluation procedures; and freeing a patient's hands and arms for signing and gesturing.

Health care facilities should take special steps to make sure that deaf and blind people know about services the hospital normally offers and about any special services to which they may be entitled because of their disabilities. For example, many hospitals provide new patients some kind of orientation to the hospital and its personnel and services. All such information should be available in writing at an English level that most people can understand. It should include an easy-to-read notice about the availability of sign language interpreters, portable TDDs, and other special services for disabled people.

If a facility gives information about its services by telephone, it should ensure that deaf people can get the same information using a TDD-equipped telephone. Hospitals also should have easy-to-read notices posted in the emergency room, outpatient clinic, and all admitting areas to inform deaf people of sign language interpreter services or other assistance and how to get them. Few deaf people realize that such services are available or know how to request them. It is the hospital's responsibility to provide this information.

Hospitals often ask patients to sign a written consent to treatment or legal waivers of rights before they will treat them. Section 504 requires hospitals to take any necessary steps so that deaf and blind people understand these rights. A deaf patient should ask the hospital to have the consent papers explained in sign language. The consent and waiver papers also should be written in language that is easy for the deaf patient to understand.

GUIDELINES FOR HOSPITALS

The following guidelines were written by NCLD to help hospital administrators develop procedures for serving the needs of their deaf patients and comply with Section 504 regulations:

- A central office should be designated to supervise services to deaf patients. This office should establish a system to obtain qualified sign language and oral interpreters on short notice twenty-four hours a day.
- The unit to which a deaf patient is admitted should immediately notify the designated office when a deaf patient is admitted.
- An interpreter, if available within the hospital, should be sent to the patient immediately to consult with the patient as to the appropriate method of communication, which may include:
  —Use of a qualified sign language and/or oral interpreter;
  —Lipreading;
  —Handwritten notes;
  —Supplemental hearing devices, or any combination of the above. The interpreter should give the patient notice of the right to a qualified sign language and/or oral interpreter to be provided by the hospital without

charge to the patient. If no interpreter is available within the hospital, the patient should be given written notice of these rights.

- The interpreter assists in communication between the patient and the staff in all situations where effective communication is necessary to ensure that the deaf patient is receiving equal services and equal opportunity to participate in and to benefit from hospital services. These situations include but are not limited to:
  —Obtaining the patient's medical history;
  —Obtaining informed consent or permission for treatment;
  —Diagnosis of the ailment or injury;
  —Explanations of medical procedures to be used;
  —Treatment or surgery if the patient is conscious, or to determine if the patient is conscious;
  —Those times the patient is in intensive care or in the recovery room after surgery;
  —Emergency situations that arise;
  —Explanations of the medications prescribed, how and when they are to be taken, and possible side effects;
  —Assisting at the request of the doctor or other hospital staff; and
  —Discharge of the patient.
  Friends or relatives of a deaf patient should not be used as interpreters unless the deaf patient specifically requests that they interpret. Deaf patients, their friends, and their families should be told that a professional interpreter will be engaged where needed for effective communication.
- The deaf patient should be informed that another interpreter will be obtained if the patient is unable to communicate with a particular interpreter.
- Any written notices of rights or services and written consent forms should be written at no higher than a fifth-grade reading level. An interpreter should be provided if the deaf patient is unable to understand such written notices.

- A telecommunications device for the deaf (TDD) should be obtained and used for making appointments, giving out information, and assisting in emergency situations. Portable TDDs should be available on request for deaf inpatients. Telephone amplifiers should be provided for hearing-impaired patients. All telephones should be compatible with hearing aids equipped with a telephone switch.
- Alternative methods to auditory intercom systems, paging systems, and alarm systems should be provided for all hearing-impaired patients.
- Ongoing efforts should be made by the hospital to sensitize staff to the various special needs of deaf patients.
- Contact with local deaf people, organizations for and of the deaf, and the community agencies serving deaf people should be maintained for assistance in drawing up a list of qualified interpreters and in developing a program of hospital services that is responsive to the needs of deaf patients.

Direct Care Staff

Hospital staff can do many things to enable communication with a deaf patient, to make the patient more comfortable with the hospital environment, and thereby to serve the patient better. Common sense and basic information about deafness will help hospital staff to provide good health care.

The deaf patient is the best resource regarding the preferred mode of communication and should be consulted about this and about any problems that arise. The isolation of deaf people can be overcome to a great extent by explaining what is happening and answering any questions the patient might have.

The importance of using a qualified interpreter to ensure effective communication cannot be overemphasized. However, there may be many routine situations—such as bringing dinner or taking temperature—where an interpreter is not necessary. The following guidelines on working with deaf patients will help compensate for the absence of an interpreter. These guidelines, if implemented, will also improve the quality of care provided.

A. Make added efforts in communication to ensure that the patient understands what is happening.
1. Allow more time for every communication, not rushing through what is said. To make sure the patient understands, some thoughts should be repeated using different phrases.
2. Lip movements should not be exaggerated. Speak at a normal rate of speed and separate words.
3. Patient's arms should not be restricted; they should be free to write and sign.
4. Make cards or posters of usual questions and responses that can be pointed to quickly.
5. Keep paper and pen handy, but be sensitive to the patient's level of English language fluency and writing skills.

B. **Be sensitive to the visual environment of deaf patients by adjusting lighting and using visual rather than auditory cues and reassurances.**
   1. Use charts, pictures, and/or three-dimensional models when explaining information and procedures to deaf patients.
   2. Do not remove a deaf patient's glasses or leave a deaf patient in total darkness.
   3. Remove any bright lights in front of the deaf person when communicating; glare makes it difficult to read signs or lips.
   4. Face the patient when speaking, without covering your face or mouth.
   5. Keep facial expressions pleasant and unworried so as not to alarm the patient.

C. **Alert all staff to the presence and needs of the deaf patient and be sensitive to those needs.**
   1. "Flag" the intercom button so that workers will know the patient is deaf and requires a personal visit rather than a response over the intercom.
   2. "Flag" the patient's charts, room, and bed to alert staff to use appropriate means of communication.

D. **Inform hospital personnel of the special needs of people with hearing aids.**
   1. Allow the patient to wear the hearing aid.
   2. Don't shout at the patient.
   3. Be sure that the patient has fully understood what is said.

Training Models

Many health care providers wonder what kind of training will best prepare their staffs to meet the needs of hearing-impaired people. Specialized training is both very important and very hard to find. Not enough attention has been paid to the needs of hearing-impaired people, let alone to ways of meeting those needs. Deafness and hearing im-

pairment are largely invisible—and therefore often neglected—handicaps. They are the most common disabilities in the United States today, and they are the most
misunderstood. To help overcome this misunderstanding,
two kinds of training for health care providers are now
being conducted.

The first is a model training concept. The National
Academy at Gallaudet University has developed a training
packet for nurses on how to care for deaf patients. The
packet has been given to a variety of hospitals across the
country and features training films, slides, and lectures.
The nurses learn how to approach their deaf patients and
how to understand the individuality of each patient.
This one-session training seminar is a model project designed to initiate continuous seminars. Nurses are encouraged to keep up their training, and their hospitals are
encouraged to keep in touch with the National Academy
for further training materials and instructions.[12]

The second kind of training is local effort to educate
health care providers and the deaf community. A two-way
educational process in maternal and child health care is
being undertaken at the community level by Deafpride of
Washington, D.C. The project was established after the
mother of a young deaf child saw the problems deaf moth-
ers had in getting medical care. The project prepares deaf
women for delivery and maternal care by holding group
sessions. It conducts workshops for both health care providers and the hearing-impaired patient. The project has
TDDs at two community health clinics plus ongoing services at Howard University Hospital in the District of Columbia and Prince George's General Hospital in nearby
Maryland.[13]

These educational programs have produced a growing
awareness among both medical providers and hearing-
impaired consumers about the importance of ongoing
education about Section 504.

For deaf people to receive effective hospital care, hospital administrators must be informed of their Section 504
obligations. Hospital personnel need to be educated and

trained to meet the special needs of deaf patients. The general community needs to understand how important it is to provide quality medical care for the deaf community. And the deaf patient needs to understand his or her rights.

NOTES

1. 45 *Code of Federal Regulations* §84.52(a)
2. 45 C.F.R. §84.21(f)
3. 45 C.F.R. §84.52(d)(1)
4. 45 C.F.R. §84.52(d)(3)
5. 45 C.F.R. §84.52(d)(2)
6. In the HHS Section 504 regulation, these rules are in Subpart F, 45 C.F.R. §84.51 *et seq.* The Office of Revenue Sharing—pursuant to Section 122(a) of the State and Local Assistance Act of 1972, as amended in 31 *United States Code* §1242(a)—has invoked the HHS Section 504 regulation for recipient state and local governments.
7. E.g., see Washington Rev. Code §70-54
8. Maryland Human Relations Code Ann. §498; Maine Rev. Stat. Tit. 5 §4591
9. 45 C.F.R. §84.52
10. "Position on the Provision of Auxiliary Aids for Hearing-Impaired Patients in Inpatient, Outpatient, and Emergency Treatment Settings," memorandum from Roma J. Stewart (Director, Office for Civil Rights, Department of Health, Education, and Welfare) to regional directors, April 21, 1980.
11. 45 C.F.R. §84.52(c)
12. The National Academy, Gallaudet University, 800 Florida Ave. NE, Washington, DC 20002
13. Deafpride, Inc., 2010 Rhode Island Ave. NE, Washington, DC 20018

Mental Health

An attendant stands in the middle of the mental health unit shouting at a patient. For thirty-five years the hospital attendants have tried to communicate by yelling at him. They still do not know that he is deaf.

This man and his situation are real. He is like many deaf people in mental health facilities who suffer from misdiagnosis or maltreatment. At the same time, the needs of many other deaf people for mental health care go unmet.

Approximately 43,000 or 10 percent of the prevocationally deaf population need mental health services, but fewer than 2 percent receive them.[1] Progressive programs exist in some states and the District of Columbia, but there are few mental health facilities functioning specifically for deaf patients. Also, few regular facilities are even modestly staffed and equipped to help deaf patients, in spite of the relative ease and minimal expense with which the patients can be aided.

The primary problem is the lack of competent mental health professionals who have skill in communicating with and understanding deaf people. Even with an interpreter present, the mental health professional must be empathetic to deaf people and their culture if therapy is to be effective.

The direct and frequent result of miscommunication is misinterpretation of the patient's deafness and speechless-

This chapter is adapted from S. DuBow, "Legal Strategies to Improve Mental Health Care for Deaf People." In L. K. Stein, E. D. Mindel, and T. J. Jabaley, eds., *Deafness and Mental Health* (New York: Grune & Stratton, 1981), pp. 195–210. Used by permission of the publisher.

ness as psychopathology or retardation. A misdiagnosis usually results in improper placement, misguided treatment and case management, unjustified exclusion of the patient from hospital programs and activities, and inappropriate aftercare. The sad result is the patient's isolation, bewilderment, and even rage, all of which run counter to the purposes of the facility and its staff.

A survey of New York state psychiatric hospitals revealed that more than one-fourth of their deaf patients had been diagnosed as mentally deficient, as contrasted with only 3.7 percent of the nondeaf.[2] McCay Vernon, a psychologist noted for his work with deaf people, observes:

> It has been established that IQ is essentially normally distributed in the deaf population. Obviously gross error had been made in the fundamental but relatively easy-to-make diagnosis of mental retardation.[3]

A study of Illinois state mental hospitals found that staff in three-quarters of the facilities had no concept of which patients were deaf. One hospital with approximately 4,000 patients provided the names of 200 patients considered to be deaf; only one of them was actually deaf. On the other hand, five deaf patients, none of whose names was on the list, were found in just one unit. Many of the deaf patients thought they were the only deaf people in the hospital. The authors of the study noted:

> Obviously, if the deaf patients were not even identified as deaf, no real effort was made to treat them. No staff members or other patients could communicate with them in the language of signs. Thus, they were total isolates. In fact, in this sense, their hospitalization was actually anti-therapeutic.[4]

Misdiagnosis can result in the deaf patient being inappropriately assigned and confined to an institution for many years before the mistake is discovered. There are numerous accounts of misdiagnosis similar to that which opened this chapter. Vernon, for example, reported the case of a patient who spent thirty-five years at Idaho's state school and hospital for the mentally retarded when deafness was the patient's primary disability.

TWO CASES

Donald Lang

A celebrated and often-cited criminal case illustrates how misdiagnosis and an absence of appropriate services can affect a deaf person's life.

Donald Lang of Chicago is unable to hear, speak, read, or write. He has been accused of two gruesome rape-murders and, for more than fifteen years, has been confined to mental hospitals and jails. For equally long, Illinois courts, lawyers, and mental health officials have struggled to decide what to do with him.

When Lang was first accused of murder in 1966, he was found to be mentally and physically incompetent to stand trial, and he was committed to a mental hospital for life. Lang appealed, and the state supreme court ruled that Lang should be given a trial to determine his guilt and, if found not guilty, released.[5] By the time of the trial, however, one of the state's principal witnesses had died. The charge was dropped, and Lang was released in 1970.

In 1972, he was again charged with a similar rape-murder. Citing the Illinois Supreme Court's decision in his first case, Lang chose to stand trial and was convicted. The state supreme court reversed the conviction, ruling that the trial was constitutionally impermissible because it had been conducted without aids that would have allowed Lang to understand the nature and object of the proceedings against him, consult with his attorney, and assist in preparing his defense.[6]

The Illinois Appellate Court ruled in June 1978 that, because Lang was neither mentally ill nor retarded, the department of mental health did not have to develop a training program to make Lang fit for trial.[7] At the same time, it criticized the state's attorney's office, the mental health department, and the Illinois legislature because of the desperate need for rehabilitation capability and for change in Illinois' law and practice.

In Illinois, contrary to the laws of some other states, the courts do not have the power to take defendants unfit to stand trial and commit them to mental health departments for proper treatment. Without such changes in Illinois, Lang cannot get treatment until he is exonerated, but he cannot be exonerated until he gets treatment.

Theon Jackson

A case similar to Donald Lang's was decided by the U.S. Supreme Court.[8] Theon Jackson, an illiterate, mentally retarded deaf person with no basic communication skills, was accused of purse snatching. An Indiana court committed Jackson to a mental institution due to his inability to understand the nature of the charges against him. His commitment was to continue until his sanity could be certified to the court.

The Supreme Court reversed the state court decision, declaring that Jackson's constitutional rights were violated since he was condemned to permanent institutionalization without the necessary showing required for commitment under the state statute. If it could not justify continued confinement after six months, the state was ordered to proceed to trial or dismiss the case.

Both of these cases raise the issues of a deaf person's fitness to stand trial for a criminal offense and the applicable standard for commitment. Both Lang and Jackson were found incompetent to stand trial. The traditional test for competence is whether the defendant understands the proceedings and charges and whether he or she can consult with a lawyer and assist actively in presenting the defense.[9]

Lang and Jackson were found incompetent to stand trial, but this stemmed from an inability to communicate, not from mental illness. A finding of incompetence usually results in commitment to a mental health facility until such time as the individual becomes competent. Yet restoration of competence for Lang and Jackson was highly unlikely. In the *Jackson* case, the Supreme Court realized that the result of this procedure—permanent institutionalization—violates the constitutional rights of the defendant.

To remedy this inequity, the Supreme Court held that any incompetency commitment must be temporary and reasonably likely to be effective in restoring the defendant to competency. If there is no substantial probability that the defendant's condition is treatable, commitment either is not allowed or must be terminated if it has already taken place. The Court thus attacked the rigid interpretation of competency and commitment standards applied by the state that resulted in the deprivation of Jackson's constitutional rights.

Presumably, the law that has developed as a result of these two cases would prevent deaf people accused of crimes from being institutionalized without proper treatment and without hope of being tried for the crime charged. Yet, practical problems remain in the implementation of these two judicial decisions. The *Lang* case demonstrates the problems in developing programs to train "incompetent" individuals to improve their communication skills and participate in their criminal defense. Who is responsible for developing these programs and what they will consist of remain unanswered questions. And although the Indiana court spoke of committing Jackson for a reasonable time until competency is restored, no guidelines were provided as to how long a reasonable period of time is.

These practical problems seriously impair any protections guaranteed by the cases of Lang and Jackson. Until judicial decisions or legislation further clarify these issues and find solutions for these problems, deaf defendants, adjudged incompetent to stand trial, will continue to suffer the loss of their constitutional rights.

PROGRAMS FOR DEAF PEOPLE

Another dismaying problem that affects deaf and deaf-blind patients is the abuse sometimes inflicted on them. Unable to summon help or to identify attackers, they and their food and property are easy targets for more aggressive patients. Even in well-managed facilities, where these abuses are rare, the deaf person may find the very process of institutionalization brutal to the psyche, because he or she can understand little or nothing of what is happening in the place.

Responding to the problems, some hospitals and mental health administrations in the states and the District of Columbia have begun to develop specific programs for deaf people.[10] Examples are St. Elizabeths Hospital in Washington, D.C., and new programs in Michigan and Maryland.

Deaf people, their hearing advocates, and the state government combined efforts in Michigan to establish a Center for Deaf Treatment Services (CDTS). Under the state department of mental health, the pilot program includes a twenty-bed inpatient unit to serve hearing-impaired patients over the age of seventeen. The philosophy behind the treatment approach is that the psychological consequences of deafness are primarily responsible for the problems in these patients' personality development. The approach is a key that opens new possibilities for intervention and treatment. Patients in the deaf unit are taught sign language, which is used in all individual and group therapy.

In addition to inpatient services, CDTS staff is available to provide education, consultation, diagnostic, and evaluation services to other institutions and community mental health programs. The center plans to set up several outpatient clinics throughout the state.

Some states fund deaf units through their departments of mental health; other states channel such funding to departments of vocational rehabilitation. Some deaf units have a mix of federal and state grants to pursue their work; because such grants are temporary, though, new ones must be sought constantly.

When no leadership exists in a state mental health system or vocational rehabilitation department, or when the legislature is indifferent, then alternate points of initiating change must be found. Courts are increasingly recognizing that mental patients have legal rights, so legal action may serve to improve mental health services for deaf patients.

LEGAL ACTION

Legal action can be on behalf of an individual or a class of people. In the first, a single person seeks relief from a situation. In the second, a person who claims to represent all people similarly situated brings a suit on their behalf. Each method has been used to achieve some impressive victories.

There are two kinds of individual action: a civil damage suit and a writ of habeas corpus. A civil damage suit is used when a patient sues physicians who neglect his or her care. A famous case of this type involved Kenneth Donaldson, who was committed to a Florida state mental hospital for fifteen years without receiving treatment. In the landmark case, *O'Connor v. Donaldson,* the U.S. Supreme Court held that it is unconstitutional to confine against their wills nondangerous people who are capable of living outside the institution and who are not receiving treatment.[11]

The second kind of individual action is the writ of habeas corpus, a traditional tool for challenging conditions of confinement, whether in jail or some other institution. It is the most appropriate legal method for patients who have been misdiagnosed or committed because proper placements were not available. It can be used to challenge overly restrictive conditions or inappropriate treatment and to obtain services or placements that are more fitting.

Habeas corpus was successfully used in the District of Columbia to challenge placement of patients in excessively restrictive treatment settings. According to District of Columbia statutes, the purpose of involuntary commitment is treatment; confinement may legally restrict liberty only insofar as it is necessary to treat the patient. For example, a patient with a mild disorder cannot be locked in a maximum security ward used to house the criminally insane. Patients have a right to the form of treatment which is least restrictive.[12] Some courts have even held that a hospital has an obligation to explore alternative placements for each of its patients and to select that placement which is least restrictive.[13]

One problem with habeas corpus is the standard used in judging whether the hospital has acted improperly. The court does not require that the hospital make the best choice of treatments but only that it make a permissible and reasonable choice in light of the relevant information it possesses.[14] It is difficult, therefore, for the patient to prove that the hospital has acted unreasonably or improperly in choosing treatment. The habeas corpus process is also expensive and time-consuming. Cases are often difficult because they are litigated individually. Also, while the case is in progress, the hospital can reassign the patient or change the terms of confinement. The court can then dismiss the patient's claim of inadequate treatment because the patient's status, even if not improved, has changed.

Class Action Suits

Because of the difficulty in bringing individual suits and the limitation of the remedy only to the patient who brought the suit, class action has proved to be a more effective means of achieving institutional change. A class action suit is filed by a patient who claims to represent all people similarly situated. Because the remedy resulting from the action applies to all such people, class action litigation often results in the definition and articulation of rights of mental patients, minimum standards for care and treatment, and responsibilities and liabilities of the treating staff.

A famous class action suit, *Wyatt v. Stickney,* later called *Wyatt v. Aderholt,* resulted in the recognition and establishment of a mental patient's constitutional right to be treated and not merely held in custodial care.[15]

The court issued a far-reaching and effective decision, ruling specifically that patients involuntarily committed through noncriminal procedures to a state mental hospital have a constitutional right to receive such individual treatment as will give them an opportunity to improve their mental condition or be cured. The court decreed minimal constitutional standards for adequate treatment, including an individual treatment plan that provides a statement of the least restrictive treatment conditions necessary to achieve the purposes of commitment. Other rights were specifically recognized: the rights to a humane psychological and physical environment, privacy, dignity, and freedom from isolation. The court also established a human rights committee to investigate violations of patients' rights and to oversee implementation of the plan. It also ordered a minimum number of treatment personnel per 250 patients and other changes to ensure more humane living conditions.

The effects of this decision for deaf people are potentially great, because current laws do not ensure that a deaf person will receive anything more than an interpreter—an accommodation that most professionals providing mental health care to deaf people agree is insufficient. The one-to-one relationship between the therapist and the patient is critical in therapy. However, under the *Wyatt* decision, an individualized treatment plan for a deaf person would probably include programs such as Michigan's Center for Deaf Treatment Services (described earlier). By including training in sign language, the program would allow the patient to participate fully in therapy and to interact with staff and other deaf patients, who themselves would know or be learning sign language. The emphasis on communication skills would be a central aspect of therapy and rehabilitation, allowing the patient the opportunity for social adjustment and eventual integration into society.

Another effective legal strategy based on constitutional law is use of the "protection from harm" theory. The principle here is that confinement by the state should not cause a person's condition to deteriorate. This principle was successfully invoked to correct overcrowded conditions in New York's Willowbrook State School.[16] The court ruled that patients of a state institution have a right to protection from such inhumane treatment as would constitute cruel and unusual punishment under the Eighth Amendment. The ruling stated that treatment is impermissibly harmful not only when there is physical harm or deterioration but also when conditions that exist frustrate the full development of one's capabilities.

State Statutes

State law is often an effective basis for suit. Many states now have statutes guaranteeing a right to treatment in their institutions, a trend that began because of a highly influential legal decision in the District of Columbia, *Rouse v. Cameron*.[17] Filing a petition for habeas corpus, the patient relied on a District law to contend that he had a right to be treated, not merely confined. The law states:

> A person hospitalized in a public hospital for a mental illness shall, during his hospitalization, be entitled to medical and psychiatric care and treatment. The administrator of each public hospital shall keep records detailing all medical and psychiatric care and treatment received by a person hospitalized for a mental illness. . . .[18]

The court construed this statute as granting the patient's contention, and other state courts have ruled similarly in interpreting their laws. One advantage of this approach is that judges in state courts will probably be more inclined to enforce state laws than to declare new constitutional rights.

In the last twenty years there has been substantial movement away from treatment in large institutions and toward treatment in the community. State reforms of their commitment procedures and policies, recent court decisions setting minimum standards for patient care, a new federal emphasis on community-based care, and the demand for appropriate treatment have all accelerated the movement toward provision of mental health services in the community.[19] By 1975 three out of every four people receiving mental health care did so as outpatients, primarily in community-based settings.[20]

Another influential ruling is *Dixon v. Weinberger*.[21] A federal court for the District of Columbia held that patients in St. Elizabeths Hospital—a federally administered mental hospital and community mental health center in Washington, D.C.—have a right to treatment that specifically includes the right to be placed in facilities outside the institution once the institution determines that such a placement is appropriate. The court ruled that the United States and District of Columbia violated the District's 1964 Hospitalization of the Mentally Ill Act when they failed to place in alternative, less restrictive facilities those St. Elizabeths inpatients determined to be suitable for community placement. Less restrictive alternatives included nursing homes, foster homes, personal care homes, and halfway houses.

Right to Habilitation

Another important case involved the state of Maine.[22] A federal district court in Maine approved a consent decree that established detailed standards for the care and treatment of mentally retarded people who are placed in community settings. In the consent decree, Maine recognized that, regardless of their age and degree of retardation or other disability, people released from institutions into the community have the right to receive "habilitation." Habilitation specifically includes the right to an individualized plan of care, education, and training and to services including physical therapy, psychotherapy, speech therapy, and medical and dental attention.

The consent agreement was the first one that obligated a state to consider specifically what was required in order for deaf people to benefit from state services. These requirements included the following: (1) hearing-impaired outpatients who could not acquire speech would be taught sign language; (2) the state would provide sign language training to staff and others working with deaf citizens; (3) screenings for hearing ability would be conducted with each patient; (4) treatment and/or further evaluation would be provided by qualified speech and hearing professionals; and (5) hearing aids, when needed, would be provided and maintained in good working order. The court appointed a master to monitor implementation of the consent agreement.

The rights of mentally retarded persons were more narrowly defined, however, in a 1981 U.S. Supreme Court decision. In the case of *Pennhurst v. Halderman*,[23] the Court held that the Developmentally Disabled Assistance and Bill of Rights Act[24] does not necessarily require states to provide treatment in community settings to mentally retarded persons. The act's bill of rights states that mentally retarded individuals have the "right to appropriate treatment, services, and habilitation" in a "setting that is least restrictive of . . . personal liberty."[25] The Court held that Congress did not intend by this language to impose massive financial obligations on states.

The Court stated that Congress must make clear to the states any obligations to be imposed upon them through the receipt of federal financial assistance. This ruling reversed a lower court decision which held that the rights of mentally retarded residents of Pennhurst State School and Hospital were violated because of unsanitary, inhumane, and dangerous living conditions.

Consciousness Raising

Any future judicial construction of a right to community treatment for mental illness will have far-reaching influence on improving the noninstitutional care of deaf people. But at present, communication and attitudinal barriers, and the lack of qualified, capable staff, prevent most existing community facilities from satisfactorily meeting the mental health needs of their deaf clients. For deaf people to be released from institutions where they receive merely custodial care is no solution if all they can look forward to is inaccessible community services.

In terms of changing the way things are done, the involvement of the mental health profession will be more important than even future litigation. The profession must produce specific and practical solutions to the problems of people put into its care, and this includes deaf people. More and better training opportunities in deaf psychology, research, information dissemination, and cultural awareness are needed within the profession The raising of consciousness should occur at every level.

State Legislation

From the point of view of increasing the number and quality of good laws and achieving effective levels of resource allocation, work with the state legislatures is absolutely necessary.* Good laws have as far-reaching an impact as legal victories. Concerned people and organizations—mental health professionals, state mental health and vocational rehabilitation administrators, legislators, jurists, and disabled advocates and activists—ought to be natural allies in the effort to produce solutions that are effective, sensible, and not merely cosmetic.

Several states have set the pace. Oklahoma has a new law establishing a comprehensive mental health care program for deaf people, including inpatient and outpatient mental health services and counseling to family members of deaf patients.[26] The law requires cooperation with other state health programs and agencies. The professional staff of this statewide program are required to have experience in working with the mental health problems of hearing-impaired individuals and their families.

Georgia, Illinois, Massachusetts, Michigan, and Penn-

---

*See chapter thirteen for more information on state legislatures and state commissions. The details of how one state legislature was persuaded to establish an outpatient mental health program for deaf people is recounted in that chapter.

sylvania have recently changed their mental health laws to require individualized treatment plans.

The Georgia legislature amended its mental health law in order to elaborate the rights of patients in state mental health facilities.[27] These include the right to refuse treatment, the right to the least restrictive alternative for every patient, the right to placement in noninstitutional community facilities and programs as appropriate, and recourse to an established complaint procedure.

A 1977 amendment to the Illinois Mental Health Code specifically mandated individual treatment plans and use of sign language with any hearing-impaired patient for whom sign language is a primary mode of communication. Unfortunately, this amendment was excluded from a comprehensive reform of Illinois' mental health law in 1978; it remains a good model, though, for states to guarantee accessibility of mental health services to deaf people.[28]

The Oklahoma statute is a good model for a legislative program that directly addresses the needs of the deaf community. Deaf people should be able to receive the entire range of housing and treatment environments: community mental health centers, nursing homes, personal care homes, foster homes, and halfway houses.

Advocacy Agencies

The enactment of progressive laws and the creation of special programs are milestones in the effort to assure accessible and effective mental health care for deaf people. To get other states to change their laws and to fund necessary services will require perseverance, coordination, and follow-through from legislative activists. In states that have not addressed the needs of their deaf citizens, federal statutes are about the only effective way to achieve even the bare minimum of accommodation—the means to communicate.

It is most important, for example, that states enact laws providing independent advocacy agencies to protect the civil rights of mental patients. Congress has required the creation of these agencies in states that receive formula grants under the Developmentally Disabled Assistance and Bill of Rights Act. Specifically, the agencies have authority to "pursue legal, administrative, and other appropriate remedies" in the protection of and advocacy for the rights of people receiving the state service. The agencies are required to be independent of the state entities that provide treatment, service, or habilitation to people with developmental disabilities.

Federal Regulations

Section 504 of the 1973 Rehabilitation Act is another statute with significant impact on the states. The federal regulations to this law require mental health facilities receiving Department of Health and Human Services' funding to provide effective benefits or services in a manner that does not limit or have the effect of limiting the participation of qualified handicapped people in the program. A recipient mental health agency or facility

> that employs fifteen or more persons shall provide appropriate auxiliary aids to persons with impaired

sensory, manual, or speaking skills, where necessary to afford such persons an equal opportunity to benefit from the service in question. . . . For the purpose of this paragraph, auxiliary aids may include brailled and taped material, interpreters, and other aids for persons with impaired hearing or vision.[29]

Mental health service providers thus bear the responsibility of providing interpreters to deaf patients. Facilities that refuse to provide them risk a withholding or cutting off of their HHS funds or a private lawsuit against them. Several successful lawsuits have been brought against universities, social service agencies, and hospitals requiring them to pay for and otherwise provide interpreter services.[30]

The difficulties in effecting change through litigation cannot be ignored. The legislative process is usually less expensive and time-consuming. In either case, links of communication and understanding must be established between all who have roles to play in mental health services for deaf people: legislators, jurists, mental health workers, concerned citizens, and deaf people themselves. They must work together to find good solutions.

Successful Lawsuits

Deaf individuals have achieved victories in several recent lawsuits.

A deaf woman committed to a Maryland mental hospital received no treatment for more than twenty years. In *Doe v. Wilzack*,[31] brought on her behalf by the National Association of the Deaf Legal Defense Fund, she won individual relief and the state of Maryland agreed to establish an inpatient treatment unit for her and other deaf inpatients in state facilities.

In a similar case in Minnesota brought by the Legal Advocacy Project for Hearing Impaired Persons, the state agreed to establish comprehensive treatment programs for deaf mental health patients. A detailed settlement agreement addresses services for the four named plaintiffs as well as staffing, program services, and obligation to secure funding in state facilities for deaf patients.[32]

In a third case, a deaf child won $1,500,000 when he proved that it was medical malpractice to diagnose him as mentally retarded when he was a normal, bright, deaf child.[33]

NOTES

1. Rehabilitation Services Administration, *Third Annual Conference on Deafness, RSA Region III, Ocean City, Md.* (Washington, D.C.: U.S. Department of Health, Education, and Welfare, 1977).
2. J. D. Rainer, K. A. Altshuler, F. J. Kallmann, and W. E. Demming, *Family and Mental Health Problems in a Deaf Population* (New York: Columbia University, New York State Psychiatric Institute, Department of Medical Genetics, 1963), p. 201.
3. M. Vernon, "Techniques of Screening for Mental Illness Among Deaf Clients," *Journal of Rehabilitation of the Deaf* 2 (1969):24.
4. R. R. Grinker, *Psychiatric Diagnosis, Therapy, and Research on the Psychotic Deaf* (Washington, D.C.: U.S. Department of Health, Education, and Welfare, Social and Rehabilitation Service, 1969), p. 24.
5. People ex. rel Meyers v. Briggs, 46 Ill. 2d 281, 263 N.E. 2d 109 (1970)
6. People v. Lang, 26 Ill. App. 3d 648 (1975), 325 N.E. 2d 305 (1975)
7. People v. Lang, 62 Ill. App. 3d 688 (1978), 378 N.E. 2d 1106 (1978)
8. Jackson v. Indiana, 406 U.S. 715 (1972)
9. Dusky v. United States, 362 U.S. 402 (1960)
10. L. Robinson, "Group Psychotherapy Using Manual Communication," *Mental Hospitals* 16 (1965): 172–174; and L. Robinson, "A Program for Deaf Mental Patients," *Hospital and Community Psychiatry* 24 (1973): 40–42.
11. O'Connor v. Donaldson, 442 U.S. 563 (1975)
12. Covington v. Harris, 419 *Federal Supplement* 617 (D.C. Cir. 1969) at 623
13. In re Henry Jones, 338 F. Supp. 428 (D.D.C. 1972) at 429
14. Covington v. Harris
15. Wyatt v. Stickney, 325 F. Supp. 781 (M.D. Ala. 1970), 344 F. Supp. 373 (1972); aff'd. sub. nom. Wyatt v. Aderholt, 503 F. 2d 1305 (5th Cir. 1974)
16. New York State Association for Retarded Children, Inc. v. Carey, 393 F. Supp. 715 (E.D.N.Y. 1975) at 718
17. 373 F.2d 451 (D.C. Cir. 1967)
18. D.C. Code §21-562 (1966)
19. Community Mental Health Centers Construction Act, 42 *United States Code* §2689

20. *Preliminary Report* (Washington, D.C.: President's Commission on Mental Health, 1977), p. 8.
21. 405 F. Supp. 974 (D.D.C. 1975)
22. Wouri v. Zitnay, No. 75-80-SD (S.D. Maine, July 14, 1978)
23. Pennhurst State School and Hospital v. Halderman, 101 S. Ct. 1531 (1981)
24. 42 U.S.C. §6000
25. 42 U.S.C. §6010
26. 43A Okla. Stat. 902, "Oklahoma Comprehensive Mental Health Services for the Deaf and Hearing Impaired Act."
27. Georgia S.B. 449, Act 1359 (1978)
28. Illinois Mental Health Code S.B. 250, 252, 253, 255; the amendment passed the Illinois legislature as H.B. 1612, Sept. 21, 1977.
29. 45 *Code of Federal Regulations* §84.52(d)
30. E.g., Camenisch v. University of Texas, 616 F.2d 127 (5th Cir. 1980), vacated as moot 451 U.S. 390 (1981); Crawford v. University of North Carolina, 440 F. Supp. 1047 (M.D.N.C. 1977); Herbold v. The Trustees of California State Universities and Colleges, C-78-1358 RHS (N.D. Cal. 1978); Riker v. Holy Cross Hospital, 78-1437 (D. Md. 1978); and Williams v. Quern, 78-C-656 (N.D. Ill. 1978).
31. U.S.D.C. Md., Civ. No. HAR 83-2409 (Stipulated Judgment Order, Feb. 26, 1986)
32. Handel et al. v. Levine et al., Ramsey County District Court File 468475
33. Snow v. State, 469 N.Y.S. 2d 959 (A.D.2 Dept 1983), aff'd 485 N.Y.S. 2d 987 (1984)

Employment

U ntil recently the rights of disabled people to employment were largely unprotected. A Senate report
accompanying the Rehabilitation Act Amendments
of 1974 noted that disabled people are "barred from employment" and "underemployed because of archaic statutes
and laws."[1]

This deplorable condition is evident in the economic
status of the deaf population.[2] A number of studies indicate that deaf people suffer underemployment and lower
incomes because of their disability.[3] They quickly reach a
plateau, and there they remain," Allen Sussman and
Larry Stewart state.

> Everywhere we find deaf men and women of normal or
> above-average abilities operating automatic ma-
> chines, performing simple assembly line operations,
> or otherwise occupied in unchallenging routines. This
> stereotyping illustrates the discriminatory attitudes
> toward the deaf job applicants that are inevitable
> among slightly informed professionals.[4]

Automation poses some very special problems for the
disabled person in the labor force. Disabled workers,
particularly deaf people, tend to be more heavily concen-
trated in occupations where automation is making its
greatest inroads. Nearly 50 percent of all deaf employees
are in manufacturing.[5]

Employer attitudes create the largest single barrier to
employment opportunities. Employers often have stereo-
typed assumptions that underestimate the capabilities of a
disabled person. One study indicated that disabled people
must generally be more qualified or competent than nondisabled people in order to overcome negative attitudes

—

and assumptions.[6] Employers often refuse to hire disabled people because of unjustified fears that a disabled person cannot perform the job safely. Studies of the safety of both mentally and physically disabled people in the employment setting indicate that these fears are groundless.[7]

Employers use communication barriers as the reason for limiting job opportunities for deaf applicants and employees. But communication difficulties "are often exaggerated, and fairly effective substitutes for oral communication are disregarded."[8] Inability to use the telephone is often given as a reason not to consider a deaf applicant, even when use of a phone is not an essential part of the job. In jobs requiring only occasional telephone communication, minor changes in assignment of job responsibiliites can accommodate the deaf worker. For example, a deaf worker assumes some of a hearing co-worker's responsibilities while the hearing person answers the phones.

If a job requires significant telephone contact with one other office a reasonable accommodation may be to install a telecommunications device in both offices, thus allowing the deaf employee to perform all job duties including those requiring telephone communication. In supervisory positions, a secretary or interpreter can answer the telephone and facilitate the conversation either through lipreading, notes, or sign language, whichever is the preferred method of the deaf person.

The requirement of attendance at various meetings or conferences is also used as a reason not to consider deaf applicants. But reasonable accommodations, such as interpreters, can enable deaf workers to participate fully in group meetings and training sessions.

TITLE V REMEDIES

Today, there are a variety of federal statutory remedies available to combat employment discrimination. Those remedies are found primarily in Sections 501, 503, and 504 of Title V of the Rehabilitation Act of 1973. While they are similar in many respects, each of these three sections of the law differs somewhat in application, scope, and quality. Each applies to different types of employers: Section 501 to the federal government, Section 503 to companies that do business with the federal government (federal contractors), and Section 504 to recipients of federal financial assistance. Each imposes varying levels of responsibility upon employers. Sections 501 and 503 require affirmative action, while Section 504 imposes only a duty of nondiscrimination. Section 504 allows an aggrieved individual to go directly to federal court to enforce his or her statutory rights, while Sections 501 and 503 require the individual to first file an administrative complaint. They also differ in the procedures to be followed in filing an administrative complaint. When faced with employment discrimination based on handicap, one must determine which of the three sections applies.

"Qualified" Disabled Person

The Rehabilitation Act does not guarantee jobs for all handicapped people. Instead, it prohibits discrimination in employment against handicapped people who are "qualified" for a job. The definition of a qualified person differs slightly under the three parts of the act:

- The Section 501 regulation for federal employees describes a qualified handicapped person as a handicapped person who, with or without reasonable accommodation, can perform the essential functions of the position in question without endangering the health and safety of the individual or others.[9]
- The Section 503 regulation for federal contractors refers to a qualified handicapped individual as one who is "capable of performing a particular job, with reasonable accommodation to his or her handicap."[10]
- The Section 504 regulation defines a qualified handicapped person as one who "with reasonable accommodation, can perform the essential functions of the job in question."[11]

In all of these definitions, the two central questions in determining whether a handicapped person is qualified for a specific position are (1) What are the essential functions of the job? and (2) Are there reasonable accommodations that will make it possible for a handicapped person to perform the essential functions of the job?

Essential Functions

The regulations for Sections 501, 503, and 504 do not define what is meant by "essential functions." The concept is critical, though, in making certain that employers do not disqualify handicapped people just because these people have difficulty with a task that is only marginally related to the job. For example, a deaf person considered for a typing position should not be disqualified because he or she has trouble using the telephone. The essential function is typing.

In practice, essential functions for a job must be determined on a case-by-case basis. This analysis is complicated by the employer's duty to restructure the job, including rewriting job descriptions, if necessary, to eliminate nonessential tasks that are barriers for handicapped workers. This is part of the employer's duty to make "reasonable accommodation" to the needs of handicapped workers. In judicial or administrative proceedings, the burden of showing what is essential is on the recipient of federal assistance.

As now written the Section 503 regulation does not use the term "essential functions" but instead considers people qualified if they are able to do a "particular job" with reasonable accommodation. This may be a more restrictive definition since it implies that handicapped people must perform all functions of the job, including those that are nonessential tasks. But Sections 501, 503, and 504 all require employers to make reasonable accommodations for handicapped employees, including job restructuring, so the difference in the definition of "qualified" may be illusory. Amendments have been proposed to bring Section 503's language into conformity with that of Section 504.[12]

Reasonable Accommodations

The regulations for Sections 501, 503, and 504 all list the following as possible reasonable accommodations in employment:

- Making facilities used by employees—work benches, parking lots, telephones, lavatories, and entrances, for example—readily accessible to and usable by handicapped people;
- Restructuring jobs in order to reassign nonessential tasks;
- Arranging part-time or modified work schedules;
- Acquiring or modifying equipment or machinery;
- Providing readers for blind employees and interpreters for deaf employees.[13]

Reasonable accommodations for deaf people might include telecommunications devices, oscilloscopes to allow them to communicate telephonically with a computer, interpreters, and telephone amplifiers. This list is not all-inclusive but merely a guide. The appropriate accommodation depends on the needs of the particular disabled worker and the particular job he or she is performing. With advances in modern technology and management science, relatively inexpensive devices and techniques for accommodating handicapped workers are increasingly available.

Reasonable accommodations are often a matter of common sense. For example, a deaf welder worked in an outdoor yard where trucks delivered fruit bins. His supervisor fired him because he believed the man could not work there safely. Later the supervisor realized that the deaf employee could be stationed to see any danger from the trucks entering the yard. With this accommodation, and with fellow employees informed of his deafness, the man could safely perform his job in a fully satisfactory manner.

Another case involved a hearing-impaired woman who had difficulty working in one part of her office because background noise interfered with her hearing aid. When she was reassigned to a quieter part of the office, her difficulty was reduced and her productivity increased.

Sometimes employers do not wish to hire deaf workers because they claim that deaf workers will not be able to hear fire alarms and warning devices on machinery. These employers can make a simple accommodation by installing a light that flashes when the alarm or buzzer sounds.

In the federal workplace, the Civil Service Reform Act of 1978 and the *Federal Personnel Manual* also provide reasonable accommodations for deaf federal employees by specifically authorizing agency heads to employ or assign interpreters to deaf employees.[14] A federal employee won a lawsuit when the judge found that his supervisors had not considered Office of Personnel Management guidelines about reasonable modifications.[15]

Employer Exemptions

Under Sections 501 and 504, a recipient employer does not have to provide a reasonable accommodation if it would cause "undue hardship" on the program's operation. The factors that determine if there is an undue hardship are

- The overall size of the recipient's program with respect to number of employees, number and type of facilities, and size of budget;
- The nature of the recipient's operation, including the composition and structure of the recipient's work force; and
- The type and cost of the accommodation needed.[16]

The "Analysis to the Section 504 Regulation" gives some examples of factors to be weighed in determining if an accommodation causes undue hardship:

> A small day-care center might not be required to expend more than a nominal sum, such as that necessary to equip a telephone for use by a secretary with impaired hearing, but a large school district might be required to make available a teacher's aid to a blind applicant for a teaching job. Further, it might be considered reasonable to require a state welfare agency to accommodate a deaf employee by providing an interpreter, while it would constitute an undue hardship to impose that requirement on a provider of foster home care services.[17]

Section 503 has a similar defense for employers but uses the term "business necessity" instead of "undue hardship." The same factors apply in determining either a business necessity or an undue hardship. Either one, if proven, excuses an employer from providing a reasonable accommodation.

Medical Examinations

Deaf people are sometimes denied particular jobs on the basis of medical criteria that disqualify any person with a hearing loss. Deaf people have been medically disqualified as bus mechanics or geologists solely on the basis of their hearing loss. These blanket medical exclusions can be challenged if they are not job related. In addition, under Section 504 regulations an employer may make offers of employment to handicapped people dependent upon the results of medical examinations only if such examinations are administered in a nondiscriminatory manner to all employees and the results are treated on a confidential basis.[18]

Job Training Programs

Sometimes deaf people are refused interpreters for training programs that are a prerequisite for employment or are essential for retaining or advancing in their jobs. This violates Sections 501, 503, and 504. The Office of Personnel Management will provide interpreters for all deaf federal employees participating in its training programs. The comptroller general for the United States also has decided that special expenses will be provided for sign language interpreters when necessary for deaf employees to participate in government training courses.

Employers with federal contracts frequently contract out to independent groups to conduct training. If the independent group does not provide interpreters, the contract can be challenged. A recipient of federal assistance cannot participate contractually or in other relationships with groups that discriminate against qualified disabled people.[19]

Some employers hire deaf people only for certain jobs such as working with loud machines. The U.S. Postal Service has encouraged this hiring practice. Section 503, however, prohibits designating certain jobs for deaf employees. Deaf workers cannot be "ghettoized" in one job category.[20]

Furthermore, Sections 501 and 503 require employers to make special recruitment efforts to comply with their affirmative action responsibilities. For deaf people, this includes advertising in newspapers directed toward deaf audiences, recruiting at schools for the deaf, and advertising with deaf clubs and organizations.[21]

Section 503 also requires companies to internally disseminate their policy of affirmatively recruiting and promoting qualified handicapped workers. The notification must be written at a language level the average deaf person can understand.[22]

Affirmative Action

The major substantive difference between the three employment sections of the Rehabilitation Act is that Sections 501 and 503 require the federal government and federal contractors to take affirmative action to hire, promote, or retain qualified handicapped persons. Section 504, however, does not require affirmative action; it simply requires nondiscrimination.

The difference between affirmative action and nondiscrimination is a fine one. Affirmative action characteristically means special programs to actively recruit, hire, train, accommodate, and promote qualified disabled people. Under Sections 501 and 503, the federal government and federal contractors must establish and implement such programs. Nondiscrimination, on the other hand, usually means a more passive obligation to treat disabled employees in the same manner as other employees.

In many situations, however, identical treatment may itself be discriminatory. An employer who holds a staff meeting for all employees has effectively excluded a deaf employee from participating if no interpreter is provided. The same is true of an employer who hires a person in a wheelchair but does not have ramps in the building to allow the employee to get to work. By treating the disabled employee the same as the nondisabled employee, the employer has acted unfairly. In all situations in which identical treatment constitutes discrimination against disabled employees, Section 504 requires recipients of federal financial assistance to take specific steps to provide equal opportunity and *equally effective* means of taking advantage of that opportunity.

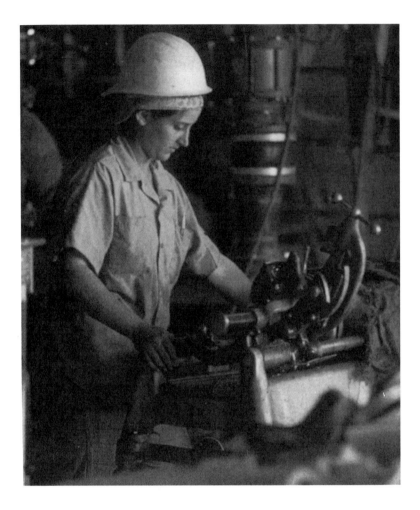

Federal Obligations

The federal government has established several policies
and programs designed to fulfill its affirmative action
obligations under Section 501. For example, the government will make special arrangements for applicants
taking the Civil Service examination when the applicant's
disability prevents him or her from competing equally.
These include provision of readers for blind applicants and
interpreters for deaf applicants, waiver of certain verbal
tests for deaf applicants, provision of enlarged answer
blocks for applicants with poor manual dexterity or motor

coordination, provision of taped and/or brailled tests, and extension of time limits for taking the tests.

The government also has special hiring programs designed to facilitate the appointment of disabled employees. One hiring program is the temporary trial appointment, which gives the disabled employee an opportunity to know what he or she can do and overcome the employer's anxieties about the person's capabilities. Under this program, physically and mentally disabled people can be hired for a four-month period without going through the normal competitive hiring procedures. As soon as the employee has demonstrated his or her ability to do the job, the appointment can be made permanent, although no guarantees are given.

Another program used to hire disabled individuals is known as the "excepted" or "Schedule A" appointment. It is available to both severely physically disabled and mentally retarded applicants. Under the excepted appointment program, disabled people can be hired for permanent jobs by federal agencies without having to take the Civil Service examination. The purpose of the program is to avoid the discriminatory effects of the examination.

There is one basic problem with the excepted appointment program: An excepted appointee lacks the same employment benefits and job security as an employee hired under the regular merit-system procedures. Although an excepted appointee's job is "permanent," he or she can be fired, demoted, or suspended without a hearing or other due process protections. Excepted appointees are also denied equal transfer rights, equal opportunity to compete for promotions, and equal protection in the event of a general job layoff (e.g., reduction-in-force).

Legal Challenges

Several lawsuits have challenged this basic inequity in the excepted appintment program. For example, on January 8, 1982, the District of Columbia federal Court of Appeals held that the federal government violated Section 501 by denying equal employment rights to an excepted service employee at the National Aeronautics and Space Administration (NASA).[23] The case was filed by the National Association of the Deaf Legal Defense Fund (NADLDF) on behalf of Edward Shirey, a deaf excepted service employee who was terminated in a reduction-in-force by NASA in January 1978. Solely because of his handicapped, excepted-service status, Shirey was not given the same rights as competitive service employees to find another job with NASA or the federal government. The appeals court ruled that it is discriminatory to deny equal rights to handicapped individuals when they are equally qualified and performing the same work as competitive service employees.

The rules applying to handicapped excepted service employees have changed in the last few years, but one change came too late to help Shirey. In March 1979, President Carter signed Executive Order 12125, which authorized handicapped excepted service employees to convert to the competitive service after two years of satisfactory performance in their jobs. But this new rule did not apply to Mr. Shirey, who was terminated in January 1978. Despite the fact that he had worked for more than four years in the same job as his competitive service co-workers and had received satisfactory ratings, he was still denied equal rights. Such a policy violates Section 501, said the appeals court. Its decision reversed a federal district court ruling that found no violation of Section 501.

Following its obligation under Section 501 and the Civil Service Reform Act of 1978, the federal government has authorized several methods of hiring interpreters for deaf employees in various work situations. Each federal agency has the option of either (1) hiring full-time interpreters, (2) using other employees who can interpret fluently, or (3) contracting out with individual interpreters or interpreter referral agencies on an as-needed basis. The best method depends on the work situation involved. If a particular deaf employee's job requires frequent use of an interpreter, or if there are several deaf employees in one agency whose combined needs require frequent service, then a full-time interpreter on staff would be the best solution. If an interpreter is needed for an occasional or regular office meeting, it might be best to contract for services of a private interpreter.

Further Assistance

More detailed information on the procedures for taking advantage of all these special federal programs and services can be obtained by contacting federal job information centers throughout the country. Also, the personnel office of each federal agency has a selective placement coordinator who is responsible for implementing these programs.

These federal selective placement coordinators want

The federal government has suggested ways that rehabilitation counselors can take the initiative to ensure that affirmative action is implemented:[24]

- Survey federal agencies to determine what types of jobs are likely to be available and which of these are likely to be in demand by disabled individuals.
- Work with other counselors and organizations to establish referral systems.
- Provide follow-up assistance to agency supervisors after a disabled person has been hired.
- Arrange for selective placement coordinators, managers, and supervisors to tour rehabilitation and independent living centers and to attend workshops and consciousness-raising programs.
- Give recognition awards and publicity to agencies that actively participate in employment programs for disabled individuals.
- Share information about federal job vacancies and personnel needs with rehabilitation counselors in the area.
- And involve selective placement coordinators in the activities of rehabilitation agencies.

---

advice and need assistance from vocational rehabilitation counselors on all issues and problems involving recruitment, hiring, and accommodations for disabled employees. Rehabilitation counselors should develop contacts with federal personnel offices; they should be thoroughly familiar with federal hiring practices and job application procedures. Continuing interaction among counselors, selective placement coordinators, managers, and supervisors is essential.

ENFORCEMENT PROCEDURES

Section 501: Federal Government

A disabled federal employee or applicant for federal employment who believes he or she has been discriminated against by a federal agency can file an administrative complaint with that agency. There are strict time limits imposed for each step of the procedure. While waiver of the time limits is sometimes allowed for good cause, a complaint can be rejected for failure to meet the deadline. The disabled person has the right to be represented by an attorney at all stages of the complaint process. If a deaf complainant needs an interpreter at any stage of the proceedings, the agency must provide and pay for one.

The step-by-step administrative complaint process is as follows:[25]

A. Informal Precomplaint Counseling
   1. An employee or applicant for employment must contact the agency's equal employment opportunity (EEO) office within thirty days of the discriminatory act. The contact may be made in person or by letter. No form is required.
   2. The EEO office will assign an EEO counselor to the case. The person bringing the complaint (complainant) must provide all the information about the discriminatory policy or action to the EEO counselor.

3. The role of the EEO counselor is to:
   a. make an inquiry into the complaint and discuss it with all the people involved;
   b. attempt an informal resolution within twenty-one days;
   c. not discourage the complainant from filing a formal complaint; and
   d. not reveal the identity of the complainant unless authorized to do so.
4. If informal resolution cannot be achieved, the EEO counselor will send the complainant a "Notice of Final Interview" informing him or her of the right to file a formal complaint.
5. The complainant has the right to file a formal complaint anytime *after twenty-one days* from the date the EEO counselor was first contacted. The complainant need *not* wait for a "Notice of Final

Interview" letter before filing the formal complaint.

6. The EEO counselor, in most cases, has no authority to force management to settle the complaint. The counselor can only try to help negotiate a settlement. Unless it appears that this pre-complaint counseling may produce a settlement, the complainant should file his or her formal complaint immediately upon expiration of the twenty-one-day settlement period.

B. Formal Complaint

1. A complainant can file a formal complaint anytime after the twenty-one-day settlement period has elapsed, but not later than *fifteen* days after receipt of the "Notice of Final Interview" letter from the EEO counselor.

2. Content of formal complaint
   a. The formal complaint is written on a form provided by the agency's EEO office and is filed with that office.
   b. The written complaint should discuss in detail all of the facts involved and should include copies of letters and other documents substantiating those facts.
   c. If there is a continuing pattern or policy of discrimination, the complainant should describe the discriminatory activity as "continuing" in order to avoid any time-deadline problems.

3. Rejection of complaint
   a. The agency may reject the entire complaint or some of the issues raised if:
      i. it is not filed on time,
      ii. the complaint raises matters identical to another complaint of the employee,
      iii. the complainant is not an employee or applicant of the agency, or

      iv. the complaint is not based on disability discrimination.
- b. If the agency rejects the complaint, the complainant must be notified in writing. The employee may then appeal to the Equal Employment Opportunity Commission (EEOC) *within fifteen days* or file suit in federal district court *within thirty days* of receipt of the rejection letter.

4. Investigation of complaint
   a. If the agency accepts the complaint, it must properly investigate. The agency will appoint an EEO investigator, a person other than the EEO counselor.
   b. The investigator will conduct an in-depth inquiry, take sworn affidavits from the people involved, and gather documents and statistics.
   c. If the complainant believes that important witnesses have not been interviewed or that important evidence has not been explored, then he or she should notify the investigator in writing.

5. Adjustment of complaint
   When the investigation is completed, the investigator writes a report. The EEO office sends copies of the report to both the complainant and the employer and provides them an opportunity to informally adjust (settle) the matter on the basis of the results of the investigation. If the complaint is informally adjusted, the terms of the adjustment must be in writing.

6. Proposed disposition
   a. If the complaint cannot be adjusted, then the agency will issue a proposed disposition (decision).
   b. If the complainant is satisfied with the proposed disposition, the agency must then implement the terms of the disposition.

    c. If the complainant is dissatisfied with the proposed disposition, he or she may request a hearing before the EEOC in writing *within fifteen days* or file suit in federal district court *within thirty days* of receipt of the proposed disposition.

  7. EEOC hearing

    a. At the hearing, as at all other stages in the process, the complainant has the right to be represented by an attorney and to have a qualified interpreter.

    b. On the basis of evidence submitted at the hearing, the examiner (judge) will issue a recommended decision that the agency can reverse.

    c. If the complainant is dissatisfied with the decision, he or she may appeal within fifteen days to the EEOC Office of Review and Appeals or file suit in federal court within thirty days of receipt of the decision.

    d. If the decision is that the agency has discriminated, i.e., if the complainant wins, he or she may be awarded back pay and attorney's fees.

C. Right to Sue in Federal Court

  1. The complainant can file suit in federal district court at any time after *180 days* from the date the *formal* EEO complaint was filed, if the agency has not yet issued a *final* decision.

  2. In addition, as noted above, the complainant can file suit within thirty days after completion of other stages of the administrative process (e.g., after receipt of the notice of proposed disposition or after receipt of final agency action).

Section 503: Federal Contractors

Section 503 of the Rehabilitation Act requires employers who have contracts with the federal government for more than $2,500 to take affirmative action to hire and promote qualified disabled people. About 300,000 private businesses are subject to Section 503. The work performed under these contracts includes construction of government buildings, repair of federal highways, and leasing of government buildings, to name a few. In addition to primary contractors, Section 503 covers companies that have subcontracted for more than $2,500 of federal business from a primary contractor.

The administrative complaint procedure under Section 503 differs significantly from that described under Section 501. Section 503 is enforced by the U.S. Department of Labor's Office of Federal Contract Compliance Programs (OFCCP). An applicant or employee who believes he or she has been discriminated against by a federal contractor can file a written complaint with the regional OFCCP office within 180 days of the date of the alleged violation. The regional OFCCP is supposed to investigate promptly and attempt to resolve the complaint. If the regional OFCCP finds no violation of Section 503, then the complainant may appeal to the national OFCCP office in Washington, D.C., within thirty days. If the regional OFCCP finds that the employer has in fact violated Section 503, then an attempt is made to resolve the matter informally and provide the appropriate relief to the complainant.

If the employer refuses to provide the appropriate relief, OFCCP can then employ more formal enforcement mechanisms. These include bringing suit in federal court, withholding payments due on existing federal contracts, termination of existing federal contracts, and/or barring the contractor from receiving future federal contracts. If OFCCP begins any of these enforcement methods, the employer can request a formal administrative hearing. While the complainant can participate in the administrative hearing, it is primarily a dispute between OFCCP and the employer. Like the Section 501 EEO complaint procedure, the OFCCP process is long and time-consuming.

An individual's right to go directly to court and enforce a Section 503 claim is not spelled out in the Section 503 regulations and has not yet been firmly established by the courts. However, strong legal arguments can be made by analogy to Section 504, where the right to sue has been established. Courts that have addressed this issue in recent years have been divided.[26]

Section 504: Federal Financial Recipients

The procedures for enforcing Section 504 are discussed in chapter three. As noted there, Section 504 applies to all recipients of federal financial assistance. "Federal financial assistance" under Section 504 differs from a "federal contract" under Section 503. It can mean grants and loans of federal money, services of federal personnel, or the lease of federal buildings for less than fair market value. Because of widespread dependence on federal money, recipients of federal financial assistance are many and varied.

Before receiving such assistance, all recipients must sign an "assurance of compliance" form agreeing to obey Section 504.

The U.S. government as well as advocacy groups for disabled people have always taken the position that Section 504 prohibits employment discrimination by all recipients of federal aid, regardless of the purpose for which their federal funds are to be used. In other words, if a hospital received federal funds to buy medical equipment, Section 504 covers that hospital's employment practices.

In 1984, a unanimous Supreme Court agreed that Section 504 covers employment discrimination in all programs receiving federal financial assistance, regardless of the purpose of the funding. The Court concluded: ". . . application of Section 504 to all programs receiving federal financial assistance fits the remedial purpose of the Rehabilitation Act to promote and expand employment opportunities for the handicapped."[27]

State Statutes

State laws sometimes provide a remedy for employment discrimination when the Rehabilitation Act does not apply. A number of states have recently acted to add some category such as "physical or mental handicap" to the list of classes protected by traditional human rights and employment discrimination laws. Formerly these laws covered only race, sex, and religion. These laws are useful because they often apply to all public and private employers, thereby prohibiting discrimination even by employers who do not have federal contracts or grants.

There is no uniformity in state human rights laws. Some protect physically disabled workers but not mentally disabled ones. Some require reasonable accommodations to disabled workers, but most do not. Some allow private causes of action—the right of individuals to sue in state court; others are limited to administrative enforcement by underfunded public agencies. In most states the agency charged with enforcement is the state civil rights commission or state employment agency. Enforcement procedures and remedies vary widely, as do the definitions of protected disabilities and of covered employers.[28]

Vocational Rehabilitation Services

Because of the chronic underemployment problems of deaf people, vocational services are widely needed and heavily used. The Rehabilitation Act is the principle federal law providing rehabilitation services for disabled people. The Rehabilitation Services Administration (RSA), part of the U.S. Department of Education, is the primary agency for implementing the section of the act that deals with disabled people.

Title I of the act provides federal grants to states for meeting the vocational needs of their disabled citizens.[29] To be eligible, a state vocational rehabilitation agency submits a state service plan for approval by RSA. The plan must comply with Title I provisions and RSA regulations.[30] To receive the grants, the state vocational rehabilitation (VR) agencies must agree to prescribe and write an individual rehabilitation plan for each person eligible under the act for the service. For deaf people, VR services include vocational counseling, education and training, medical services, job placement, job support, and provision of interpreters and telecommunication devices.

Amendments to the Rehabilitation Act in 1978 broadened the services available to deaf people.[31] The RSA Office of Handicapped Individuals was given authority to fund twelve programs for interpreter training.[32] The secretary of education was authorized to set minimum standards for interpreter certification, and the programs were also permitted to train teachers of deaf students. Congress appropriated $900,000 for the first year of this program. Ten programs have been funded.

The amendments also provided for use of discretionary funds from the RSA commissioner to set up information and interpreter referral centers in each state. The centers may be run by public agencies or nonprofit organizations that provide services to deaf people. The centers must serve the whole state and be centrally located.

Any public agency serving deaf people can use the interpreter referral services. The funds of these referral centers may also be used for the purchase or rental of telecommunications devices. When the program needs outside help for its operation, it is required to seek it from private, nonprofit organizations either comprised primarily of hearing-impaired people or having the primary purpose of providing services to hearing-impaired people.

Comprehensive rehabilitation centers were also authorized. Their purpose is to provide a broad range of services to disabled people: information and referral, counseling, job placement, health, education, and social and recreational services.[33] Information and technical assistance, including interpreter services, are to be provided by these centers to other public and nonprofit organizations or agencies in the area to help them fulfill their responsibilities under Section 504 of the Rehabilitation Act.

These amendments expand the rehabilitation services available to deaf people and increase the number of public agencies existing to serve their needs.

NOTES

1. S. Rep. No. 1297, 93d Cong., 2d Sess. 43 (1974); reprinted in *Congressional and Administrative News* (1974): 6400.
2. See S. Fisher, *An Assessment of the Occupational Status and Training of Former Model Post-Secondary Deaf Students,* unpublished thesis (Washington, D.C.: Gallaudet College, 1974); A. Crammatte, *The Formidable Peak: A Study of Deaf People in Professional Employment* (Washington, D.C.: Gallaudet College, 1965); and E. Boatner, E. Stuckless, and D. Moores, *Occupational Status of the Young Deaf Adult of New England and the Need and Demand for a Regional Technical Vocational Training Center* (West Hartford, Conn.: American School for the Deaf, 1964).
3. A 1978 study showed a significant economic decline for deaf people between 1972 and 1977. Jerome Schein, Director of the Deafness Research and Training Center at New York University, noted that the percentage of deaf people who were working dropped from 65.5 percent in 1972 to 61.3 percent in 1977. These declines ran counter to national trends; for the same period, the national percentages of both men and women who were in the labor force increased. Unemployment for deaf people increased from 9.6 percent in 1972 to 10.9 percent in 1977. Personal income of deaf people as a proportion of the national per capita average declined substantially from 1971 to 1976. In 1971 the average deaf person's personal income was 74.6 percent of the national per capita average; by 1976 this average had dropped to 64.2 percent. This data is from J. Schein, *Economic Status of Deaf Adults* (unpublished study, 1978).
4. A. Sussman and L. Stewart, "Social and Psychological Problems of Deaf People," in *Counseling of Deaf People,* Sussman and Stewart, eds. (New York: New York University School of Education, 1971), p. 25.
5. Schein and Delk, *Deaf Population,* p. 81.
6. Richard, Triandis, and Patterson, "Indices of Employer Prejudice Toward Disabled Applicants," *Journal of Applied Psychology* 45 (1953): 52.
7. See Wolfe, "Disability Is No Handicap for Dupont," *The Alliance Review* (Winter, 1973–74): 13; and Kalenick, "Myths About Hiring the Physically Handicapped," *Job Safety and Health* 2(1974): 9, 11.
8. Crammatte, *The Formidable Peak,* p. 118.
9. 29 *Code of Federal Regulations* §1613.702(f)
10. 29 C.F.R. § 32.3
11. 45 C.F.R. §84.3(k)(1)
12. 45 *Federal Register* 86,208, December 30, 1980
13. 45 C.F.R. §84.12(b)(2); 29 C.F.R. §1613.704(b)
14. 5 U.S.C. §5331
15. Crane v. Dole, 617 F.Supp. 156 (1985)
16. 45 C.F.R. §84.12(c)

17. 42 Fed. Reg. 22,688, May 4, 1977
18. 45 C.F.R. §84.14(c, d)
19. 45 C.F.R. §84.11(a)(4)
20. 41 C.F.R. §60-741.5(i)(2); see also A. Hermann and L. Walker, *Handbook of Employment Rights for the Handicapped: Sections 503 and 504 of the Rehabilitation Act of 1973* (Washington, D.C.: George Washington University, 1978).
21. 41 C.F.R. §60-741.5(f)
22. 41 C.F.R. §60-741
23. Shirey v. Devine, 670 F.2d 1188 (D.C. Cir. 1982)
24. See Office of Personnel Management, "Handbook of Selective Placement of Persons with Physical and Mental Handicaps," OPM Doc. 125-11-3 (March 1979).
25. For more detailed information, see 29 C.F.R. §1613.201 through 1613.806.
26. For court rulings that there is no private right to sue under Section 503, see Rogers v. Frito-Lay, 611 F.2d 1074 (5th Cir. 1980); Simpson v. Reynolds Metal Co., 629 F.2d 1226 (7th Cir. 1980); Simon v. St. Louis County, 656 F.2d 316 (8th Cir. 1981); and Davis v. United Air Lines, No. 81-7093 (2nd Cir. 1981). For court rulings that an individual may bring suit under Section 503, see Hart v. County of Alameda, 485 F. Supp. 66 (N.D. Cal. 1979); and Chaplin v. Consolidated Edison of New York, 482 F. Supp. 1165 (S.D. N.Y. 1980).
27. Consolidated Rail Corp. v. Darrone, 465 U.S. 624 (1984)
28. *Amicus* 3 (1978): 39.
29. 29 U.S.C. §720 *et seq.*
30. 45 C.F.R. §1361.1 *et seq.*
31. Rehabilitation, Comprehensive Services, and Developmental Disabilities Amendments, Public Law 95-602 (1978), 29 U.S.C. §701 *et seq.*
32. 29 U.S.C. §777(e)
33. 29 U.S.C. §775(a)(1)

Architectural Barriers

Congress passed Section 502 of the Rehabilitation Act of 1973 to make sure that federally funded buildings are accessible to disabled people.[1] Specifically, Section 502 created an independent federal agency, the Architectural and Transportation Barriers Compliance Board (ATBCB), to enforce the Architectural Barriers Act of 1968. The 1968 law requires most buildings and facilities designed, constructed, altered, or leased with federal money after 1968 to be accessible to disabled people.

This means that buildings cannot have barriers to people who are in wheelchairs or on crutches or who are blind or deaf. Everyone must be able to enter and use these buildings. The potential impact of this law is great. As of 1980, there were 400,000 federally owned and 50,000 federally leased facilities in the United States.

Buildings covered by the Architectural Barriers Act must meet the minimum standards for accessibility established by the American National Standards Institute (ANSI).[2] These standards have also been adopted by the federal government's General Services Administration (GSA).

If a person knows of a federal building that violates these accessibility standards, he or she may file a written complaint with ATBCB, which has the authority to conduct investigations and to attempt to achieve voluntary compliance. If this is not possible, the board's general counsel can file a citation against the federal agency accused of violating the standards. A hearing is held before an administrative law judge to determine if there has been a violation of the barriers act. The judge can order the violating agency to obey the act or withhold or suspend its funding. The judge's order is final and binding on any federal department or agency.

THE ATBCB

Amendments to Section 502 changed the size and composition of the ATBCB board from only nine federal agency members to ten federal agency members and eleven public members, five of whom must be disabled.[3] The board was also given authority to investigate communication barriers, including the absence of telecommunication devices; to provide technical assistance to make buildings and transportation vehicles accessible; and to adopt its own accessibility standards to replace the ANSI standards.

While ATBCB has achieved voluntary compliance in most of its cases, a number of alleged violations have gone through the citation process. In June 1978 the board ordered the Department of the Interior and the Department of Transportation to re-install two elevators in Washington, D.C.'s Union Station/National Visitors Center to make it accessible to disabled people.

Cases involving pedestrian overpasses and underpasses were successfully settled in St. Louis, Missouri, and Omaha, Nebraska. The St. Louis case marked the first time that federal funds were withheld from the construction of a facility until the question of accessibility was resolved. The Omaha settlement was the first time an agency entered into an agreement to go beyond the requirements of the Architectural Barriers Act and correct existing problems on an agency-wide basis.

In another case, the Department of Health, Education, and Welfare and the General Services Administration were ordered by an administrative law judge to make Alabama's largest office building accessible to disabled persons. The restrooms and elevators in the Birmingham building violated GSA's own ANSI accessibility standards. In his order, the judge stated that cost was no defense for noncompliance. These cases represent the beginning of ATBCB's capacity to ensure accessibility.

Ambiguous Standards

The inadequacy of the twenty-year-old ANSI standards is a serious problem. Although present ANSI standards require accessible and usable public telephones for hearing-impaired individuals, it is not clear whether this entails such specific solutions as amplifiers, telecommunications devices, adapted pay telephones, or adapted telephones in business offices. The requirement of visual warning signals is also unclear. Where should they be? Are flashing exit signs sufficient?

The ATBCB board and GSA are now considering a revised set of accessibility standards that should address the problems of deaf people more specifically. Until new standards are adopted, however, these agencies will continue to use the ANSI standards.

The ambiguity of the ANSI standards lessens the effectiveness of Section 502 for deaf people. However, complaints to the ATBCB board can be used to compel the installation of telecommunication devices. Administrative complaints led to an order that TDDs be installed in post office buildings in several locations. Section 502 can also be used to require the installation of doorbells with flashing-light relays, visual warning systems such as fire alarms, and security sytems that are not wholly dependent on operation of an auditory intercom.

The law may also apply to other architectural barriers to communication. For example, this law might be used to compel builders of auditoriums and meetings rooms to install appropriate spotlighting for interpreters and audio "loops" to assist persons with hearing aids.

Complaints about architectural, transportation, and communications barriers can be sent to:

Architectural and Transportation Barriers
   Compliance Board
Switzer Building, Room 1010
330 C Street SW
Washington, DC 20201
(202) 245-1801 (Voice or TTY)

In your letter of complaint, identify yourself, the barrier to which you object, the federal agency that is responsible for the building, and the owner and occupant of the building.

Section 504 Compliance

In addition to Section 502, Section 504 can be invoked to remove architectural barriers in structures used by recipients of federal financial assistance. Section 504 regulations at the Departments of Health and Human Services and of Education require each new facility or new part of a facility to be designed and constructed to be readily accessible to and usable by disabled people.[4] Alterations and new construction will comply with Section 504 if they meet the ANSI standards discussed above.

Other federal agencies have adopted the ANSI standards by referring to them in their own Section 504 regulations. If a building is constructed, altered, or leased by the federal government, complaints about architectural barriers could be filed with either the particular federal agency involved under Section 504 or with the ATBCB board under Section 502. If the federal financial assistance was given to a program for some purpose other than construction, alteration, or lease, then, under Section 504, complaints about architectural barriers can only be filed with the particular agency providing the assistance.

Because the ANSI standards do not specifically address many of the communication barriers confronted by deaf people, a person with a complaint about an architectural or communication barrier may have to rely on the general nondiscrimination and program accessibility provisions of Section 504 discussed in chapter three.

State Laws

State architectural barrier laws can be used to remove obstructions. Some of these laws are broader in application than the Rehabilitation Act because they are not limited to buildings that receive federal funding. For example, a state or local law may require all newly constructed places of public accommodation to be accessible. If so, this would include restaurants and stores as well as state structures.

Other state laws specifically deal with the problems of deaf people. Some states require apartment buildings to install both auditory and visual smoke detectors and alarms. If a state does not have such a law, deaf people might want to lobby for one.

NOTES

1. 29 *United States Code* §792
2. 45 *Code of Federal Regulations* §84.23(c)
3. See Public Law 95-602: The Rehabilitation, Comprehensive Services, and Developmental Disabilities Amendments of 1978; 29 U.S.C. §701 *et seq.*
4. 45 C.F.R. §84.23(a)

CHAPTER TEN

The Legal System

D eaf people experience numerous difficulties with the legal system because of communication barriers. They may be unjustly committed to mental institutions because they are misdiagnosed by people who do not know how to work and communicate with them. They often cannot afford a lawyer; if they can, they often are unable to find one who is able to communicate with them and understand their needs. If they have to go to court, they often do not understand the proceedings and cannot adequately explain their side of the story. More than fifty years ago, a judge wrote:

> [I]n the absence of an interpreter, it would be a physical impossibility for the accused, a deaf [defendant], to know or understand the nature and cause of the accusation against him and . . . he could only stand by helplessly . . . without knowing or understand[ing], and all this in the teeth of the mandatory constitutional rights which apply. Mere confrontation would be useless.[1]

Today's courts still deny equal access and due process to hearing-impaired people. Most of the state interpreter laws are inadequate. They fail to ensure that deaf defendants understand fully the charges against them and participate effectively in their own defense. A number of state interpreter laws fail to provide interpreters for arrest and civil and administrative proceedings. These laws also permit judges to assess the cost of interpreters as "court costs."

In recent years, however, considerable progress has been made at both federal and state levels to make courts more accessible to deaf people. The Americans with Disabilities Act requires all state and local courts to be accessible to

—

deaf individuals, and requires the provision of interpreters, transcription, or other appropriate auxiliary aids for deaf persons in court.[2] The cost of these services cannot be assessed against deaf litigants.[3] State laws on interpreter services and qualifications for jury duty are being rewritten to ensure necessary access.

SIGNS OF PROGRESS

In 1979 Congress enacted the Bilingual, Hearing, and Speech-Impaired Court Interpreter Act.[4] This law requires that, in any criminal or civil action *initiated by the federal government,* the court must appoint a qualified interpreter. The director of the Administrative Office of the U.S. Courts determines the qualifications required of court-appointed interpreters. Each district court must maintain on file in the office of the clerk of the court a list of certified interpreters, both oral and manual, for deaf people. The history of the legislation shows that the director of court administration must consult organizations of and for deaf people in preparing such lists. These organizations include the National Association of the Deaf (NAD) and the Registry of Interpreters for the Deaf (RID).

If any interpreter is unable to communicate effectively with the defendant, party, or witness, the court's presiding officer must dismiss that interpreter and obtain the services of another. The service is paid for by the government, whether or not the person needing the service is indigent. In his or her discretion, however, a judge can apportion the interpreter fees among the parties or tax their costs to the losing party.

The shortcoming of this law is that an interpreter is not provided for a deaf person who initiates an action, for example, to challenge a denial of federal rights. Only criminal and civil cases initiated by the federal government require appointment of interpreters.

Many states will provide an interpreter to a deaf defendant in a criminal proceeding, but very few provide one at the time of arrest, even though it is during pretrial proceedings that a deaf person is most often denied his or her constitutional rights. Few states provide interpreters in civil cases.

However, the Department of Justice's analysis of its Section 504 regulation specifically requires the appointment of interpreters in civil and criminal proceedings:

> Court systems receiving Federal financial assistance shall provide for the availability of qualified interpreters for civil and criminal court proceedings involving persons with hearing or speaking impairments. . . . Where a recipient has an obligation to provide qualified interpreters under this subpart, the recipient has the corresponding responsibility to pay for the services of the interpreters.[5]

Interpreters for indigent deaf defendants are also specifically provided:

> [In cases where the courts appoint counsel for indigents, they] are also required to assign qualified interpreters (certified, where possible, by recognized certification agencies) in cases involving indigent defendants with hearing or speaking impairments to

aid the communication between client and attorney. The availability of interpreting services to the indigent defendant would be required for all phases of the preparation and presentation of the defendant's case.[6]

Miranda Advice of Rights

In the landmark decision *Miranda v. Arizona,* the Supreme Court recognized that questioning by police in the stationhouse or jail is inherently coercive and undermines the privilege against self-incrimination.[7] As a result of this decision, police are now required to "effectively inform" the accused person of his or her constitutional rights before any questioning can take place. Without use of a qualified interpreter, most deaf people would not be able to understand their rights fully, and any waiver of their rights would not meet the Supreme Court's standard of being voluntary, knowing, and intelligent.

Depending upon which reading-level formula is used, the standard written advice of rights form given to suspects before questioning requires a sixth-to-eighth-grade reading comprehension level. The ability of the hearing person to understand the rights set forth in this form is not seriously impaired by a reading deficiency, because they can be told out loud what is written on the form. The listening comprehension level of people with normal hearing and of people with reading problems usually exceeds their reading comprehension level.[8] However, the reading level required by the *Miranda* warnings and advice of rights forms remains far above the comprehension of most prelingually deaf people. These people require a careful explanation of the rights by a qualified sign language interpreter.

The conceptual and linguistic difficulties posed by the *Miranda* advice of rights cannot be overcome by a direct translation into sign language. Sign language uses everyday rather than formal concepts. Critical concepts that are unfamiliar to many deaf people include "right" and "Constitution." Some deaf people would not understand the term "lawyer" in the full sense of understanding a lawyer's

Mary Furey, an educator, observed that the standard advice of rights form poses serious problems for the average deaf person.

A great number of deaf adults would find the language of this [*Miranda*] warning strange and incomprehensible because of the many idioms used in it. True, each word in and of itself is simple, but when two or more are put together in a special sense, they can be totally unintelligible to a deaf individual because many deaf adults give each word narrow or literal meaning. . . . The idiom "can be used against" would also be difficult to understand. Even the word "rights" could be perplexing.

Infinitives, verbs used in the passive voice, gerunds, and other verbals such as . . . "without a lawyer present," etc., would not be readily comprehended by the usual deaf adult. The meaning of "if" at the beginning of a clause usually is not understood. . . .

I find that . . . the warning itself . . . as presently written, would be difficult for the usual deaf adult to read with understanding and indeed could be misunderstood or not comprehended at all.[9]

function. There are not many signs to express legal terms. The sign for "Constitution" is newly created; most American Sign Language users would be unfamiliar with either the sign or the English word, let alone the concept behind it.

Fingerspelling of important legal terms would not necessarily increase understanding, especially if the accused deaf person has a low reading level.[10] To be understood, the terms and their meanings must be carefully explained in clear concepts. A qualified interpreter is fundamental at this point. Acting out and other demonstrative approaches might be needed.

Moreover, deaf people are accustomed to questions that are direct and concrete. Several of the rights described in the *Miranda* warning are mentioned as if implied to exist. The word "if" is frequently used.

Examples of the Problem

In a recent case, a Maryland circuit court addressed the problem of communicating the *Miranda* advice of rights to a deaf defendant. David Barker, a congenitally deaf man with a reading comprehension level of grade 2.8, was charged with murder in 1975. The charges were dropped, but in 1976, while Barker was in custody for unrelated charges, police questioned him extensively about the murder by means of written notes. They did so without providing him either a sign language interpreter or advice of counsel. After several hours of being questioned, Barker signed the *Miranda* waiver of rights and then a confession.

When Barker was interrogated a month later with an interpreter, he showed confusion in answering questions. Asked if he had understood the *Miranda* advice of rights, he replied in sign language, "a little bit." He also referred to promises allegedly made by the police guaranteeing hospitalization.

The court suppressed the first confession as being involuntary and suppressed a second confession on the grounds that the original promise of hospitalization continued to influence him, making the second confession involuntary. The court wrote:

> There was additionally offered testimony by experts in the field of sign language for the deaf that the expression "Constitutional Rights," being an abstract idea, is extremely difficult to convey to the deaf, especially, as in this case, when the educational level of the individual is so curtailed. There was testimony that the warning, "Do you understand that you have the right to have an attorney present at all times during the questioning?," may well have been signalled, and understood as "Do you understand it is *all*

right to have an attorney present?," which obviously is far from the actual portent of the warning.[11]

Extra Jail Time

Without the assistance of an interpreter at the time of their arrest, deaf people often spend excessive time in jail, unaware of their right to counsel and to post bail; sometimes they are unaware even of the charges against them.

Oklahoma state law requires that interpreters be provided to deaf defendants upon arrest. In one instance, however, a deaf man arrested for a misdemeanor was in jail for two days without being given an interpreter. In this case, the Oklahoma Supreme Court found that the state law applies to city police departments and that, because the deaf man could not understand his rights or communicate with those who could help him, he was forced to stay in jail longer than a hearing person would have.[12]

In another case, a deaf man remained in a St. Louis, Missouri, jail for five days after arrest without being provided an interpreter. The St. Louis police department had no written policy on the matter. The National Center for Law and the Deaf (NCLD) filed a complaint against the police department with the U.S. Department of Treasury Office of Revenue Sharing (ORS). The ORS had proposed Section 504 regulations requiring that agencies receiving revenue sharing funds "provide appropriate aids to individuals with impaired sensory, manual, or speaking skills, where necessary to afford such individuals equal opportunity to obtain the same result or to gain the same level of achievement as that provided to others."[13]

After an investigation by ORS, the police department issued a written policy stating that the arresting officer should decide when an interpreter would be provided. Because police officers dealing with deaf people frequently try to get by with notewriting, ORS found this policy inadequate and directed the St. Louis police department to provide a qualified interpreter to any deaf person upon arrest and prior to interrogating or taking a statement.

According to the directive, the interpreter should be appointed to serve throughout the arrest procedure in order to make certain that the deaf person is fully aware of the charges. The police department must also make known this policy to its officers by including a written directive in the department's procedure book. St. Louis's police department was required to take these steps or face a possible suspension of federal revenue sharing funds.

Qualified Interpreters

The Department of Justice's Section 504 regulation is specific in the requirements it makes of police departments receiving financial assistance:

> A recipient that employs fifteen or more persons shall provide appropriate auxiliary aids to qualified handicapped persons with impaired sensory, manual, or speaking skills where a refusal to make such provision would discriminatorily impair or exclude the participation of such persons in a program receiving Federal financial assistance. Such auxiliary aids may include . . . qualified interpreters. . . . Department officials may require recipients employing fewer than fifteen persons to provide auxiliary aids when this would not significantly impair the ability of the recipient to provide its benefits or services.[14]

The Justice Department's analysis of the regulation explains this requirement in more detail:

> Law enforcement agencies should provide for the availability of qualified interpreters (certified, where possible, by a recognized certification agency) to assist the agencies when dealing with hearing-impaired persons. Where the hearing-impaired person uses American Sign Language for communication, the term "qualified interpreter" would mean an interpreter skilled in communicating in American Sign Language. It is the responsibility of the law enforcement agency to determine whether the hearing-impaired person uses American Sign Language or Signed English to communicate.

If a hearing-impaired person is arrested, the arresting officer's *Miranda* warning should be communicated to the arrestee on a printed form approved for such use by the law enforcement agency where there is no qualified interpreter immediately available and communication is otherwise inadequate. *The form should also advise the arrestee that the law enforcement agency has an obligation* under Federal law *to offer an interpreter* to the arrestee *without cost and that the agency will defer interrogation pending the appearance of an interpreter* (our emphasis).[15]

Neither the regulation nor its analysis limits the provision of interpreters to arrested hearing-impaired people. Victims and complainants are also entitled to them. In addition, hearing-impaired people who attend programs and functions sponsored by a law enforcement agency, such as informational workshops and educational programs, must be provided qualified interpreters upon request.

The analysis stresses the critical importance of the interpreter's qualifications. Quality can be ensured by contacting the local or state chapter of the Registry of Interpreters for the Deaf (RID) for a list of certified and qualified interpreters. If the interpreter is inadequate—as judged by either the hearing-impaired person, the interpreter, or a law enforcement or court official—another interpreter must be secured. The analysis places specific responsibility on the recipient agency to ascertain what kind of sign language the deaf person feels most comfortable with and then to secure an interpreter who is competent in that language.

Competence Is Critical

Making the effort to secure a competent interpreter is critical. The existence of a federal or state law providing interpreters is in itself no guarantee that they are actually provided and that they function appropriately.

In Virginia, where state law requires the appointment of qualified interpreters, an unskilled and uncertified interpreter was provided to a deaf rape victim. Although the interpreter told the court that he was not skilled at reading sign language, the judge proceeded with the trial. When the prosecutor asked the victim what had happened, she gave the sign for "forced intercourse." The interpreter said that her reply was "made love," the sign for which is completely different. The legal effect of the interpreter's mistake was devastating because, in rape, force is the essential element. Later, when she answered, "blouse," to the prosecutor's question of what she was wearing, the interpreter told the court, "short blouse," creating the impression that she had dressed provocatively.[16]

Effective enforcement of the right to a qualified interpreter is extremely important. It will require a continuing effort to raise the awareness of judicial and administrative judges and court clerks about relevant laws and the communication patterns of deaf people.

The obligation of law enforcement agencies to provide interpreters is founded not only in regulation and statute but in constitutional law as well. Courts have suppressed evidence obtained from hearing-impaired defendants when it was found that the *Miranda* advice of rights was not adequately communicated.[17] In each case in which the confession was suppressed, the *Miranda* warning was conveyed in sign language beyond the defendant's level of comprehension.

Securing an interpreter with an RID legal skills certificate for a timely explanation of rights, accompanied by a careful explanation of every legal term and sign, is one way police departments can both prevent objections to the adequacy of the communication and comply with the Department of Justice's Section 504 regulations. Presentation of a printed advice of rights form without providing interpretation will seldom if ever be sufficient. Some police departments videotape all communications with hearing-impaired defendants in order to verify for the court that the rights warning was effectively communicated and that the interpreter acted properly.

Pre-Trial Preparation

The period between arrest, arraignment, and subsequent trial is critical for the defendant. A defense is formulated at this stage. Under the sixth amendment to the Constitution, every accused person has the right to have an attorney and to be effectively represented. In *DeRoche v. United States,* the Court of Appeals for the Ninth Circuit held that effective assistance of counsel means adequate opportunity for the accused and his or her attorney to consult and prepare for arraignment and trial.[18] No attorney can effectively represent a client without a full understanding of the client's case. The Justice Department's Section 504 regulation requires that interpreters be provided to indigent deaf defendants for all phases of case preparation.[19] Interpreters also should be provided when, in preparation of pre-sentence or probation reports, it is necessary to interview a convicted deaf person. A Florida state judge used the authority of the Revenue Sharing Act and Section 504 of the Rehabilitation Act to convince a probation officer to provide an interpreter to a deaf defendant.

Due Process and Access in Prison

Once in jail to serve their terms, deaf people are frequently denied basic due process rights and access to rehabilitation programs simply because prison staff cannot communicate with them. A deaf and blind prisoner in a state prison in Arizona could not communicate effectively with prison guards and other prison personnel. He could not talk to prison counselors or medical staff when he was ill. He was charged with breaking a prison rule, but he could not understand the testimony against him at the disciplinary hearing or explain his version of what had happened. When he sued the state prison system, the case was dismissed by the trial judge. But the federal Court of Appeals for the Ninth Circuit held that he could bring his complaint in court under Section 504 or the Fourteenth Amendment of the U.S. Constitution. The court upheld the regulations of the U.S. Department of Justice, which require prison systems to provide auxiliary aids for deaf individuals to give them equal access to prison programs and activities.[20]

A deaf inmate of Maryland's prison system was denied an interpreter at a disciplinary hearing and was therefore unable to present a defense. The disciplinary board took away "good time" days that would have led to earlier release, and it transferred him for psychological evaluation from a minimum-security camp to a maximum-security house of corrections. The state psychologist there could not communicate with him and, therefore, could not competently evaluate him.

The deaf man filed a lawsuit in federal district court in Baltimore requesting a court order requiring the state of Maryland to provide an interpreter to any deaf inmate who faces administrative charges. The suit argued that, without a qualified interpreter, a deaf inmate who depends on sign language cannot testify or question witnesses and is thereby denied his or her constitutional right to a fair hearing.

The federal judge approved a consent decree that provided interpreters for deaf prisoners in many situations of prison life: at adjustment team hearings; when officials give notice that a disciplinary report is being written; whenever a deaf inmate is provided counseling or psychiatric, psychological, or medical care; and in any on-the-job or vocational training or any educational program. This consent agreement is a model of how to provide deaf prisoners their basic due process rights and access to needed counseling, medical services, and rehabilitation programs.[21]

The Department of Justice's Section 504 regulation analysis specifically states that prisons

> Should provide for the availability of qualified interpreters (certified, where possible, by a recognized certification agency) to enable hearing-impaired inmates to participate on an equal basis with non-handicapped inmates in the rehabilitation programs offered by the correctional agencies (e.g., educational programs).[22]

State Civil and Administrative Proceedings

In criminal proceedings, the constitutional rights to notice, confrontation, and effective assistance of counsel have compelled the right to an interpreter. Traditionally these rights have not been recognized as fundamental in civil proceedings, and many states lack statutes providing interpreters to deaf people in such settings.

However, the U.S. Supreme Court increasingly has required the observance of constitutional due process rights in certain civil proceedings and administrative hearings. These include juvenile hearings,[23] parole and probation revocation hearings,[24] prison disciplinary proceedings,[25] and passport reviews.[26]

In addition, the Department of Justice's analysis of its Section 504 regulation (quoted on pages 175–176) specifically requires the appointment of interpreters in civil proceedings when the court system receives federal financial assistance. Section 504 can provide a remedy if the state or local government receives federal financial assistance from the Department of Treasury's Office of Revenue Sharing or other federal agencies.

Few states have laws providing interpreters for deaf people in administrative proceedings that deal with matters such as worker's compensation, welfare, immigration, tax, licensing, school placement, employment disputes, and zoning hearings. These hearings affect many areas of our lives, and deaf citizens should neither be prevented from participating in them nor fail to get justice simply because a state refuses to provide interpreters.

Interpreter Privilege

States have begun to recognize that interpreters in a confidential attorney-client situation are covered by the attorney-client privilege. The privilege means that interpreters cannot be forced to reveal any information based on that confidential interview. The privilege exists to ensure that clients will freely discuss their problems with their lawyer without fear of disclosure. Kentucky, New Hampshire, Tennessee, and Virginia have laws explicitly applying this privilege to sign language interpreters.[27] In other states, laws and precedents pertaining to the status of translators should be applied also to sign language interpreters.

A Maryland circuit court ruled that interpreters could not be ordered to disclose statements that a deaf suspect made to his attorney. An interpreter with legal-specialist certification was subpoenaed to testify before a grand jury about a jailhouse interview between a deaf defendant, his attorney, and the defendant's relatives. The judge stated: "When both attorney and client depend on the use of an interpreter for communicating to one another, the interpreter serves as a vital link in the bond of the attorney-client relationship."[28] The judge also stated that the presence of close relatives at such interviews may be helpful in aiding the accuracy of the communication, thereby "enabling the attorney to provide meaningful assistance to his client."

The case was appealed. The Maryland Court of Special Appeals did not deal with the question of whether the communication was confidential. It reversed the decision saying that the lower court lacked the jurisdiction to issue the decree.[29]

Telephone Access

Section 504 regulations of each of the federal executive departments and the Office of Revenue Sharing require installation of telecommunication devices for deaf people (TDDs) in all federally assisted agencies with which the public has telephone contact. In the analysis of its regulation, the Justice Department refers specifically to the obligation of police departments:

> Law enforcement agencies are also required to install TTYs or equivalent mechanisms . . . to enable people with hearing and speaking impairments to communicate effectively with such agencies.[30]

The installation of TDDs at police stations can help protect the lives and property of hearing-impaired citizens. Moreover, the general public benefits from the ability of an additional segment of the local population to make police reports by telephone. Many cities across the country have already installed TDDs in their police departments and other offices.

Equal Justice

Although recent state and federal legislation has greatly advanced the rights of deaf people involved with the legal system, much remains to be done if they are to achieve full access and equal justice.

First, states without laws should adopt model statutes that provide qualified interpreters to any deaf party or witness in any judicial action.* In criminal cases, interpreters should be provided to the deaf person during any police interrogation. Civil and administrative proceedings

---

*See Appendix D: "A Model Act to Provide for the Appointment of Interpreters for Hearing-Impaired Individuals for Administrative, Legislative, and Judicial Proceedings."

should also require interpreters paid for by the government.

Second, laws such as the Rehabilitation Act of 1973 must be fully enforced. The Department of Justice must ensure full compliance with its regulation if the rights of deaf people involved with the legal system are to be protected.

Third, judges, court administrators, lawyers, and law enforcement officers must become more aware of the communication problems of deaf people.

Good laws, thorough enforcement, and enlightened attitudes will ensure that deaf people obtain equal justice under law.

NOTES

1. Terry v. State of Alabama, 105 So. 386 (1925)
2. 28 C.F.R. §35.160(b)
3. 28 C.F.R. §35.130(f). See analysis by the Department of Justice at 56 Fed. Reg. 35,705 (July 26, 1991). (Imposition of the cost of courtroom interpreter services as court costs is impermissible under Section 504.)
4. 28 *United States Code* §1827
5. 45 *Federal Register* 37,630 (1980)
6. Id.
7. Miranda v. Arizona, 384 U.S. 436 (1966)
8. M. Vernon, "Violation of Constitutional Rights: The Language-

Impaired Person and the Miranda Warnings," *Journal of Rehabilitation of the Deaf* 11 (1978): 4.

9. Mary Furey, personal communication, June 1976
10. Vernon, "Violation of Constitutional Rights," p. 6
11. State of Maryland v. Barker, Crim. Nos. 17,995 and 19,518 (Md. Cir. Ct., Dec. 8, 1977)
12. Kiddy v. City of Oklahoma City, 576 P.2d 298 (S. Okla., 1978)
13. Section 51.55(c)(1) of Office of Revenue Sharing regulation to Section 122(a) of the State and Local Fiscal Assistance Act of 1972, as amended; 31 U.S.C. §1242(a)
14. 28 *Code of Federal Regulations* §42.503(f)
15. 28 C.F.R. §42, Subpart G
16. Commonwealth v. Edmonds, Cir. Ct. Staunton, Va. (1975)
17. See, for example, State of Maryland v. Barker (Note 9) and State of Oregon v. Mason, Crim. No. C-80-03-30821 (Ore. Cir. Ct., May 27, 1980)
18. 337 F.2d 606 (9th Cir. 1964)
19. 45 Fed. Reg. 37,630 (1980)
20. Bonner v. Lewis, 857 F.2d 559 (9th Cir. 1988)
21. Pyles v. Kamka, Civil No. K-79-1864 (unreported decision), Feb. 20, 1980
22. 45 Fed. Reg. 37,630 (1980)
23. In re Gault, 387 U.S. 1 (1967)
24. Wolff v. McDonnell, 418 U.S. 539 (1974)
25. Gagnon v. Scarpelli, 411 U.S. 778 (1973); and Morrissey v. Brewer, 408 U.S. 471 (1972)
26. Trop v. Dulles, 356 U.S. 86 (1958)
27. Kentucky Rev. Stat. §304.064 (Supp. 1976); New Hampshire H.B. 870, Ch. 521.1–521.5 (1977); Tennessee Code Ann. §24-108; and Virginia Code Ann. §2.1-560 through §2.1-563, §19.2-164, §8.01-400.1, and §63.1-85.4
28. Touhey v. Duckett, 19 Crim. L. Rptr. 2483 (Cir. Ct. Anne Arundel County, Md., 1976)
29. Duckett v. Touhey, 36 Md. App. 238 (1977)
30. 45 Fed. Reg. 37,630 (1980)

Television

Television has become our major source of entertainment, news, and information. Though televised images are powerful, much of the information accompanying these images is presented through sound, making the content of the transmission inaccessible to deaf and hard of hearing people. Technological advances, such as open- and closed-captioning, have made it possible for deaf and hard of hearing viewers to have access to prime-time and sports programming. However, not until the passage of federal legislation was television truly accessible to all hearing-impaired people.

The Television Decoder Circuitry Act ensures that the benefits of closed-captioning will reach every American home. In addition, the Federal Communications Commission (FCC) requires broadcasters to open-caption emergency bulletins and to consider the deaf community's needs when preparing their programming. This chapter explains the federal laws and how the new technology will make television available to all deaf and hard of hearing viewers.

EMERGENCY CAPTIONING

Before 1977, when the FCC adopted a rule requiring television broadcasters to present emergency bulletins in visual as well as oral form, deaf people were more vulnerable to danger because they could not hear televised disaster warnings.[1] In an emergency, the television station would interrupt the sound portion of the signal to make oral announcements, but the picture would continue without any indication that something was wrong. Sometimes "Emergency Bulletin" would appear on the screen, and an off-camera announcer would read the details of the emergency. The deaf viewer, unable to hear what was said, could not make realistic plans for safety.

When fires ravaged wide sections of California in 1970, officials used loudspeakers and radio and television broadcasts to warn residents to evacuate threatened areas. Several hearing-impaired people burned to death because they could not hear the loudspeakers or the radio bulletins and because the television announcements gave no visual information about the danger. Their deaths could have been prevented except for simple thoughtlessness.

This and similar tragedies prompted appeals to the FCC. Thousands of letters from people all over the country convinced the FCC to adopt a visual warning rule. The "Operation During Emergency" section states:

> Any emergency information transmitted in accordance with this Section shall be transmitted both aurally and visually or only visually. Television broadcast stations may use any method of visual presentation which results in a legible message conveying the essential information. Methods which may be used include but are not limited to slides, electronic captioning, manual methods (e.g., hand printing) or mechanical printing processes. However, when emergency operation is being conducted under a National, State, or Local Level Emergency Broadcast System (EBS) Plan, emergency announcements shall be transmitted both aurally and visually.[2]

Under the Communications Act of 1934, the FCC is authorized to make such rules to protect the safety of life and property through the use of electronic media and to improve the quality of those media in ways that promote the public interest.[3]

Even though the visual warning rule has been in effect for many years, many television stations still do not comply. A person should contact the station and explain to the station manager the need for the visual emergency bulletin, citing the above FCC rule. If the station still refuses to provide visual emergency warnings, then a person can file a complaint with the FCC. Complaints are considered when a station applies to renew its FCC license.

THE GROWTH OF CAPTIONING

Captioned television has made it possible for millions of people with hearing losses to see what television has to say. Captioning has taken two forms—*open-captioning*, which involves broadcasting captions on a regular television signal to all receivers, and *closed-captioning*, which involves transmitting the caption on a special television signal that requires the use of a decoder-adapter on the receiver. Today, almost all captions are closed.

The Public Broadcasting Service (PBS), a nonprofit, noncommercial television network, first introduced captioning. The first nationally broadcast captioned program was the cooking show, "The French Chef." The captioning was done by WGBH, the PBS station in Boston, Massachusetts. This program, and a few others available only on public television, had open captions. In December 1973, WGBH began captioning the "ABC Evening News," a half-hour program that daily took five staff people five hours to caption. This program also had open captions.

Open captions appear on all television sets and cannot be turned off by the viewer. Because of concerns that hearing viewers would object to widespread open captioning, PBS began developing a closed-captioning system in 1972.[4] In 1975, PBS filed a petition with the FCC to reserve a segment of the television signal known as "Line 21" for transmitting closed-captions.[5] Closed-captions are included in a video signal as invisible data. Presently, only viewers with a special device called a decoder can see the captions.

Since 1976, the FCC has reserved Line 21 of the television broadcast signal for transmitting closed-captions.

Nevertheless, the FCC has not imposed mandatory captioning requirements.[6] In 1979, Congress created the National Captioning Institute, a nonprofit corporation, to offer closed-captioning services to the broadcast television industry using Line 21.[7] In 1980, closed-captioned television services began as a cooperative agreement between the National Captioning Institute (NCI), the American Broadcasting Company (ABC), the National Broadcasting Company (NBC), PBS, and Sears, Roebuck & Company.[8/15] ABC, NBC, and PBS each agreed to caption up to 16 hours of their programming per week, and Sears agreed to manufacture and sell decoders.[9] In 1984, the Columbia Broadcasting System, Inc. (CBS) agreed to transmit closed-captions using both Line 21 and its own teletext technologies.[10] By 1989, all prime-time television programs and most major sports events were closed-captioned.[11] In 1990, there were approximately 290 hours of closed-captioned programming each week.[12]

Need for Legislation

Despite the growth in the number of closed-captioned programs, the benefits of television still are not fully accessible to millions of deaf and hard of hearing Americans or to millions of people who could use television to learn the English language. This lack of full access is primarily due to the small number of separate decoders currently in use. The separate decoder is a heavy piece of equipment, similar to a VCR, that must be attached to the television. NCI has estimated that since decoders first became available on the market, and as of June 1990, only about 300,000 have been sold.[13]

The Commission on Education of the Deaf has explained that because consumers purchase so few separate decoders, commercial incentives for private funding of captioning services are lacking.[14] The absence of funding has been one of the main impediments to a self-sustaining captioning service.

Because there is no market incentive, a great number of television programs, as well as movies on videocassette (both current and classic), are not being closed-captioned. In addition, commercial cable TV channels rarely caption any of their programs. In 1990, few network daytime and late night shows were closed-captioned. Moreover, in 1991, only 150 out of 1450 broadcast affiliates closed-captioned local news programs.[15] Yet, access to such local news programs is essential to deaf and hard of hearing people. For example, during the 1989 San Francisco and Los Angeles earthquakes and hurricane Hugo, local stations failed to provide captions to accompany their reports.[16]

Part of the reason that few programs other than prime-time television shows and major sports events are captioned is that it is more costly for broadcasters to caption programs with only a limited viewing audience. NCI estimates it costs $2,500 and takes between 20 and 30 hours to close-caption a one-hour program.[17] NCI explained to the Commission on Education of the Deaf that to maintain the current level of closed-captioned programming, 500,000 homes must be able to receive closed-captioned broadcasts.[18] The president of CBS Sports, Neil Pilson, in a letter to Senator Harkin discussing the threat to closed-captioning, stated:

> As a businessman and broadcaster, I am concerned about this imbalance between the cost of captioning programming and the very limited number of viewers. This gap makes it difficult to justify the expansion of captioning beyond those widely viewed kinds of programming being captioned today. Furthermore, some in the industry who have demonstrated their growing support of captioning through funding may begin to re-evaluate their commitment and, I fear, gradually reduce that commitment.[19]

ABC told the Commission that decoder usage must be increased to ensure a self-sustaining captioning service:

> [If] decoders were more widely used and viewership to grow, the marketplace can be relied upon to increase captioning because more viewers would be reached at a decreased per capita cost. Increased decoder ownership—not just more captioning—is required for a strong, self-sustaining captioning service.[20]

Congress recognized that it was necessary to enlarge the audience for captioned services to provide market incentives for an increased level of captioning. The potential audience that can benefit from closed-captioning is very significant—it includes 24 million deaf and hard of hearing persons.[21] In addition, by the year 2000, it is estimated that there will be more than 11 million senior citizens with a significant hearing loss who could benefit from closed-captioning.[22]

The potential audience includes more than just individuals with hearing impairments, however. Studies have shown that closed-captioning is an effective tool in teaching literacy skills. Captioning has been used successfully in the classroom with adults who have literacy problems,[23] those learning English as a second language, and children with and without disabilities. A study by the National

Assessment of Educational Progress estimates that 23 to 27 million American adults are functionally illiterate.[24] Another three to four million are learning English as a second language.[25] NCI reported that "forty percent of the 60,000 closed-captioning decoders sold in 1989 were to people for whom English is a second language."[26] These sales confirm research that shows closed-captioning benefits those learning English as a second language.

Closed-captioning has also been shown to benefit children who can hear. A report commissioned by the Pew Charitable Trust in Philadelphia found that closed-captioning has "a startling effect" on non-English-speaking children's ability to learn English words.[27] Most of the students in the study were from Southeast Asia. Results of a study at the University of Maryland showed that captioning improved word recognition for students with learning disabilities.[28] In addition, a Los Angeles teacher has been using closed-captioning in high-school English classes and reports marked improvement in student literacy skills.[29] The teacher turns off the sound on closed-captioned programs to force the students to read the captions to understand the television shows.[30]

Technology offers a way to provide this large potential audience with easy access to the benefits of closed-captioning. Decoder circuitry could be built into new television sets at a nominal cost. Two decoder chip designers estimated that the cost of each chip could be below three dollars if mass produced.[31]

The Commission on Education of the Deaf has recommended that all new televisions have build-in decoder circuitry so that they are capable of receiving closed-captioned programming.[32]

THE TELEVISION DECODER CIRCUITRY ACT

The Television Decoder Circuitry Act (TDCA) was signed into law in October 1990.[33] The TDCA requires that all television sets with screens 13 inches or larger, manufactured or imported into the United States, have the ability to display closed-captioned television transmissions without the aid of external equipment.[34] In 1988, 96 percent of new televisions had 13-inch or larger screens.[35]

In addition, the TDCA requires the FCC to establish performance and display standards for built-in decoder circuitry. The FCC has adopted final closed-caption display standards.[36] These standards will ensure that the television viewer can enjoy the benefits of both the latest innovative technologies and proven methods to provide quality closed-captioning. For example, the FCC requires the use of new technology that will allow captions to appear anywhere on the screen.[37] Today's closed-caption decoders can place text only at the top and bottom of the TV picture. Captions sometimes cover important parts of the picture, particularly in news programs where name and place identifications appear at the bottom of the screen. The new feature will allow captions to be moved out of the way when identifications appear and more precise placement to indicate who is speaking.

Several features that have proven effective in the separate decoder, such as a black background, are required in

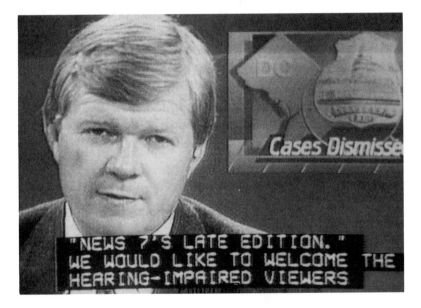

the new televisions containing decoders. The FCC pointed out that "it is essential that television receivers display captions that are readable. By providing a black background, the legibility of the caption is assured."[38] Further, the FCC has encouraged television manufacturers to develop other methods that can ensure legibility without obscuring as much of the video picture.[39]

Because of the rapid changes in television technology, the drafters of the TDCA were concerned that any new television technologies, such as high definition TV, be capable of transmitting closed-captions. A section was included in the TDCA requiring the FCC to take appropriate action to ensure that as new technologies are developed, closed-captioning will continue to be available to television viewers without the need of a separate decoder.[40]

As a result of the passage of the TDCA, almost all new televisions will contain decoder circuitry, greatly expanding the audience for closed-captioned programming. This, in turn, will provide the market incentive for a stronger, self-sustaining captioning service. It will then be possible for *all* people—hearing, deaf, and hard of hearing—to have easy access to television programming.

NOTES

The sections of this chapter on the Television Decoder Circuitry Act are adapted from an article on the TDCA written by Sy DuBow in the *Temple Law Review* ADA Symposium Issue, Volume 64 (1991). It is reprinted with permission of the *Temple Law Review*, copyright © 1991 Temple University of the Commonwealth System of Higher Education.

1. FCC Docket No. 20,659, RM 2502 (1977)
2. 47 *Code of Federal Regulations* §73.1250(h)
3. 47 *United States Code* §151 *et seq.*
4. In the early 1980s the Greater Los Angeles Council on Deafness, Inc., brought a class action suit against Community Television of Southern California to mandate open-captioning. Greater Los Angeles Council on Deafness, Inc. v. Community Television of Southern Calif., 719 F. 2d 1017, 1019 (9th Cir. 1983), *cert. denied* Gottfried v. United States, 467 U.S. 1252 (1984). Affirming the district court's ruling that public television stations were not required to provide open-captioning, the United States Court of Appeals for the Ninth

Circuit ruled that § 504 of the Rehabilitation Act does not mandate that federally funded television programs be produced and broadcast with open-captions rather than closed-captions. *Id.* at 1023. The court noted that the U.S. Department of Education helped originate closed-captioning and requires all programs it funds to be produced with closed-captions. Further, as a condition of its grants, the Department requires that public stations broadcast with closed-captions those programs produced with closed-captions. *Id. See also* Community Television v. Gottfried, 459 U.S. 498 (1983) (§ 504 of the Rehabilitation Act does not require the FCC to impose greater obligation on public licensees than on commercial licensees to provide special programming for the hearing-impaired population).

5. FCC Docket No. 20,793, RM 2616 (1975)
6. Commission on Education of the Deaf (C.O.E.D.), *Toward Equality: Education of the Deaf* (1988) at 113
7. *Id.*
8. *Id.*
9. *Id.*
10. *Id.*
11. S. Rep. No. 393, 101st Cong., 2d Sess. 2 (1990)
12. H. Rep. No. 767, 101st Cong., 2d Sess. 5 (1990)
13. *TV Decoder Circuitry Act: Hearings on S. 1974 Before the Subcomm. on Communications,* 101st Cong., 2d Sess. (1990) [hereinafter *Hearings*] at 67 (statement of John Ball, president, National Captioning Inst.)
14. C.O.E.D., *supra* note 6, at 114–115
15. S. Rep. No. 393, *supra* note 11, (citing CAPTION CENTER TELEVISION STATION, WGBH, Boston, Mass., SURVEY (1990))
16. *Id.*
17. *Id.* (citing National Captioning Inst., FYI Report (July 1987)).
18. C.O.E.D., *supra* note 6, at 119 (500,000 homes must be able to receive closed-captioning for it to become economically self-sustaining)
19. S. Rep. No. 393, *supra* note 11 at 4
20. C.O.E.D., *supra* note 6, at 119
21. S. Rep. No. 393, *supra* note 11, at 1
22. U.S. Congress, Office of Technology Assessment, "Hearing Impairment and Elderly People—A Background Paper," OTA-BP-BA-30, U.S. Govt. Printing Office 3 (May 1986)
23. Wilson, "Using Closed-Captioned Television to Teach Reading to Adults," *Reading Research and Instruction* 28(4)(1989): 27–37.
24. F. Chisman, *Jump Start, The Federal Role in Adult Literacy, Final Report on the Project of Adult Literacy* (1989).
25. *Id.* at iv
26. "TV Closed-Captions Fight Illiteracy," *USA Today,* July 11, 1990, at 6D, col. 6.
27. *Id.* at 6D, col. 1

28. Koskinen, Wilson, Gambrell, & Jensema, "Closed-Captioned Television: A New Technology for Enhancing Reading Skills of Learning Disabled Students," *E.R.S. Spectrum, Journal of Scholarly Research & Information* (1986).
29. *USA Today, supra* note 26
30. *Id.*
31. Letter from EEG Enterprises, Inc. to Sy DuBow (Mar. 1, 1990); *Hearings, supra* note 13 (statement of John Ball, president, National Captioning Inst.)
32. C.O.E.D. *supra* note 6 at 120
33. Television Decoder Circuitry Act of 1990, Publ. L. No. 101–431, 104 Stat. 960 (1990) [hereinafter TDCA]. The Senate unanimously passed Senate Bill 1974 on August 2, 1990; the House unanimously passed it on October 1, 1990. President Bush signed it into law on October 16, 1990.
34. TDCA, *supra* note 33, § 3, 104 Stat. at 960
35. 12 TV Digest (September 11, 1989).
36. *Report and Order,* in the Matter of Amendment of Part 15 of the Commission's Rules to Implement the Provisions of the Television Decoder Circuitry Act of 1990, General Docket No. 91–1, FCC 91–119, 38151 (adopted April 12, 1991) (released April 15, 1991). The standards cover, inter alia, the use of color characters, italics, upper and lower case characters, smooth scrolling, caption size, and the compatibility with cable scrambling technology.
37. *Id.* at 5–8
38. *Id.*
39. *Id.*
40. TDCA, *supra* note 33, § 4(a), 104 Stat. at 960

Telephone Service

Society has isolated deaf people for centuries. Today such exclusion is perhaps most obvious in the area of telecommunications. Rapid and efficient telecommunications services, readily available to almost all hearing Americans, have been largely denied to those who cannot hear. The telephone network has placed unnecessary barriers of expense and difficulty on deaf people, limiting their ability to communicate with family, friends, businesses, government, and social services. For deaf people to participate fully in our society, telecommunications must be made as rapid, efficient, and reasonably priced for people who cannot hear as it is for those who can.

Significant developments have been made in the area of telecommunications for deaf and hard of hearing individuals in the past few years. Telecommunications relay systems have spread across the country, giving TDD users new telephone access to all voice telephone users. Requirements for hearing-aid-compatible telephones have grown, as have requirements for TDD-equipped public pay phones. These and other changes have come about as a result of work with federal and state legislative bodies and regulatory agencies.

REGULATION OF TELECOMMUNICATIONS

Telephone companies are public utilities whose rates and practices are regulated by federal and state agencies. The federal agency that regulates interstate telephone practices is the Federal Communications Commission (FCC). Each state has its own agency with power to regulate most

---

of the operations of telephone companies within the state (intrastate). The state agencies are usually called public utility commissions (PUCs) or public service commissions. The FCC was established by Congress and the PUCs by the state legislatures to ensure that telephone companies operate in the public interest. In other words, telephone companies must provide adequate service to the public for a fair price, and they must comply with applicable laws and regulations.

The state agencies set the rates that telephone companies can charge. They allow the companies enough revenue to operate, provide the service, and make a reasonable profit. The telephone companies must justify their requests for rate changes at public hearings. For example, at a rate hearing, an individual phone company gives the state PUC detailed financial information about its expenses and equipment. Consumers and other interested people can participate in the hearings. They can tell the agencies about the services they need and the rates they consider fair. The final decision about the rate or "tariff" is made by the PUC.

TELECOMMUNICATIONS RELAY SERVICES

Telecommunications relay services enable people who use TDDs or other nonvoice terminal devices to have conversations with people who use conventional voice telephones. The call is relayed back and forth by a third party who reads what the TDD user types and types what the voice telephone user speaks. In the early 1980s, private relay systems began to develop around the country, offering some link for TDD users to the public telecommunications network. Most of these private programs were funded with donations and staffed with volunteers.

In 1987, California became the first state to open a 24-hour, 7-day-a-week relay system. Several other states followed California's example, establishing both private and state-run services. Unfortunately, funding shortages caused most of these state and private programs to impose restrictions on relay users. Few programs relayed interstate calls, and many placed limitations on the length, number, and time of day that calls could be made. Even with these restrictions, the demand for relay services was overwhelming. In California, for example, 50,000 calls were relayed the first month of its operations. That number has now reached 260,000. The tremendous need for relay services eventually resulted in the passage of Title IV of the Americans with Disabilities Act (ADA), which requires all telephone companies to provide intra- and interstate relay services across the United States by July 26, 1993.[1]

In addition to the ADA, Congress took other action to expand relay services for TDD users. Specifically, on October 28, 1988, Congress passed the Telecommunications Accessibility Enhancement Act (TAEA). This Act expanded the federal relay system. The federal system is used for relaying calls to, from, and within the federal government. It has been in existence since 1986. It was originally established by the Architectural and Transportation Barriers Compliance Board and operated by the U.S. Treasury Department. Unfortunately, before the passage of TAEA, the federal relay system had been poorly publicized and understaffed. The new law transferred authority for its operations to the General Services Administration and added relay operators to accommodate many more TDD users. In addition to enlarging the federal relay program, the TAEA ordered the publication of federal TDD numbers in a government-wide directory and directed each house of Congress to develop a policy with respect to the placement of TDDs in members' offices.

EQUIPMENT DISTRIBUTION PROGRAMS

The cost of owning a TDD can be prohibitive for deaf people, most of whom have below-average incomes. In addition to the initial cost, the TDD user must also pay for repair, maintenance, and, if needed, paper supplies. Expense is the main reason that only about 200,000 TDDs are in use today in the United States. The cost of TDDs and other specialized telephone equipment has prompted many states to develop equipment distribution programs. These programs distribute specialized equipment to deaf and other disabled individuals free of charge or at a discount. Some states set income qualifications for individuals wishing to receive such equipment; other states merely require certification that the individuals are hearing-impaired or otherwise disabled.

To date, approximately twenty-five states have equipment distribution programs. As the number of relay programs increases, the number of these programs, too, is expected to increase to fill the increased need for TDDs.

One issue, however, has arisen with respect to these distribution programs. Many fear that these programs are promoting the use of archaic technology. Research and development in the field of TDDs is advancing rapidly. Newer TDDs can now use a transmission code called ASCII—the American Standard Code Information Interchange. ASCII-coded TDDs can "talk" with computers and transmit words faster than conventional TDDs, thus requiring less time and money to complete a call. The advantages of the ASCII format have caused several deaf advocacy groups to pass resolutions to have the entire TDD network switch to the ASCII format within the next few years.

The problem with many, if not most, of the TDD distribution programs is that they distribute TDDs that use an incompatible and older code—the Baudot code. Many fear that these programs are saturating the markets with Baudot equipment that will soon be obsolete. If a state or company is required to furnish a TDD to a deaf customer now, it may feel little or no obligation to replace the TDD with a more advanced model within a few years. One solution is for states and companies to distribute TDDs with dual-mode capacity, that is, the ability to switch from Baudot to ASCII and back.

LONG-DISTANCE RATE REDUCTION

The charge for a long-distance call is usually based on the number of minutes the telephone line is used, the distance between the callers, the day of the week, and the time of day the call is placed. Because TDD calls take much longer than voice calls to communicate the same message, long-distance TDD calls are very expensive.

Although basic TDDs can transmit at a maximum speed of sixty words per minute, most TDD calls are transmitted at a much slower rate. One reason is that some deaf people have below-average skills with written, as well as spoken, English vocabulary and syntax. The language they are most comfortable with is American Sign Language (ASL). They communicate in English more slowly than they communicate in sign language. Even among skilled English-language users, only a small percentage can type sixty words per minute. By contrast, the estimated average speaking rate for native users of American English is 165 words per minute. Thus, a typical TDD user pays $6.50 to have the same long-distance telephone conversation that a hearing person could have for only $2.50.

In August 1981, AT&T petitioned the FCC for a reduction of interstate long-distance rates for hearing-impaired TDD customers. The FCC approved the petition and the rates went into effect in November 1981.[2] AT&T rates are now reduced 35 percent for daytime and 60 percent for evening calls. Late night and weekend rates remain the same. Recently, Sprint, another long-distance telephone company, also began procedures to offer TDD discounts.

Deaf customers have used two means to request rate reductions for intrastate long-distance calls. In some states, they have petitioned the state PUC for a rate reduction and presented evidence at an administrative PUC hearing about the need for the discount. In other states, they have asked the legislature to pass a law requiring the state PUC to adopt the rate reduction. The choice between these two approaches depends on where deaf customers have the best contacts and most influence. It also depends on whether or not the state PUC is willing to grant a reduction without getting specific authority from the state legislature.

Numerous methods have been adopted by states and telephone companies to administer rate reductions. Some states, such as New York, require deaf customers to submit a statement from a doctor, audiologist, or public agency certifying that they are hearing impaired. Other states merely ask deaf customers to apply for the reduced rate, without requiring certification. In some states a reduction applies to the deaf person's entire household; in other states the discount is only applied to calls made with a TDD.

A new issue regarding TDD discounts has come up with the ADA's new requirement for relay services. Because long-distance calls that are relayed take longer than direct voice-to-voice calls, deaf individuals believe that the FCC should order a rate reduction for all long-distance relayed calls. Indeed, some relay providers and state relay systems already offer such discounts. For the present time, the FCC has rejected this request, but has encouraged long-distance companies to voluntarily offer rate reductions as a competitive feature of relay service.

Telephone charges should be based on the value of the service to the customer rather than on the cost to the telephone company of providing the service. For example, if homes in rural or mountainous areas were charged the actual cost to the telephone company of running telephone lines and installing equipment, their rates would be very high. Yet all residential telephone customers, urban and rural, are charged the same fee for basic telephone service. This is done because the value of that service is the same for everyone and because the telephone system is more useful for everyone if it reaches as many people as possible. The cost of providing service to all households is averaged, and the cost is spread among all customers. The telephone system is supposed to provide access to universal communication services at fair and reasonable rates. Reduced rates for TDD calls will help to ensure that deaf people have access to the telephone system on the same basis as other telephone users.

TDD-EQUIPPED PAY TELEPHONES

Public telephones have an important communication function. Deaf people who cannot afford their own telephones or TDDs or who are away from home need to use pay phones. Most deaf individuals do not own TDDs that are truly portable. Even those individuals who do purchase portable TDDs are unable to use them at pay phones that do not have electrical outlets to supply the necessary power.

Only recently have public places begun to install TDD-equipped pay phones. New developments designed to make these phones less susceptible to vandalism have prompted some airports, subway transit systems, and malls to install them.

Guidelines issued by the Architectural and Transportation Barriers Compliance Board (ATBCB) pursuant to the ADA will also increase the availability of TDD-equipped public telephones.[3] These guidelines apply to new construction and alterations in places of public accommodations and commercial facilities, as covered by Title III of the ADA[4]. The requirements are as follows:

1. If the total number of pay phones at a given location is four or more, and at least one of these phones is located inside a building at that location, a TDD-equipped pay phone must be provided inside the building.
2. If a public pay telephone is provided in a stadium or arena, a convention center, a hotel with a convention center, or a covered mall, at least one public TDD-equipped pay phone must be provided in the facility.
3. If a public pay phone is located in or next to a hospital waiting room, recovery room, or emergency room, one public TDD-equipped pay phone must be provided at each location.

The ATBCB rules also require that TDD-equipped pay phones be identified by the international TDD symbol. In addition, if a facility has a TDD-equipped pay phone, it must place a sign (using the international symbol) directing individuals to that phone next to banks of pay phones that are not equipped with TDDs. If a facility has no banks of telephones, it must place the directional sign at the entrance to the facility.

Many deaf individuals feel that in addition to requiring TDD-equipped telephones in the above situations, public pay telephones should be designed to accommodate portable TDDs. This is especially important in larger facilities where individuals would have to walk long distances to locate the TDD-equipped phones. Responding to this concern, the ATBCB regulations require that new construction or alteration of public accommodations covered under Title III of the ADA must include at least one public pay telephone in each bank of three or more telephones that can accommodate portable TDDs. These telephones will have a shelf for the TDD, an electrical outlet, and a telephone handset cord long enough to reach the TDD.

HEARING AID COMPATIBILITY

Hearing-aid-compatible telephones enable individuals who use hearing aids with a telephone switch to block out background sounds and high-pitched squeals that can occur with incompatible telephones. The hearing aid switch enables the wearer to pick up sound waves generated by the electromagnetic field of the telephone receiver. Telephones with the required amount of electromagnetic leakage are considered to be compatible with hearing aids.

Until the early 1980s most telephones manufactured in this country had strong electromagnetic fields. This is because prior to this time, AT&T rented telephones to most Americans. These telephones were all hearing aid compatible. Around this time, however, new equipment companies here and abroad were given permission to manufacture and distribute telephones that could be purchased by consumers. Many of these telephones did not have enough electromagnetic leakage to be compatible with hearing aids.

In 1982, Congress took steps to rectify this situation. At that time, Congress passed the Telecommunications for the Disabled Act,[5] which made clear that compatibility between telephones and hearing aids was necessary to accommodate the needs of individuals with hearing loss.

In the 1982 Act, Congress took several steps. First, it directed the FCC to establish uniform technical standards for hearing aid compatibility. Second, it set forth a requirement that all "essential telephones" be equipped for use with hearing aids. Congress defined "essential" phones as coin-operated phones, phones for emergencies, and phones frequently needed by individuals with hearing impairments. Finally, Congress also directed the labelling of telephone equipment so that consumers would be aware of the compatibility between telephones and hearing aids.

In the years following passage of the Telecommunications for the Disabled Act, individuals with hearing losses insisted that the definition of essential telephones was far too narrow to meet the needs of hearing aid users. As a consequence, Congress finally passed the Hearing Aid Compatibility Act of 1988 (HAC Act).[6] The HAC Act required that all telephones manufactured after August 16, 1989, be compatible for use with hearing aids.[7] On May 18, 1989, the FCC promulgated regulations directing compliance with the new law.[8]

After the HAC Act was passed, hearing aid wearers were still concerned that the FCC had not taken steps to reduce the number of incompatible telephones that had been installed in workplaces and other institutions prior to the 1989 manufacturing deadline. As a result of consumer persistence in this area, in 1990, the FCC finally issued a rule to again expand the availability of HAC telephones. The new rule changed the definition of essential telephones, to require that telephones located in common areas of the workplace and all credit-card-operated telephones be compatible with hearing aids by May 1, 1991.[9]

Some individuals can also benefit from telephones that amplify the speaker's voice. These telephones have volume controls, which allow the telephone user to control the loudness of the other person's voice. A new ATBCB rule issued under the ADA will expand the number of public pay phones with volume control in places of public accommodation. The new rule requires that 25 percent of all public pay telephones in newly constructed buildings and facilities be equipped with volume control. All of these telephones shall be identified by a sign containing a telephone handset radiating sound waves.

CUSTOMER AND OTHER TELEPHONE SERVICES

In the past, deaf telephone subscribers paid for many telephone services that they could not use. For example, many types of calls, such as person-to-person and collect long-distance require operator assistance. Directory assistance is necessary for new listings and for long-distance and other calls for which no telephone directory is available. When people desire telephone service repairs or installations or have questions about telephone bills, they must call the telephone business office.

After July 26, 1993, access to most of these services should no longer be a problem. After that time the relay requirement of the ADA will go into effect mandating, in part, relay access to all operator services.

A few problems remain, however. To begin with, many operators do not have a directory of TDD numbers. To date, most conventional telephone directories do not note whether a number is accessible via a TDD. Even those directories that do contain this information typically charge consumers an extra fee for such "additional lines of information." This is an issue that deaf advocacy groups will have to address in order to gain full access to the telephone directory system.

Another problem with regard to customer services occurs when telephone companies use recorded "intercept" messages. Typically, these messages are used for telephone numbers that have been changed, disconnected, or for some other reason are not functioning. These messages do not register with TDD equipment. When TDD users encounter a recorded message, they know their call has not been completed but they do not know why. They either wait on the line for extended periods or continue trying to reach the number, even though it is not in service.

While TDD users may use the new relay systems to ascertain why they are not getting through to a number, this will cause added phone calls for both the TDD callers and the relay systems. Deaf advocacy groups have sought to require that routine recorded messages be encoded for TDD users. Telephone companies have opposed this proposal, arguing that it is technologically difficult and prohibitively expensive. However, deaf customers pay for and need this service just as hearing customers do. It is a basic service that should be available to all telephone subscribers.

A more recent problem regarding telephone services has arisen with the development of audiotext services. These services provide a recorded message that gives the caller a choice of options as to how to direct the call. Banks, educational institutions, and transportation information lines are only a few of the places that now routinely use audio-text services. TDD callers have access to this service only through relay operators; however, relay operators have a difficult time keeping up with the speed of the recorded messages, making this service virtually inaccessible to TDD users.

NEW DEVELOPMENTS

Telephone accessibility is extremely important for deaf and hard of hearing people, just as it is for hearing people. Lack of access to the telephone system dramatically increases isolation. This chapter provides only a summary of the major issues and some of the approaches that advocacy groups have taken to expand telecommunications access.

New and dramatic advances in telephone technology are expected within the next few years. For example, new services such as speech-to-text may eliminate the need for an operator to relay calls between TDD and voice telephone users. Similarly, new devices may become available that can provide better and cheaper communication for deaf people. New methods of providing services and competition in the telephone manufacturing and service industries have and will continue to alter service rates and equipment prices. The role of regulatory agencies will also continue to change. Deaf people and their advocates should become knowledgeable about these telecommunications developments in order to take advantage of the changes when they occur.

NOTES

1. ADA Title IV requirements are discussed in detail in chapter two.
2. FCC Transmittal No. 13,822 (August 1981)
3. 56 Fed. Reg. 35408 (July 26, 1991), to be codified at 36 C.F.R. Part 1191
4. See chapter two for a detailed explanation of the regulations and requirements included in Title III of the ADA.
5. 47 U.S.C. §610
6. P.L. 100–394 (1988), codified at 47 U.S.C. §610
7. The HAC Act does exempt radio and secure telephones from this requirement.
8. 54 Fed. Reg. 21429 (May 18, 1989), codified at 47 C.F.R. Part 68
9. 55 Fed. Reg. 28762 (July 13, 1990)

State Legislatures and Commissions

S ince the 1980 elections, the federal government has sought to cut drastically both the budgets and the regulations for numerous programs that have assisted the poor and other minority groups, including the disabled. The policy of the Reagan administration has been to reduce the role of the federal government and to funnel lump sums of less money to the state governments. The states thus have a larger role in funding and regulating—or deciding not to fund or regulate—such programs.

One result of this policy is that hearing-impaired people and their advocates must increasingly turn to state governments to provide not only services but access to those services. This requires increased awareness of the state legislative process and of the purposes that can be served by state commissions. Those two factors are the substance of this chapter. First, however, there is a true story about the patience and persistence required to get one state government to approve a bill benefiting hearing-impaired people.

Maryland enacted legislation in 1980 establishing an outpatient mental health program for deaf people. The requirements for staff expertise are spelled out in the law: Staff must be fluent in receptive and expressive sign language, including American Sign Language, or become so within one year of being employed. The professional staff must have experience in assessment techniques, individual psychotherapy, and group psychotherapy with hearing-impaired people. They must also have practical knowledge of deaf psychology.

The problems of hearing-impaired people under treatment in Maryland's mental health facilities were first brought to light by psychologist Allen Sussman in a presentation at the 1977 convention of the Maryland Association of the Deaf (MAD). Sussman pointed out that several deaf persons in Maryland hospitals were largely being neglected because there was no regular staff trained in aspects of deafness or fluent in sign language. The association responded by establishing a task force to meet formally with officials of the Maryland Department of Health and Mental Hygiene (DHMH) to discuss the problems and suggested solutions. The department responded to the proposed solutions by saying that it lacked money to pay for the specialized mental health services that hearing-impaired patients needed.

Members and officials of MAD worked with the staff of the National Center for Law and the Deaf (NCLD) to develop a legal strategy. They concluded that litigation would be expensive, time-consuming, and probably not result in the needed services.

THE STORY OF ONE BILL

A legislative approach was adopted, with MAD and NCLD working closely to draft a bill. Delegate Raymond Beck sponsored the bill in the Maryland House of Delegates, and DHMH supported the legislation. After hearings that committee chairperson Torrey Brown characterized as among the better ones he had seen in his years in the general assembly, the bill passed quickly in the house but got stuck in the senate's finance committee. Late in the legislative session, confusion arose in committee hearings over the composition of the proposed advisory committee and the statutory definition of who is eligible for the proposed service. Amendments were made that required house approval.

Bill supporters were frustrated and disappointed when the 1979 legislative session expired with no action on

the bill. They regrouped before the next session and resolved all differences of opinion about the definition of a
person qualified for the service and about the composition
of the advisory committee. They sought bipartisan support, and identical bills were introduced simultaneously in
both the house and the senate to speed action. The agreed-
upon definition of an eligible person was "an individual
whose hearing impairment is so severe that the individual
is impaired in processing linguistic information through
hearing, with or without amplification."

The measure was one of the first introduced in the 1980
session and, backed by the organized and demonstrated
support of the deaf community, passed both houses
quickly. Governor Harry Hughes received a large delega-
tion of deaf people in the capitol and, on May 6, 1980,
signed the bill.[1]

Seven months later, however, the governor indicated
that he would cut funding for the new program because of
budgetary problems. A coalition of deaf organizations
quickly responded by meeting with the governor and
organizing a rally which helped convince the governor not
to cut the program. The outpatient program is now operating at Family Service of Prince George's County, Maryland.

LOBBYING IN YOUR STATE LEGISLATURE

The above account points out some of the triumphs and
frustrations of the state legislative process. Attention to
organization, timing, and detail are important before,
during, and after a bill is processed. All of these factors
are discussed in more detail in the following guide to
working effectively with state governors and legislators.[2]

Preparing for Action

1. State organizations of and for hearing-impaired people
   must set priorities. What specific services or protections do deaf citizens of your state need most?

2. Concentrate on these basic goals.
3. Can you achieve your goals through state agencies and the governor's office without legislative action, or do you need a state law?
4. Develop contacts with the heads of state agencies and find out if there are existing funds in the state agency to provide the services you need. Work with the governor's staff on the possibility of the governor issuing an executive order to provide you the protection you want. In Virginia the head of the state human resources agency required all state agencies and institu-

tions to pay for qualified interpreters for deaf citizens seeking access to their services. In Illinois the governor issued an executive order to require interpreters, when requested, at all state meetings and conferences.

5. If you need a state law, first try to get support from the state agency that would administer the program. Encourage them to recommend to the governor that your proposal be included in their budget.

6. If the agency refuses, work directly with the governor's staff to include your priority in the governor's budget. In most states, legislators approve most of the governor's budget. The governor's full-time, professional staff and the state agency personnel have the data and expertise that often persuade part-time legislators with limited staff. Legislators will more often support, amend, or reject the governor's budget items than initiate their own proposals. If you try to approach a legislator directly and independently, the executive branch may oppose your proposal. Even if the governor's staff considers your proposal worthwhile, they may oppose it because it upsets the governor's budget. This is especially true given tough economic times and the pressure for balanced budgets.

7. Sometimes the governor will not agree to support your proposal. Do not give up! Seek out influential legislators who are sympathetic to your goal. Try to get them to introduce a bill.

8. One big plus is to get a legislator—preferably one who sits on the committee that will hear the bill—to sponsor your bill. A legislator who knows the committee members well is best situated to move your bill through the committee.

9. Before you and other bill supporters meet with your legislative sponsor(s), *work out your differences*. It is important for leaders of all state organizations of and for hearing-impaired people to meet and agree on all parts of the bill before it is filed. Too often some organizations have not been consulted or involved in planning a bill because of philosophical, political,

or personality differences. After a bill is introduced, these organizations sometimes object to parts of the bill due to misunderstanding the bill's purpose or because of major or minor errors or omissions. These objections create confusion in legislators' minds and lead to delay, withdrawal, or defeat of a bill. It is imperative that a united front be presented to the legislators.

10. *Do your homework*. Gather facts on why the bill is needed. Document with actual experiences. The most important question the legislators will want answered is "how much will the bill cost the taxpayers?" Advocates for the hearing-impaired in North Carolina effectively answered this question in support of a comprehensive interpreter bill. First they compiled the number of times interpreters were used in court cases county-by-county; then they multiplied by the standard state interpreter fee for the hours involved. They calculated the actual costs for interpreters paid out by interpreter referral agencies. Data were also collected from other states that had state funds available for interpreter services; this showed the costs per year for providing interpreters in criminal, civil, and administrative proceedings.

Such detailed information should be provided to the legislative office that develops the fiscal note (calculates the annual cost of implementing the bill). These offices frequently have no idea how to estimate the fiscal cost for interpreters. Any hard data you can provide them, especially if they total a low but realistic figure, can help sway votes to support your bill. Also, find out how many hearing-impaired people in the state could benefit from the law. Will it help people throughout the state or only in one or two counties or cities? Collect data on how often the service will be needed. For example, if you want an interpreter bill to cover civil proceedings, how many cases were there in the state last year in which a deaf person requested interpreter services for a civil trial (such as a car accident case)?

11. When you meet with your legislative sponsor, present him/her with as complete a bill as possible, including your supporting research. The state legislator will frequently have limited time and staff resources. Your sponsor can help on the bill's wording and will refer the bill to the legislative drafting office for a final draft that meets all legal requirements. Urge your sponsor to prefile the bill if possible that year. Prefiling helps ensure an early hearing on your bill and gives you time before the legislative session begins to sign up cosponsors. Having both Democrat and Republican sponsors is helpful.

12. If a state legislature meets only for a few months, try to arrange for sponsors in both the house and senate to introduce identical bills. This will ensure hearings in both houses and a legislative advocate for your bill in each chamber.

13. Form coalitions with other organizations with similar interests. Coalitions give you clout with both the legislators and the governor. Senior citizen organizations are very powerful in many states due to their experience, their high voter turnout, and their invaluable time to lobby. They are an ally worth cultivating. Many of their interests coincide with yours. Parents' groups and professionals working for hearing-impaired children and adults should be part of your network. Finally, develop ties with organizations representing other disabilities and work together on common objectives. Coalitions are needed throughout the legislative process to ensure passage and implementation of needed laws and services.

When the Legislative Session Begins

1. The most crucial step in the legislative process is getting your bill reported favorably out of committee. The house and senate usually support a bill approved by a

committee. If a committee votes down your bill, getting the full house or senate to vote on it is very difficult. In Maryland, for example, a bill rejected by a committee can be brought to a floor vote only by petition of three senators or fifteen delegates. A bill frequently is amended or killed in committee. You must, therefore, devote considerable effort to

- presenting persuasive testimony,
- having answers for committee members, and
- demonstrating wide support for the bill through speakers representing different groups and by having many supporters at the hearing.

The job of persuasion must continue after the hearing.

2. Encourage letter writing to members of the committee and individual lobbying with legislators. An individualized letter discussing a relevant personal experience from a person in the legislator's home district is most effective. Try to organize a network of people in your state who can be mobilized quickly before the vote on your bill.

3. Remember that a legislator's time is valuable. You are competing with people who lobby for a living. You must be prepared on short notice to meet a legislator and explain concisely why your bill is needed.

4. Try to avoid amendments of your bill in the second chamber that considers it. If the senate amends a bill that passed the house, the amended bill must go back to the house for approval. There may not be time left for a house vote. A sad example of this procedure occurred in the Maryland General Assembly in 1979; as described early in this chapter, an amended bill to set up an outpatient mental health program died when time ran out.

5. Compromise is often necessary to gain passage and the governor's approval. Remembering your basic goal, however, you should staunchly resist amendments that cut funds, staff, or coverage necessary for the law to be effective. Legislators frequently find it easier simply to

pass a beautifully worded resolution or set up a voluntary commission that has no power.

Approval, Implementation, and Monitoring

1. Once a bill passes both houses, efforts must be directed to getting the governor to sign it into law. Sometimes a governor will sign a bill but later try to cut funding to your new program because of budgetary problems. Also, agencies responsible for implementing a law sometimes perform unsatisfactorily and need to be monitored.
2. A full- or part-time person working in the capitol is invaluable for keeping organizations aware of legislative and executive activities that may affect hearing-impaired people. Those states that have set up commissions or councils for deaf people have been extremely successful in developing friendly, working relationships with executive staffs and legislators. But it is you, the committed voters, who will make the difference.
3. Use the media. Newspaper and television stories can bring public attention and support to your bill and increase legislative awareness.
4. Work with the National Center for Law and Deafness (NCLD) on drafting the bill and comparing what other states have done. The NCLD is a free resource to help you at every step of the legislative process.

   Working with public officials can be a stimulating, rewarding, yet frustrating experience. They are elected by you and are accountable, finally, to you. So make your views known. Remember Benjamin Franklin's advice: "We must all hang together, or assuredly we shall all hang separately."

STATE COMMISSIONS

Deaf people have worked with state legislatures to see that agencies are established to provide necessary services.

The agencies currently in existence take various forms; usually they are constituted as state commissions or councils for deaf people.

At least twenty states now have commissions, councils, or other agencies specifically concerned with providing services to deaf people.* These commissions usually advocate for the needs of deaf citizens by advising the state legislature and by providing liaison with various agencies to secure and coordinate services. Another purpose is to collect and disseminate information about deafness, especially demographic and other data that serve to raise public consciousness about deaf people. Some agencies also coordinate or provide services, including information, referral, individual advocacy, counseling, and interpreters. A goal of some commissions is to create service projects such as job development programs.

The typical commission has from nine to twenty members, including deaf citizens, parents of deaf children, and

*See Appendix E for the titles and addresses of the state commissions or councils that have been established to date.

representatives of various state agencies, professions serving deaf people, and organizations of deaf people.

There are three basic organizational structures for state commissions: Commissions directly funded by the state, those with independent budgets within their agency or department, and those with no separate budget within their agency or department.

Independent Commissions

The independent commissions report to the governor and submit their budgets directly to the legislature or governor. Connecticut, Texas, and Virginia have commissions on this model.

Connecticut's commission is a statewide coordinating and advocacy agency that provides information, 24-hour-a-day interpreter services in a complete range of settings, interpreter training, counseling, referral, consultation on communication problems in mental health facilities, and representation of deaf citizen interests before public agencies and private industry.

The Texas commission, the first in the nation, was created in 1971 and is responsible for providing all services that are not the responsibility of other state agencies. It serves as an information clearinghouse; provides interpreter services in courts, hospitals, and government offices at no charge; and hires deaf senior citizens to visit other elderly deaf people.

The Virginia Department for the Deaf and Hard of Hearing coordinates a statewide interpreter service, consults with state agencies and institutions on the unique problems of deafness, evaluates state programs for their relevance and effectiveness, and provides information to the state government on the rights and needs of deaf Virginians. Recognizing that underemployment is a major problem of deaf workers, the department established an Industrial Relations Committee to identify and suggest ways to meet needs of deaf workers.

The director of Massachusetts's Office of Deafness is appointed by the state secretary of human services. The office studies the service needs of deaf people and then advises and recommends priorities to state officials and agencies. It acts as an information clearinghouse and reviews budget requests from state agencies, making comments and recommendations on them. It evaluates and monitors state services for deaf people and suggests necessary changes to improve their quality. And it coordinates interpreter services to deaf people and state programs. The office also monitors all bills in the state legislature that affect deaf people.

Commissions Within Other Agencies

Some of the state commissions are independent parts of another agency and are directly responsible to the head of the umbrella agency. North Carolina is an example of this kind of commission.

Established in 1977, North Carolina's Council for the Hearing Impaired acts as an advocate for deaf people, a bureau of information, and an advisor to the secretary of the state department of human resources. The council plans and implements services for deaf people through community service centers, informs deaf people of their rights and available services, makes referrals, coordinates communication between service agencies and deaf clients, and promotes accessible public community services and the training of interpreters. All of its community service programs are administered by the state Division of Vocational Rehabilitation Services.

Commissions that are part of another state agency have no separate budget and operate under the authority of the head of that agency. Minnesota, New Jersey, and Wisconsin have commissions of this type.

In addition to the usual information and advisory functions, the Minnesota Department of Public Welfare has a direct service component for deaf people. The Deaf Services Division works to ensure that all services available to hearing people are also available to deaf people. It negotiates for client's rights and does short-term case management, counseling, and referral. It advises welfare departments and other agencies and programs and, in conjunction with the Division of Vocational Rehabilitation, maintains eight regional service centers, each of which is an entry point for deaf people who need the services. Each center has an advisory committee of eight people appointed by the state commissioner of economic security; four advisors are deaf persons or parents of deaf children and four are representatives of county and regional human service agencies.

A Division of the Deaf within the New Jersey Department of Labor and Industry provides information and referral services, coordinates interpreter services, and provides interpreter training and TDD services for public agencies. It is establishing regional community service centers and works with other state agencies to coordinate services. For example, it has a formal, job-related services agreement with the state division of employment services and the state division of vocational rehabilitation.

Wisconsin's State Service Bureau for the Deaf has a forty-year history. From the beginning, state funds were granted to and administered by a private organization, the Wisconsin Association of the Deaf. In 1979 the service bureau was made into a state agency, the Bureau for the Hearing Impaired, as part of the community services division of the Wisconsin Department of Health and Social Services. The new entity will carry out its advisory and service functions with new authority and a greatly expanded staff.

Specific Needs of Deaf People

In some other states, the commission responsible for deaf concerns also represents other physically and mentally handicapped people. Such commissions may be satisfactory if they have a broad base of support. The advantage gained in not dividing community support on accessibility and discrimination issues may be lost, however, if the commission is not fully aware of the problems of deafness and attentive to the special service needs of deaf people.

When a state legislature establishes a commission, it should specifically address deafness in the enabling legislation.* If the commission is to exist for the entire range of physical and mental disabilities, then all disabled groups should be represented on the commission. The enabling legislation should have a clear and comprehensive definition of eligibility and broad application to the entire range of available programs and settings. The HHS regulations to Section 504 are excellent models.[3] Once established, the commission should be carefully monitored to make sure that its offices, services, and staff are fully accessible to deaf people. The offices should have TDD-equipped telephones, and commission members, staff, and clients should be provided with interpreters and other necessary accommodations. The interpreters should be qualified and certified.

The histories of existing state commissions indicate that those set up specifically for hearing-impaired citizens do not duplicate services already provided by other departments. The commission is simply a central office with special knowledge of the problems and needs of hearing-impaired people. It provides a center for vital information, consultation, and advocacy. It also raises public awareness about deafness and communication barriers.

The primary need of a council or commission is adequate means to perform its task. Funding must be sufficient and stable so that planning may have a predictable and realistic scope. A full-time, paid staff with wide experience in deafness is vital.

---

*See Appendix F for the (amended) enabling legislation that established Virginia's Council for the Deaf. Note the clear and comprehensive definition of eligibility and the adequate degree of authority given to the agency.

NOTES

1. Maryland Code Ann., Art. 59, §70–75 (1980)
2. Adapted from S. DuBow, "Communicating with Your Legislators," *Deaf American* 34(3): 34–35. Used by permission of the publisher.
3. 45 *Code of Federal Regulations* §84.2(j)

APPENDIX A

Reference Publications
on Deafness and PL 94-142

The Deaf Child and Regular Education (Mainstreaming)

Benderly, B. *Dancing Without Music*. Garden City, N.Y.:
Anchor Press/Doubleday, 1980. Reprint. Washington,
D.C.: Gallaudet University Press, 1990.

Birch, J. W. *Hearing-Impaired Children in the Mainstream*.
Reston, Va.: Council for Exceptional Children, 1975.

Bishop, M. E., ed. *Mainstreaming: Practical Ideas for
Mainstreaming Hearing-Impaired Students*. Washington,
D.C.: Alexander Graham Bell Association for the Deaf,
1979.

Brill, R. G. *Mainstreaming the Prelingually Deaf Child*.
Washington, D.C.: Gallaudet College Press, 1978.

Garretson, M. "Concept of the Least Restrictive Environment." *Gallaudet Alumni Newsletter* 11(16) Special
Issue, June 15, 1977, pp. 10–11.

Jacobs, L. M. *A Deaf Adult Speaks Out*. 3rd ed. Washington, D.C.: Gallaudet University Press, 1989.

Jensema, C., and Trybus, R. J. *Who Are the Deaf Children
in 'Mainstream' Programs?* Washington, D.C.: Gallaudet
College, 1977.

Karchmer, M. A., and Trybus, R. J. *Reported Emotional/
Behavioral Problems Among Hearing Impaired Children
in Special Education Programs; United States, 1972–73*.
Washington, D.C.: Gallaudet College, 1975.

Katz, L.; Mathis, S. L.; and Merrill, E.C. *The Deaf Child in
the Public Schools: A Handbook for Parents of Deaf
Children*. Danville, Ill.: Interstate Printers and Publish-
ers, 1978.

—

Mindel, E. D., and Vernon, M. *They Grow in Silence*. Silver Spring, Md.: National Association of the Deaf, 1971.

Moores, D. F. *Educating the Deaf: Psychology, Principles and Practices,* Boston: Houghton Mifflin, 1977.

Nix, G. W., ed. *Mainstream Education for Hearing-Impaired Children and Youth*. New York: Grune and Stratton Inc., 1976.

Northcutt, W. H. *The Hearing-Impaired Child in the Classroom: Pre-School, Elementary, and Second Years*. Washington, D.C.: Alexander Graham Bell Association, 1973.

Spradley, J. P., and Spradley, T. S. *Deaf Like Me*. New York: Random House, 1978. Reprint. Washington, D.C.: Gallaudet University Press, 1985.

Vernon, M., and Prickett, H. "Mainstreaming: Issues and a Model Plan." *Audiology and Hearing Education* 2(2): 5–11.

PL 94-142

Alexander Graham Bell Association for the Deaf. *Rights of Hearing-Impaired Children*. Washington, D.C.: Alexander Graham Bell Association for the Deaf, 1977.

Council on Exceptional Children. *Primer on Due Process in Education*. Reston, Va.: Council on Exceptional Children, 1977.

Council on Exceptional Children. *Primer on IEP for Handicapped Children*. Reston, Va.: Council on Exceptional Children, 1977.

DuBow, S. "P.L. 94-142." *American Annals of the Deaf* 122(5) (1977): 468–469.

DuBow, S. "Application of Rowley by Courts and SEAs." *Education of Handicapped Law Reporter,* SA-107 (1983).

DuBow, S. "Mainstreaming or Residential Schools for Deaf Students." *Gallaudet Today* (Spring 1985).

DuBow, S. "Into the Turbulent Mainstream—A Legal Perspective on the Weight to Be Given to the Least Restrictive Environment in Placement Decisions for Deaf Children." *Journal of Law and Education* 18 (1989): 215–228.

DuBow, S., and Geer, S. "Special Education Law Since Rowley." *Clearinghouse Review* 1001 (January 1984).

Gallaudet College. *Parents' Guide to Individualized Education Program.* Washington, D.C.: Gallaudet College, 1978.

Geer, S. "How Hearing-Impaired Children Fare in the Courts and Due Process Hearings Under PL 94-142." *Gallaudet Today* (Special Issue 1986).

Kendall Demonstration Elementary School. *Kendall Guide to Assessment: A Handbook for Parents.* Washington, D.C.: Kendall Demonstration Elementary School, Gallaudet College, 1978.

"PL 94-142 and Deafness." *Gallaudet Today* (Winter 1986).

Appropriate Public Education: Sample Letters of Request

I. Request for Evaluation

(Your Address)
(Date)

Superintendent of Schools
(Local Education Agency)
(Address)
(City, State, Zip Code)
    Re: (Name of Child)   Date of Birth: (Date)

Dear (Sir or Madam):

    This is to advise you that I have been (retained) (requested) to represent Mr. and Mrs. (name) in connection with their efforts to obtain a free appropriate public education for (child's name). My clients suspect that their (son) (daughter) is (describe suspected handicapping condition) and desire an immediate evaluation leading to an individualized education program meeting for placement in a program appropriate for their child's abilities. (Name of child) was born on (month, day, year) and is currently (describe present educational placement).

    Would you please schedule (child's name) for an evaluation as soon as possible pursuant to Public Law 94-142 and the implementing federal and state regulations. Please advise me when and where Mr. and Mrs. (name) should bring their child for (his) (her) evaluation.

    Thank you very much. With best wishes, I am,

Very truly yours,

(Your name)

    We join in this request for the purpose of consenting to the requested evaluation.

_____*(signature)*_____
Mr. (name)

(date)

_____*(signature)*_____
Mrs. (name)

II. Request and Authorization for Records

(Your Address)
(Date)

Superintendent of Schools
(Local Education Agency)
(Address)
(City, State, Zip Code)
     Re: (Name of Child)   Date of Birth: (Date)

Dear (Sir or Madam):

    This is to advise you that I have been (retained) (requested) to represent Mr. and Mrs. (name) in connection with their efforts to obtain a free appropriate public education for (child's name). In connection with this representation I wish to secure copies of all the school records, tests and reports on this child and (will be at your office on (date) at (time) to examine and secure copies of these records) (would like copies of these records sent to me at my office along with any bill for copying as soon as possible).

    These records are sought pursuant to the provisions of Public Law 94-142 and the "Buckley Amendment" and their implementing regulations. Mr. and Mrs. (name) have joined in this letter to authorize release of the records to me. With best wishes, I am,

Very truly yours,

(Your name)

    We, the parents of (child's name) hereby authorize the release of our child's complete school records to (your name) as our (representative) (attorney).

                           (signature)
                           Mr. (name)

(date)

                           (signature)
                           Mrs. (name)

III. Request for Local Due Process Hearing

(Your Address)
(Date)

Chairman, School Board
(Local Education Agency)
(Address)
(City, State, Zip Code)
    Re: (Name of Child)   Date of Birth: (Date)

Dear (Sir or Madam):

This is to advise you that I have been (retained) (requested) to represent Mr. and Mrs. (name) in connection with their efforts to obtain a free appropriate public education for (child's name). Mr. and Mrs. (name) do not agree with the (evaluation) (placement recommended pursuant to the IEP meeting) of (child's name) and wish to request a hearing on this matter pursuant to Public Law 94-142 and its implementing State and federal Regulations. We would like this hearing to be scheduled as soon as possible. Please advise me of the name, address, and telephone number of the hearing officer as soon as his or her identity is ascertained. I would also request that a verbatim written transcript be prepared of the hearing when held.

Please notify Mr. and Mrs. (name) and me of the time, date and place for the hearing when it is scheduled, and it might be (desirable) to check with me regarding the proposed date prior to sending out any notices so as to avoid a conflict that would require rescheduling the hearing. Mr. and Mrs. (name) have joined in this letter to confirm their request for a hearing. Thank you very much. With best wishes, I am,

Very truly yours,

(Your name)

We, the parents of (child's name) join in and affirm this request for a hearing regarding our child's education.

                    _(signature)_____

                    Mr. (name)

(date)

                    _(signature)_____

                    Mrs. (name)

IV. Request for State Review

(Your Address)
(Date)

(Superintendent of Public Instruction)
(State Department of Education)
(Address)
(City, State, Zip Code)
    Re: (Name of Child)   Date of Birth: (Date)
       (Locality)

Dear (Sir or Madam):

This is to advise you that I have been (retained) (requested) to represent Mr. and Mrs. (name) in connection with their efforts to obtain a free appropriate public education for (child's name) in the (local school division) schools. Mr. and Mrs. (name) do not agree with the decision reached on (date) by (name of local hearing officer), the hearing officer for the (local school division) and desire a review of (his) (her) decision pursuant to Public Law 94-142 and its implementing State and Federal Regulations. We would like this review hearing to be scheduled as soon as possible as we request the opportunity to present both written and oral arguments to the hearing officer. Please advise me of the name, address, and telephone number of the hearing officer assigned as soon as his or her identity is ascertained.

Please notify Mr. and Mrs. (name) and me of the time, date and place for the hearing when it is scheduled, and it might be desirable to check with me regarding the proposed date prior to sending out any notices so as to avoid a conflict that would require rescheduling the hearing. Mr. and Mrs. (name) have joined in this letter to confirm their request for a review hearing. Thank you very much. With best wishes, I am,

Very truly yours,

(Your name)

We, the parents of (child's name) join in and affirm this request for a review of the local hearing officer's decision of (date) in (local school division) regarding our child's education.

                (signature)
                Mr. (name)

(date)

                (signature)
                Mrs. (name)

NOTE

Appendix B is adapted from R. Shepard, "The Repudiation of Plato: A Lawyer's Guide to the Educational Rights of Handicapped Children," *University of Richmond Law Review* 13(83) Summer 1979, pp. 842–845. Used by permission of the publisher.

Providing Interpreter Service: One Agency Example

Memorandum

DATE: Nov. 15, 1979

TO: All Associate Commissioners
All Acting Associate Commissioners
All Regional Commissioners
All Assistant Regional Commissioners, Field
    Operations
All Area Directors
All DO's/BO's/TSC's

FROM: Acting Director for Civil Rights and Equal
        Opportunity
Social Security Administration
Department of Health, Education, and Welfare

SUBJECT: Providing Interpreter Service for the Hearing-
        Impaired in Social Security Administration
        Proceedings—ACTION

Pursuant to Section 504 of the Rehabilitation Act of 1973 as amended, SSA has an obligation to make sure that all programs and facilities are accessible to handicapped persons. This includes making certain that there is accurate communication with the hearing-impaired.

In October of 1978 the Associate Commissioner for Program Operations issued a see below [*sic*] outlining the circumstances under which SSA could purchase interpreter service. However, some organizations of the hearing-impaired have now requested more specific guidelines. In addition, we have had many recent contacts indicating that there is some confusion as to how our policy is to be implemented, and that some district and branch office employees are unaware that interpreters can be hired by SSA.

Accordingly, this memorandum will outline in greater detail the procedures to be followed. A Claims Manual section will be issued on this subject in the near future.

Provision of Interpreters

It is the policy of the Social Security Administration to ensure maximum accessibility of social security programs to the hearing-impaired in all agency proceedings concerning application for, or receipt, suspension, revocation, underpayment or overpayment of benefits under the Social Security Act. At times, this will include the local purchase of interpreter services for the hearing-impaired. This procedure is authorized within the local purchase authority delegated to district and branch office managers when it is necessary for effective communication. The claimant shall be informed immediately by the appropriate district or branch office employee that he or she has the right to interpreter service in accordance with the options listed below, and may request an interpreter at the agency's expense at any stage of agency proceedings, if he or she feels that effective communication is not occurring.

Several options for the provision of interpreter service exist:

1. The hearing-impaired person may provide his or her own interpreter at no cost to SSA;
2. A district or branch office may use its own employee who is proficient in sign language, or may borrow a qualified SSA employee from another office;
3. A qualified interpreter may be borrowed from another HEW component or from another Federal agency;
4. Free community service may be secured; or
5. SSA may purchase the needed service.

Note: An SSA or other Federal employee is considered to be qualified to sign if he or she is able accurately and simultaneously to *express* (send signs to the hearing-impaired person) and *receive* (understand signs from a hearing-impaired person) in sign language.

Conditions for Purchase of Interpreter Services

Initial Claims Proceedings

The above discussion will help to determine when the purchase of interpreter services is needed. The purchase of the services of an interpreter may be made when the following conditions are met:

1. There are no available SSA or other Federal employees who are able to communicate effectively with the hearing-impaired claimant.

   Normally, effective communication will require the use of an employee who is able to sign rather than written communication. If either the employee-interpreter or hearing-impaired claimant indicates he or she has difficulty communicating, then a non-SSA interpreter shall be obtained. In no event shall a hearing-impaired person be required to use an interpreter with whom he or she is unable to communicate.

2. There are no available community organizations that offer free interpreter services for the hearing-impaired.

   The district or branch office management shall initially survey the appropriate local agencies to determine the availability of free services. If free community services are available, the district or branch offices shall maintain a listing of available resources containing information such as the number of available interpreters and the timeliness with which a volunteer would be available in the office to interpret an interview. It shall be the primary responsibility of the office employee to secure the free outside service if the hearing-impaired individual has none of his or her own.

   If community services are not available or become unavailable, there shall be periodic checks (about every six months) to see if free interpreter services are available. These periodic checks should be part of the normal community relations activities of the district or branch office.

3. Approval for the purchase of service has been secured in advance.

    Purchase may be made via issuance of SF-147 or the use of imprest funds in accordance with ADS Guide OPO F:130–34, Small Purchase Procedures. Both require approval before a service can be utilized.

    When an office is notified that a hearing-impaired person wishes to come in for an interview and does not have his or her own interpreter, a determination must be made as to the availability of free community service. If none is available, and if no SSA or other Federal employee is available, the appropriate district or branch office employee shall make arrangements for the purchase of service, shall secure the necessary approval described herein, and shall notify the hearing-impaired individual and the interpreter as to the time and place of the interview. Every effort shall be made to conduct the interview as quickly as possible.

    If a hearing-impaired person comes to an office with an interpreter without prior arrangement for the interview, and if the hearing-impaired person requests SSA to pay for the interpreter's service, every effort shall be made to secure approval of the purchase immediately so that the interview can be conducted while the hearing-impaired person is in the office (naturally the other criteria must also be met).

4. A "qualified interpreter" is available.

    An interpreter shall be deemed qualified if he or she is certified by the National Registry of Interpreters or by a state registry of interpreters, or if he or she is on a list of qualified interpreters compiled by the National Association of the Deaf or any state association of the deaf.

    It is recognized that qualified interpreters are not available everywhere in the country. In the event that a qualified interpreter as described above is unavailable,

the agency shall provide an interpreter who is acceptable to both the hearing-impaired person and the
agency.

Appeal Proceedings

A hearing-impaired individual has the right to have an
interpreter available at all stages of the appeals procedure.
If the hearing-impaired individual does not have his or her
own interpreter, SSA shall purchase such service in
accordance with the conditions outlined above.

Interpreters—Appointment; Compensation

District and branch office employees shall assist the claimant in locating an interpreter and arrange for the purchase of an interpreter whenever this is requested by the
claimant.

Any interpreter, other than a Federal employee, appointed under this policy shall be paid a reasonable fee by
the agency for his or her services. The fees should be based
on prevailing rates and should reflect input from associations for the deaf or hearing-impaired.

SSA Notification to the Hearing-Impaired Community Concerning the Availability of Interpreter Service

In order to ensure maximum accessibility to all SSA
programs by the hearing-impaired, district and branch
offices shall take all possible steps to notify hearing-
impaired persons of the policies contained herein. Wher-
ever possible, public service announcements shall be made
through the news media on an ongoing basis. In addition,
district and branch office personnel shall provide the
information contained herein to local organizations of the
hearing-impaired, community service organizations, or
social service agencies as part of their ongoing community
relations effort.

Each district and branch office shall maintain a notice
to the public on its bulletin boards containing the policies
outlined herein.

Note: In making arrangements for an interpreter where the interview is in connection with filing a claim, care must be taken to ensure that there is no loss of benefits because an application is not filed timely.

(Signed)

Peter F. Velasquez

A Model Act to Provide for the Appointment of Interpreters for Hearing-Impaired Individuals for Administrative, Legislative, and Judicial Proceedings

I. Public Policy

It is the policy of this state to secure the rights of hearing-impaired persons who, because of impaired hearing, cannot readily understand or communicate in spoken language and who consequently cannot equally participate in or benefit from proceedings, programs, and activities of the courts, legislative bodies, administrative agencies, licensing commission, departments, and boards of the state and its subdivisions unless qualified interpreters are available to assist them.

II. Definitions

As used in this chapter, the following terms have the following meanings:

1. "Appointing authority" means the presiding officer or similar official in any court, board, commission, authority, department, agency, or legislative body, or in any proceeding of any nature where a qualified interpreter is required pursuant to this Act.
2. A "hearing-impaired person" means a person who, because of a hearing impairment, has difficulty understanding oral communication.
3. "Qualified interpreter" means a sign language or oral

---

interpreter as provided in Sections IV and VII of this Act.

4. "Intermediary interpreter" means any hearing-impaired person who is able to assist in providing an accurate interpretation between spoken English and sign language, or between variants of sign language, by acting as an intermediary interpreter.

III. Interpreter Required in the Following Situations

1. Whenever a hearing-impaired person is a party or witness at any stage of any judicial or quasi-judicial proceeding in this state or in its political subdivisions—including but not limited to civil and criminal court proceedings, grand jury proceedings, proceedings before a magistrate, juvenile proceedings, adoption proceedings, mental health commitment proceedings, and any proceeding in which a hearing-impaired person may be subjected to confinement or criminal sanction—the appointing authority shall appoint and pay for a qualified interpreter to interpret the proceedings to the hearing-impaired person and to interpret the hearing-impaired person's testimony.

2. Whenever a juvenile whose parent or parents are hearing-impaired is brought before a court for any reason whatsoever, the court shall appoint and pay for a qualified interpreter to interpret the proceedings to the hearing-impaired parent's testimony.

3. In any hearing, proceeding, or other program or activity of any department, board, licensing authority, commission, or administrative agency of the state or of its political subdivisions, the appointing authority shall appoint and pay for a qualified interpreter for the hearing-impaired participants.

4. Whenever a hearing-impaired person is a witness before any legislative committee or subcommittee, or legislative research or study committee or subcommittee or commission authorized by the state legislature or legislative body of any political subdivision of the

state, the appointing authority shall appoint and pay for a qualified interpreter to interpret the proceedings to the hearing-impaired person and to interpret the hearing-impaired person's testimony.

5. Whenever a hearing-impaired person is arrested for an alleged violation of a criminal law, including a local ordinance, the arresting officer shall procure a qualified interpreter for any interrogation, warning, notification of rights, or taking of a statement. No hearing-impaired arrestee otherwise eligible for release shall be held in custody pending arrival of an interpreter. No answer, statement, or admission, written or oral, made by a hearing-impaired person in reply to a question of a law enforcement officer or any other person having a prosecutorial function in any criminal or quasi-criminal proceeding may be used against that hearing-impaired person unless either the statement was made or elicited through a qualified interpreter and was made knowingly, voluntarily, and intelligently or, in the case of waiver, unless the court makes a special finding that the statement made by the hearing-impaired person was made knowingly, voluntarily, and intelligently.

6. Where it is the policy and practice of a court of this state or of its political subdivision to appoint counsel for indigent people, the appointing authority shall appoint and pay for a qualified interpreter for hearing-impaired indigent people to assist in communication with counsel in all phases of the preparation and presentation of the case.

IV. Preliminary Determination of Interpreter's Qualifications

Before appointing an interpreter, the appointing authority shall make a preliminary determination, on the basis of the hearing-impaired person's testimony, that the interpreter is able to accurately communicate with and translate information to and from the hearing-impaired person involved. If the interpreter is not able to provide effective communication with the hearing-impaired person, the appointing authority shall appoint another qualified interpreter.

V. Intermediary Interpreter to Be Used

If a qualified interpreter is unable to render a satisfactory interpretation without the aid of an intermediary interpreter, the appointing authority shall appoint an intermediary interpreter to assist the qualified interpreter, subject to the same provisions that govern a qualified interpreter under this Act.

VI. Interpreter in Full View

Whenever an interpreter is required to be appointed under this Act, the appointing authority may not commence proceedings until the appointed interpreter is in full view of and spatially situated to assure effective communication with the hearing-impaired participants.

VII. Coordination of Interpreter Requests

1. [The Department of Human Resources] shall establish, maintain, update, and distribute a list of qualified interpreters. The Department shall obtain the names of interpreters for this list from the state association of the deaf, state registry of interpreters for the deaf, and state schools for the deaf.
2. Whenever an interpreter is required under this Act, the appointing authority shall use one of the interpreters on the [Department of Human Resources] list. If none of the listed interpreters is available or if an interpreter is unable to provide effective communication with the particular hearing-impaired person, then the appointing authority shall appoint any other person who is able to accurately and simultaneously communicate with and translate information to and from the particular hearing-impaired person involved.

VIII. Oath of Interpreter

Before he or she begins to interpret, each interpreter appointed under this Act shall take an oath that he or she will make a true interpretation in an understandable manner to and for the person for whom he or she is appointed to the best of his or her skills and judgment.

IX. Compensation

An interpreter appointed under this Act is entitled to a reasonable fee for his or her services, including waiting time, reimbursement for necessary travel, and subsistence expenses. The fee shall be based on any fee schedule for interpreters recommended by the [Department of Human Resources] or prevailing market rates. Reimbursement for necessary travel and subsistence expenses shall be at rates provided by law for state employees generally.

X. Waiver

The right of a hearing-impaired person to an interpreter may not be waived except by a hearing-impaired person who requests a waiver in writing. Such waiver is subject to the approval of counsel to the hearing-impaired person, if existent, and is subject to the approval of the appointing authority. In no event is the failure of the hearing-impaired person to request an interpreter deemed a waiver of that right.

XI. Privileged Communications

Whenever a hearing-impaired person communicates through an interpreter to any person under such circumstances that the communication would be privileged and said person could not be compelled to testify as to the communications, said privilege shall apply to the interpreter as well.

XII. Visual Recording

The appointing authority, on his or her own motion or on the motion of a party to the proceedings, may order that the testimony of the hearing-impaired person and the interpretation thereof be electronically recorded (visually) for use in verification of the official transcript of the proceedings.

State Commissions and Councils for Deaf People

Arizona
Arizona Council for the Hearing Impaired
1300 West Washington Street, Second Floor
Phoenix, AZ 85007
(602) 542-3323 V/TDD
(800) 352-8161 in AZ V/TDD

Arkansas
Office of the Deaf and Hearing Impaired
300 Donaghey Plaza, North
7th and Main Streets
Little Rock, AR 72203
(501) 682-6697 VTDD

California
State Office of Deaf Access
Department of Social Services
744 P Street, MS 15-10
Sacramento, CA 95814
(914) 445-3039 V
(914) 445-8445 TDD

Connecticut
Connecticut Commission on the Deaf and Hearing
    Impaired
141 North Main Street
West Hartford, CT 06107
(203) 566-7414 V/TDD

Florida
Florida Council for the Hearing Impaired
Florida Education Center
Suite 622-C
Tallahassee, FL 32399-0401
(904) 488-5087 V/TDD
(800) 451-4327 in FL V/TDD

Indiana
Office of the Deaf and Hearing Impaired Services
Indiana Department of Human Services
150 West Market Street
Box 7083
Indianapolis, IN 46207
(317) 232-1143 V/TDD

Iowa
Deaf Services Commission of Iowa
Iowa Department of Human Rights
Lucas State Office Building
Des Moines, IA 50319
(515) 281-3164 V/TDD

Kansas
Kansas Commission for the Deaf and Hearing Impaired
Biddle Building
300 Southwest Oakley
Topeka, KS 66606
(913) 296-2874 V/TDD
(800) 432-0698 in KS V/TDD

Kentucky
Kentucky Commission on the Deaf and Hearing Impaired
Suite 9
Versailles Road
Frankfort, KY 40601
(502) 564-2604 V/TDD
(800) 372-2907 in KY V/TDD

Louisiana
Louisiana Commission for the Deaf
P. O. Box 3074
Baton Rouge, LA 70821-3074
(504) 769-8160 ext. 340 V/TDD
(800) 256-1523 in LA V/TDD

Massachusetts
Massachusetts Commission for the Deaf
    and Hard of Hearing
600 Washington Street, Suite 600
Boston, MA 02111
(617) 727-5106 V/TDD
(800) 882-1155 in MA V/TDD

Michigan
Michigan Department of Labor
Division on Deafness
201 North Washington Square
Box 30015
Lansing, MI 48909
(517) 373-0378 V/TDD

Missouri
Missouri Commission for the Deaf
505 East 5th Street
Fulton, MO 65251
(314) 592-4000 V/TDD

Nebraska
Nebraska Commission for the Hearing Impaired
4600 Valley Road
Lincoln, NE 68510
(402) 471-3593 V/TDD

New Hampshire
Program for the Deaf and Hard of Hearing
Division of Vocational Rehabilitation
78 Regional Drive, Building 2
Concord, NH 03301
(603) 271-3471 V/TDD

New Jersey
Division of the Deaf and Hard of Hearing
Department of Human Services
CN 074
Trenton, NJ 08625-0074
(609) 984-7281 V/TDD

North Carolina
Division of Services for the Deaf and Hard of Hearing
Department of Human Resources
695-A Palmer Drive
Anderson Building, Dorothea Dix Campus
Raleigh, NC 27603
(919) 733-5199 V
(919) 733-5930 TDD

Oklahoma
Services to the Deaf and Hearing Impaired
Rehabilitation Service Division
RS #24
P. O. Box 25352
Oklahoma City, OK 73125
(405) 424-4311 ext. 2920 V
(405) 424-2794 TDD

Oregon
Oregon Disabilities Commission
Deaf and Hearing Impaired Access Program
1880 Lancaster Drive NE, Suite 106
Salem, OR 97310
(503) 378-3142 V/TDD
(800) 358-3117 in OR V/TDD

Pennsylvania
Office for the Deaf and Hearing Impaired
1308 Labor and Industry Building
7th and Forster Streets
Harrisburg, PA 17120
(717) 783-4912 V/TDD
(800) 233-3008 in PA V/TDD

South Dakota
Communication Services for the Deaf
3520 Gateway Lane
Sioux Falls, SD 57106
(605) 339-6718 V/TDD

Tennessee
Tennessee Council for the Hearing Impaired
400 Deaderick Street, 11th Floor
Nashville, TN 37219
(615) 741-5644 V/TDD

Texas
Texas Commission for the Deaf
P. O. Box 12904
Austin, TX 78711-2904
(512) 444-3323 V/TDD

Virginia
Department for the Deaf and Hard of Hearing
Washington Building
Capital Square
1100 Bank Street, 12th Floor
Richmond, VA 23219–3640
(804) 225-2570 V/TDD
(800) 552-7917 in VA V/TDD

West Virginia
West Virginia Commission for the Hearing Impaired
4190 West Washington Street
Charleston, WV 25313
(304) 348-2175 V/TDD

Wisconsin
Office for the Hearing Impaired
Department of Health and Social Services
1 West Wilson Street
P. O. Box 7852
Madison, WI 53707
(608) 266-8081 V/TDD

Enabling Legislation for a State Commission: The Example of Virginia

Virginia Council for the Deaf

Va. Code §63.1-85.1.   Council established; appoint-
                       ment, terms and qualifications of
                       members; meetings; chairman.

§63.1-85.2.   Director.

§63.1-85.3.   Deaf persons defined and classi-
              fied.

§63.1-85.4.   Powers and duties of Council.

§63.1-85.4:1   Statewide interpreter service.

§63.1-85.5.   Register of the deaf to be main-
              tained by Department of Health;
              further duties of Department.

§63.1-85.6.   [Repealed.]

§63.1-85.7.   Gifts and donations; disposition
              of moneys received.

§63.1-85.1. Council established; appointment, terms and qualifications of members; meetings; chairman.— (a) There is hereby established a Virginia Council for the Deaf, hereinafter in this chapter referred to as the Council.

(b) The Council shall be composed of fourteen members from the Department of Health; one member from the Department of Education; one member from the Department of Mental Hygiene and Hospitals; one member from the Department of Vocational Rehabilitation; one member from the Department of Welfare; one member from the Virginia School for the Deaf and Blind at Staunton; one member from the Virginia School at Hampton; and seven other members, one of whom shall be an audiologist, and one of whom shall be an otolaryngologist, and of the remaining five members at least two shall be persons who are deaf and the remaining three shall be representatives of professions, community agencies or organizations concerned with the health, education, rehabilitation and welfare of the deaf. No person shall be eligible to serve more than two successive terms (other than the representatives of the above named State agencies and institutions), except that a person appointed to fill a vacancy may serve two additional successive terms. The Council shall meet at the call of the chairman, who shall be selected by the Council from among its membership, but no less than four times a year. (1972, c. 543; 1974, cc. 44, 45.)

§63.1-85.2. **Director.**—The director may be either a deaf person or one with normal hearing, but shall be a trained professional who is experienced in problems of the deaf and skilled in the use of manual communication, commonly referred to as sign language. (1972, c. 543; 1978, c. 603.)

§63.1-85.3. **Deaf persons defined and classified.**— For the purposes of this chapter, deaf persons are defined as those in whom the sense of hearing is nonfunctional for the ordinary purposes of life, including two distinct classes based on the time of the loss of hearing: (1) the congenital deaf—those who were born deaf; and (2) the adventitiously deaf—those who were born with normal hearing but in whom the sense of hearing becomes nonfunctional later through illness or accident. (1972, c. 543.)

§63.1-85.4. **Powers and duties of Council.**—The Council shall act as a bureau of information to the deaf, to State agencies and institutions providing services for the deaf, local agencies of government, and other public or private community agencies and programs. In this respect the Council shall:

(a) Inform the deaf of the availability of the provisions of the Virginia Council for the Deaf and such other services available for the deaf at all levels of government;

(b) Establish a framework for consultation and cooperation among the State agencies and institutions represented on the Council;

(c) Advise the several agencies and institutions represented on the Council concerning the administration of,
preparation of regulations for and operation of their programs;

(d) Continuously study the handicapping problems of
deaf of all ages, review the administration and operation of
the various programs for deaf in the Commonwealth and
make recommendations with respect thereto to the several
agencies and institutions represented on the Council as
the Council deems necessary and proper;

(e) Make and submit to the Governor and the General
Assembly annual reports of its finding and recommendations;

(f) Conduct independent evaluations of programs for the
deaf in the Commonwealth and publish and distribute the
results thereof;

(g) The Council may obtain the services of such professional, technical and clerical personnel as may be necessary to enable them to carry out its function under this
section and to contract for such services as may be necessary to carry out its evaluation functions;

(h) The Council shall cooperate with the schools for the
deaf as provided for in chapter 19 (§23-254 et seq.) of
Title 23 of the Code insofar as may be practicable. (1972, c.
543; 1977, c. 668.)

§63.1-85.4:1. Statewide interpreter service.—The
Council is authorized to establish, maintain and coordinate a Statewide service to provide courts, State and local
legislative bodies and agencies, both public and private,
and deaf persons who request the same with qualified
interpreters for the deaf out of such funds as may be
appropriated to the Council for these purposes. Those
courts and State and local agencies which have funds
designated to employ qualified interpreters shall pay for
the actual cost of such interpreters. The Council is further
authorized to establish and maintain lists of qualified

interpreters for the deaf to be available to the courts, State and local legislative bodies and agencies, both public and private, and to deaf persons. (1978, c. 603.)

§63.1-85.5. Register of the deaf to be maintained by Department of Health; further duties of Department.—(a) The Department of Health shall prepare and maintain a complete register of the deaf in the State which shall describe the condition, cause of deafness and such other facts as may be of value. Each physician or other person who, upon examination of the hearing of any person, determines that such person is a deaf person shall immediately report the name and address of such person to the Department of Health.

(b) The Department of Health shall make inquiries concerning the cause of deafness, ascertain what portion of such cases are preventable and adopt and enforce proper preventive measures.

(c) The Department of Health shall make information contained on the register available to the several agencies and institutions directly connected with the administration of programs providing services to the deaf; or for research purposes may make the information available to an organization or individual engaged in research only for purposes directly connected with the administration of programs relating to the deaf, including research for the development of new knowledge or techniques, which would be useful in the administration of the program, but only if the organization or individual furnishes satisfactory assurance that the information will be used solely for the purposes for which it is provided; that it shall not be released to persons not connected with the study; and that the final product of the research will not reveal any information that may serve to identify any person about whom the information has been obtained without the written consent of such person and the Department of Health. (1972, c. 543.)

§63.1-85.6. Repealed by Acts 1980, c. 728.

(Cross reference.—For present provisions as to compensation of members of boards, commissions, committees, councils and similar bodies, see §2.1-20.2 et seq.)

§63.1-85.7. Gifts and donations; disposition of moneys received.—The Council is authorized to receive such gifts and donations, either from public or private sources, as may be offered unconditionally or under such conditions as in the judgment of the Council are proper and consistent with this chapter. All moneys received as gifts or donations or State appropriations shall be deposited in the State treasury to be used by the Council to defray expenses in performing its duties. A full report of all gifts and donations accepted, together with the names of the donors and the respective amounts contributed by each, and all disbursements therefrom, shall be submitted annually to the Governor by the Council. (1972, c. 543.)

Index

A

ABC. *See* American Broadcasting Company
Accessible federally funded buildings, 167–170
  Americans with Disabilities Act provisions, 36–37
Accessible meetings, HHS Section 504 regulation, 57–58
Accessible programs, HEW Section 504 regulation, 51–53
Accommodation of handicapped persons
  Americans with Disabilities Act, 17–18
  employment of deaf persons, 141–142
  exemptions for employers, 147
  HEW Section 504 regulation, 52–53
  hospitals, 111–113
  mental health services, 129–131
  "reasonable accommodation," 17–18, 145–146
  undue hardship for employer, 147
Activists for legislative change, 135–136
ADA. *See* Americans with Disabilities Act
Administrative Office of the U.S. Courts, 174
Advertising job openings, 148–149
Advice of rights. *See Miranda v. Arizona*
Affirmative action
  federal agencies, 143, 149
  federal contractors, 149, 158–160
  Section 501, Rehabilitation Act of 1973, 143, 149
  Section 503, Rehabilitation Act of 1973, 143, 149, 159
Alabama, University of, 93
Alarms. *See* Lights as signals for auditory systems
Alexander v. Choate, 97
American Broadcasting Company (ABC), 193–194
  Evening News, 193
American National Standards Institute (ANSI), 167–170
  inadequacy of standards, 169
American Sign Language (ASL), 2–5
  difficult concepts expressed, 177
  instruction method, 77–78
American Society for Deaf Children, 78
American Standard Code Information Interchange (ASCII), 206
Americans with Disabilities Act, 15–45
  accessibility guidelines for new construction and building alterations, 36–37
  acquisition or modification of equipment, 17–18

auxiliary aids, 32–37
  provided by state and local governments, 26–29
captioning, 27, 44
complaint, filing, 37, 43
conferences and performances in public accommodations, 34
courts, accessibility provisions, 173–174
"direct threat" to health or safety, 20–22
effective date of public accommodation provisions, 37
employer defenses, 20–23
employers covered, 15–16
employment discrimination provisions, 15–23
enforcement provisions, 23, 37, 43
examinations and courses, 35–36
hiring provisions, 15–23
Justice Department enforcement, 49
medical examinations prior to hiring, 20
public accommodations, 32–37, 210, 212–213
public service announcements, 27
public transportation provisions, 24
qualifications for employment, 19–20
"qualified" individuals, defined, 16–17
reasonable accommodation, 17–18
reassignment of position, 18
relay services, 37–43, 205, 213
remedies, 23, 43
restructuring of job, 18
selection criteria for hiring, 19–20
service animals, use in public accommodations, 35
state and local government provisions, 23–31
TDD services, 37–43. *See also* Telecommunications device for the deaf
  employment setting, 17–18
  operator and customer services, 213
  public accommodations, 36–37, 210
  public agencies, 33–34
tests for employment, 19–20
undue hardship on operation of business, 22–23
American Telephone and Telegraph Co. (AT&T).
  See Telephone services
Amplifiers for telephone receivers, 10, 213
AMTRAK, Americans with Disabilities Act provisions, 24
ANSI. *See* American National Standards Institute
Appeals
  due process hearings, 82–83
  federal employee discrimination suits, 157

261

Architectural and Transportation Barriers
Compliance Board (ATBCB), 167–170, 205,
209–210
address, 170
composition of, 167–170
Architectural barriers, 167–170
ambiguous standards, 169
complaint procedure, 167, 170
public and pay phones. *See* Telephone services
Section 502, Rehabilitation Act of 1973, 168–
170
Section 504, Rehabilitation Act of 1973,
compliance, 170–171
state laws, 171
Architectural Barriers Act of 1968, 167
Arizona, provision of interpreters for prisoners,
184
Arrests of deaf persons, 179
ASCII. *See* American Standard Code Information
Interchange
ASL. *See* American Sign Language
Assistive devices. *See* Auxiliary aids
AT&T. *See* Telephone services
ATBCB. *See* Architectural and Transportation
Barriers Compliance Board
Attorney-client privilege, interpreters covered by,
186–187
Attorney General suits, 37
Auditory method of teaching, 76
Auxiliary aids. *See also* Interpreters; Telecom-
munications device for the deaf
Americans with Disabilities Act provisions, 26–
28, 32–35
colleges and universities, 90–91
hospitals, 101, 108–110
legal system to provide, 174
libraries, 101
service agencies, 102–104

B

Background noise, 7. *See also* Hearing aids
Barker, David, 178
Baudot code for TDDs, 206
Beck, Raymond, 218
Bilingual, Hearing, and Speech-Impaired Court
Interpreter Act, 174
Broadcasting. *See* Federal Communications
Commission; Television
Brown, Torrey, 218
Brown v. Board of Education, 67
Building construction, accessibility guidelines,
167–170
Americans with Disabilities Act, 36–37
Bureau for Education of the Handicapped, 83
*Burlington, Town of v. Massachusetts Department
of Education*, 75

C

Cable television, 194
California, telecommunication relay services,
204–205
Camenisch v. University of Texas, 93–94
Captioning. *See also* Television Decoder Circuitry
Act
Americans with Disabilities Act provisions, 27,
44

college and university course films or
videotapes, 90
television, 191, 193–194
benefits to nondeaf persons, 197
cable television, 194
decoders, 195–196
emergency captioning, 191–193
funding needs, 195
"Line 21," 193–194
news programming, 193, 195
standards, 197–198
CBS. *See* Columbia Broadcasting System, Inc.
Childbirth, interpreter present during, 105
Civil damage suits, 128
Civil rights laws, state. *See* State laws; *specific
states*
Civil Service examinations, 150
Civil Service Reform Act of 1978, 146, 152
Class action suits, 129–131
Clinics
Americans with Disabilities Act provisions, 24
Closed captioning, 191, 193–194. *See also
generally* Captioning
Coin-operated phones. *See* Telephone services
Colleges and universities
admissions, 87–89
auxiliary aids, 90–91
interpreters, 87–89
pre-admission inquiries, 88
recruitment, 87–89
Section 504, Rehabilitation Act of 1973,
applicability, 87
tests for admissions, 88
treatment of disabled students, 88
vocational rehabilitation deaf students, 87–89
Columbia Broadcasting System, Inc. (CBS), 193–
194
Commission on Education of the Deaf, 195–197
Commissions, state, 225–229
directory (Appendix E), 251–255
enabling legislation, Virginia as example
(Appendix F), 256–260
Communication barriers, 5–8
Americans with Disabilities Act provisions, 15–
45
employment, 142
HEW Section 504 regulation, 55–57
hospitals, 105–106
prisons, 183–185
Communications Act of 1934, 191
Communications assistants for telephone use. *See*
Telecommunications device for the deaf
Communication with hearing impaired, 1–12. *See
also* Interpreters; Lipreading; Notewriting;
Telecommunications device for the deaf
Community-based care for mental illness, 133–
134
Commuter transportation. *See* Public transporta-
tion
Complaint procedures
Americans with Disabilities Act provisions, 37,
43
architectural barriers in federally funded
buildings, 167, 170
Federal Communications Commission, 193

federal contractors' employee claiming discrimination, 158–160
federal employees, discrimination complaints, 154–158
PL 94–142, 83
Section 501, Rehabilitation Act of 1973, 143, 154–158
Section 503, Rehabilitation Act of 1973, 143, 158–160
Section 504, Rehabilitation Act of 1973, 50–51, 59–62, 83, 143, 160
Conferences in public accommodations, Americans with Disabilities Act provisions, 34, 210
Connecticut, commission for the deaf, 227
Consent to medical treatment, 88, 113–115
Constitutional rights
  Fourteenth Amendment, 184
  interpreter for deaf party in court proceedings, 173, 175–176, 185–186
  mental health patients when institutionalized, 129–131
  Sixth Amendment, 183
Continuing education classes, 83
Contractors
  federal. *See* Federal contractors
  state and local governments, Americans with Disabilities Act provisions, 24
Convention centers, TDD service, 210
Counseling
  Americans with Disabilities Act, counseling center provisions, 24
  Section 501, Rehabilitation Act of 1973, informal pre-complaint counseling provisions, 154–156
  vocational rehabilitation counselors, 153–154
Courts. *See* Criminal proceedings; Legal system
Criminal proceedings
  arrests of deaf persons, 178–182
  confessions of deaf defendants, 178
  interpreters for, 174–176, 178–184
  jail time of deaf defendants, 178–180
  Miranda rights, 176–178, 182
  pre-trial preparation, 183
  victims, interpreters for, 181
Cued speech, 77

D

Damages. *See* Remedies
Davis, Frances, 94–96
Davis v. Frank, 17
"Deaf and dumb," as insult, 8
Deaf-blind persons
  definition under PL 94–142, 69
  interpreters for, 2–5
"Deaf-mute," as insult, 8
Deaf parents, interpreters for, 80–84
Deaf persons
  definition under PL 94–142, 69
  postlingually deaf, 106
  prelingually deaf, 5, 106, 176
  statistics, 1, 6, 121–122, 141
Deafpride, Inc., 118
Decoders. *See* Captioning; Television Decoder Circuitry Act

DeRoche v. United States, 183
Developmentally Disabled Assistance and Bill of Rights Act, 133, 136
Disabled persons. *See* Accommodation of handicapped persons; Handicapped persons
Discrimination
  employment. *See* Employment of deaf persons
  federal contractors' employees charging, 158–160
  federal employees, 154–158
  health care and social services, 103–104
District of Columbia
  Hospitalization of the Mentally Ill Act, 132
  involuntary commitment, 131
  programs for deaf persons when institutionalized, 126
  right of treatment for institutionalized patients, 129–131
  St. Elizabeths Hospital, 126, 132
Dixon v. Weinberger, 132
Doe v. Wilzack, 137
Donaldson, Kenneth, 128
Due process hearings, 80–83
  appeals, 82–83
  decisions, 82–83
  letters of request (Appendix B), 235–238
  preparation for, 80–82
  record of hearing, 82

E

Education, U.S. Department of (ED)
  architectural barriers, Section 504 regulation, 170–171
  college and university violations of Section 504, Rehabilitation Act of 1973, 75
  Office for Civil Rights, 83, 87
  Rehabilitation Services Administration (RSA), 161–162
  Section 504, Rehabilitation Act of 1973, regulation, 48, 87
Educational institutions. *See* Schools and educational institutions
Education for All Handicapped Children Act. *See* Public Law 94–142
EEOC. *See* Equal Employment Opportunity Commission
Emergency broadcasting, 191–193
Emergency medical care, communication with deaf persons, 108–111
Employer attitudes, 141–142
Employer defenses, 147
  Americans with Disabilities Act provisions, 20–23
Employment of deaf persons, 141–142. *See also* Section 501, Rehabilitation Act of 1973; Section 503, Rehabilitation Act of 1973; Section 504, Rehabilitation Act of 1973
  accommodation. *See* Accommodation of handicapped persons
  advertising job openings, 148–149
  affirmative action. *See* Affirmative action
  Americans with Disabilities Act, discrimination provisions, 18–20
  communication barriers, 142

complaint procedures for discrimination under Title V, Rehabilitation Act of 1973, 154–158
"essential functions," defined, 144
exemptions for employers, 147
federal jobs. *See* Federal employees
"ghettoizing" prohibited, 148
interpreter services, 145–146
medical examinations, 147–148
state discrimination laws, 160–161
statistics, 141
training programs, 148–149
undue hardship, 147
vocational rehabilitation services, 161–162
English language and deaf persons, 2–7
college admission tests, 88–89
incomprehensibility of *Miranda* warnings, 176–178
Equal Employment Opportunity Commission (EEOC)
Americans with Disabilities Act, powers and regulation, 17, 18, 21
federal employee appeal to, 154–158
Equal justice, 187–188
Equal opportunity, HEW Section 504 regulation, 53–54
Executive Order 12125, 152

F

FCC. *See* Federal Communications Commission
Federal agencies
discrimination complaints against, 154–158
employees of. *See* Federal employees
Section 504, Rehabilitation Act of 1973, applicability, 49–51
Federal Communications Commission (FCC)
Americans with Disabilities Act relay services, regulation, 38–43
complaint procedure, 193
HAC Act regulations, 212
telecommunications regulation, 203–204
television broadcasters to consider deaf community's needs, 191–195
Television Decoder Circuitry Act standards, 197–198
Federal contractors. *See also* Section 503, Rehabilitation Act of 1973
affirmative action, 149, 159
complaint procedure for employee claiming discrimination, 158–160
job training for deaf persons, 148–149
Federal employees. *See also* Section 501, Rehabilitation Act of 1973
affirmative action, 149
Civil Service. *See* Civil Service examinations
discrimination suits, 154–158
excepted appointments, 151
Executive Order 12125, 152
legal challenges, 151–152
interpreter services, 149, 152
job information centers, 153
rehabilitation counselors, 153–154
Schedule A appointment, 151
selective placement coordinators, 154
temporary trial, 151

Federal funding
"assurance of compliance" form, 160
defined, 49–50
mental health programs, 126–127
Section 504, Rehabilitation Act of 1973, 48–64
vocational grants, 161
Federally funded buildings
accessibility, 167–170
Americans with Disabilities Act provisions, 36–37
Federal Personnel Manual, 146
Fingerspelling, 5
instruction method, 76
Miranda warnings, 176–178
Fire departments, Americans with Disabilities Act provisions, 24
FOIA. *See* Freedom of Information Act
Food stamp offices
Americans with Disabilities Act provisions, 24
auxiliary aids, 102
Fourteenth Amendment, 184
Freedom of Information Act (FOIA), 50
Furey, Mary, 177

G

Gallaudet University, National Academy, 118
General Services Administration, 168–169, 205
Georgia, mental health services, 134–135
Grievance procedures. *See* Complaint procedures
Guide dogs, Americans with Disabilities Act provisions, 35

H

Habeas corpus actions, 128–129
HAC Act. *See* Hearing Aid Compatibility Act of 1988
Handicapped persons. *See also* Americans with Disabilities Act; Rehabilitation Act of 1973
accommodation. *See* Accommodation of handicapped persons
definition, HEW Section 504 regulation, 51
"Hard of hearing," definition under PL 94–142, 69
Health, Education, and Welfare, U.S. Department of. *See now* Education, U.S. Department of; Health and Human Services, U.S. Department of
Health and Human Services, U.S. Department of
Section 504, Rehabilitation Act of 1973, regulations, 48
architectural barriers, 170–171
hospitals, 107–110
interpreters, 56
mental health services, 136–137
TDDs, 56
Health care services. *See also* Hospitals; Mental health services
agency responsibilities, 103–104
agency rules prohibiting discrimination, 103–104
Americans with Disabilities Act provisions, 24
consent to medical treatment, 109, 113–115
emergency medical care, 108–111
HHS Section 504 regulation, 107–110
interpreters, 101–103

Section 504, Rehabilitation Act of 1973,
  applicability, 101–119
  state laws prohibiting discrimination, 104–105
  training for staff, 117–119
Hearing Aid Compatibility Act of 1988 (HAC
  Act), 212
Hearing aids
  employees with, 146
  hospital patients with, 112
  mental health services providing, 133
  Section 502, Rehabilitation Act of 1973, audio
    loops in public buildings, 170
  telephone compatibility, 211–213
  telephone switches, 10
Hearing officers, 80, 82
Hearings. *See* Due process hearings
Hendrick Hudson School District v. Rowley, 74–75
HEW Section 504 regulation. *See* Section 504,
  Rehabilitation Act of 1973
HHS Section 504 regulation. *See* Health and
  Human Services, U.S. Department of
Hiring. *See* Employment of deaf persons
Hospitals
  accommodation of deaf persons, 111–113
  Americans with Disabilities Act provisions, 24
  auxiliary aids, 101, 107–110
  care staff, 115–116
  childbirth, interpreter present during, 105
  communication barriers, 105–106
  consent to medical treatment, 109, 113–115
  emergency medical care, 108–111
  hearing aids, patients with, 112
  HHS Section 504 regulation, 107–110
  intercom systems, 112
  interpreter services, 105–111
  NCLD guidelines, 113–115
  notice to patients, 109
  staff awareness, 112, 117–119
  TDD service, 101, 210
  training for staff, 112, 117–119
Hotels. *See* Public accommodations
Howard University Hospital, 118
Hughes, Harry, 219

I

IDEA (Individuals with Disabilities Education
  Act). *See* Public Law 94–142
IEP. *See* Individualized Education Program
Illinois
  Institute of Technology, 92–93
  Mental Health Code, 133–134
  mental health services, 122, 134–135
  rehabilitation legislation, 123–124
  Rehabilitation Services Department, 92
Incompetent to stand trial, 123–124
Indigent deaf defendants, interpreters for, 175–
  176, 183
Individualized Education Program (IEP), 70–74
  aids and services for deaf children, 73
  contents, 72
  development of, 70–71
  due process hearings, 80–83
  letters of request, samples (Appendix B), 235–
    238
  manual language components, 77–78

  methods of instruction, 76
  notice of change in, 80
  parental role, 71, 79–80
  teacher experience and educational level, 78–79
  writing, 75–77
Individuals with Disabilities Education Act
  (IDEA). *See* Public Law 94–142
Information referral centers for deaf persons,
  161–162
Interior, U.S. Department of, 168
International Association of Parents of the Deaf.
  See now American Society for Deaf
  Children
Interpreters
  accessible meetings, HHS regulation, 56
  Americans with Disabilities Act provisions, 19,
    24, 32
  arrest of deaf defendants, 178–182
  Bilingual, Hearing, and Speech-Impaired Court
    Interpreter Act, 174
  certification, 3, 162
  Code of Ethics, 4
  colleges and universities to provide, 87–88, 90–
    94
  courts to provide, 174–176
  criminal proceedings, for, 174–176, 178–184
  deaf-blind, for, 2–5
  deaf parents, for, 80, 84
  EEOC hearing, 158
  employers to provide, 145–146
  federal employees, 149, 152
  guidelines for use, 4
  HEW Section 504 regulation, 56–58
  hospitals to provide, 105–111
  indigent deaf defendants, for, 175–176, 183
  inexperienced, 5
  model state act to provide for interpreters for
    government and judicial proceedings
    (Appendix D), 245–250
  oral, 2
  police departments to provide, 178–182
  prisoners, for, 183–185
  privileged communications in court proceed-
    ings, 186–187
  referral centers, 161–162
  Registry of Interpreters for the Deaf (RID), 2–4
  schools to provide, 80, 84
  Social Security Administration, 103–104, 239–
    244
  social service agencies to provide, 101–103
  state commissions to provide, 230
  training, federal funding for, 162
  victims of crimes, for, 181
Irving Independent School District v. Tatro, 75

J

Jackson, Theon, 124–126
Jails
  Americans with Disabilities Act provisions, 24
  incarceration time of deaf criminal defendants,
    178–180
Job applicants. *See* Employment of deaf persons
Job information centers for federal employees,
  153–154
Job training for deaf persons, 148–149

Justice, U.S. Department of
Americans with Disabilities Act, enforcement, 49
Section 504, Rehabilitation Act of 1973, enforcement, 49, 175
interpreters, provision by police departments, 179–181
interpreters, provision for civil proceedings, 186
TDD services, provision by police departments, 187

K

Kean College, 91
Kentucky, interpreter privilege in, 186

L

Labor, U.S. Department of, 159
Lang, Donald, 123–124
Law enforcement agencies. *See* Police departments
Legal Advocacy Project for Hearing Impaired Persons, 137
Legal system, 173–188. *See also* Constitutional rights; Criminal proceedings
costs of interpreters, 174
equal justice, 187–188
indigent deaf defendants, 175–176
interpreters, 174–176
state, civil, and administrative proceedings, 186
Legislation, state. *See* State governments; State laws
Libraries
Americans with Disabilities Act provisions, 24
auxiliary aids and TDDs, 101
Lights, flashing, 10, 146, 170
Americans with Disabilities Act provisions, 36
"Line 21," 193–194
Lipreading, 6–7, 113
instruction method, 76
Lobbying, 219–225
Local governments
Americans with Disabilities Act provisions, 23–31
contractors with, Americans with Disabilities Act coverage, 24

M

Maine, community-based mental health services, 132–133
Mainstreaming, 70
reference publications (Appendix A), 232–233
Manual language components. *See* American Sign Language; Fingerspelling; Sign language
Maryland
Association of the Deaf, 218
Department of Health and Mental Hygiene, 218
mental health services for deaf persons, 137
outpatient mental health program for deaf persons, 217–218
prisoners, provision of interpreters for, 184

privileged communications between deaf persons and interpreters, 186–187
Massachusetts
mental health services, 134–135
Office of Deafness, 228
Massachusetts Department of Education; Burlington, Town of v., 75
Mass transit, Americans with Disabilities Act provisions, 24–31
Medical examinations
Americans with Disabilities Act, pre-employment examinations, 20
job disqualification of deaf persons due to, 147–148
Medical malpractice, misdiagnosis of deaf child as mentally retarded, 138
Medical services. *See* Health care services; Hospitals
Meeting accessibility, HHS Section 504 regulation, 57–58
Mental health services, 121–139
abuse of patients, 126–127
accommodation of deaf persons, 129–131
advocacy agencies, 135–136
civil damage suits, 128
class action suits, 129–131
community-based care, 133–134
consciousness raising for community-based services, 133–134
constitutional rights of patients, 129–131
federal funding, 126–127
federal regulation, 136–137
habeas corpus actions, 128–129
HHS Section 504 regulation, 136–137
less restrictive alternatives, 128, 132
litigation by deaf persons, 137–138
Maryland outpatient program for deaf persons, 217–218
misdiagnosis, 121–123, 138
"protection from harm" theory, 131
right of treatment for institutionalized patients, 129–131
right to rehabilitation, 132–133
sign language, 130, 133
state laws, 131–132, 134–135
statistics of deaf persons in mental health facilities, 121–122
Michigan
Center for Deaf Treatment Services, 126
Handicapper's Civil Rights Act, 105
mental health services, 134–135
Minnesota
Department of Public Welfare, Deaf Services Division, 228–229
mental health services for deaf persons, 137–138
Miranda v. Arizona, 175
advice of rights, 176–178, 181, 182
incomprehensibility of warnings by deaf persons, 176–178
Misdiagnosis, mental health, 121–123, 138
Motor vehicle departments, Americans with Disabilities Act provisions, 24
Municipalities. *See* Local governments

N

National Academy, Gallaudet University, 118
National Aeronautics and Space Administration, 152
National Assessment of Educational Progress, 196–197
National Association of the Deaf, 174
  Legal Defense Fund, 91, 137, 152
National Broadcasting Company (NBC), 194
National Captioning Institute (NCI), 194–196
National Census of Deaf Population, 6
National Center for Law and the Deaf (NCLD)
  hospital guidelines, 113–115
  interpreters for deaf defendants upon arrest, 179
  legislative drafting assistance, 225
  litigation, 108
  Maryland legislation, 218–219
NBC. *See* National Broadcasting Company
NCI. *See* National Captioning Institute
NCLD. *See* National Center for Law and the Deaf
Neo-oralism, 76
New Hampshire, interpreter privilege in, 186
New Jersey
  Department of Labor and Industry, Division of the Deaf, 229
  Vocational Rehabilitation Services Division, 91–92, 102
New Mexico, provision of interpreters, 104
New York
  mental health services, 122
  telephone rate reductions for TDD users, 208
  Willowbrook State School, 131
North Carolina Council for the Hearing Impaired, 228
Notetakers, colleges and universities, 90
Notewriting, 5–6, 113
Nurses. *See* Health care services; Hospitals

O

O'Connor v. Donaldson, 128
OFCCP. *See* Office of Federal Contract Compliance Programs
Office for Civil Rights, U.S. Department of Education, 83, 87
Office of Federal Contract Compliance Programs (OFCCP), 158–160
Office of Handicapped Individuals, 162
Office of Personnel Management, 148
Office of Revenue Sharing (ORS), 179, 187
Oklahoma
  interpreters for deaf defendants upon arrest, 178–182
  mental health services for deaf patients, 134, 135
Open captioning, 193
Oral interpreters, 2
Oral method of teaching, 76
ORS. *See* Office of Revenue Sharing

P

Parents
  IEP role, 71, 79–80
  interpreters for deaf parents, 80, 84
Parks and recreation programs, Americans with Disabilities Act provisions, 24

Pay phones. *See* Telephone services
PBS. *See* Public Broadcasting Service
Pennhurst v. Halderman, 133
Pennhurst State School and Hospital, 133
Pennsylvania, mental health services, 134–135
Pew Charitable Trust, 197
Pilson, Neil, 196
PL 94–142. *See* Public Law 94–142
Police departments
  Americans with Disabilities Act provisions, 24
  arrests of deaf persons, 178–182
  interpreters, provision of, 179–181
  TDD services, 104, 187
  videotaping of communications with deaf persons, 182
Postal Service, U.S.
  hiring of deaf persons, 148
  Section 504, Rehabilitation Act of 1973, applicability, 51
Postsecondary education. *See* Colleges and universities
Pre-admission inquiries
  colleges and universities, 88
Prince George's General Hospital (Maryland), 118
Prisoners, deaf, 183–185
  Americans with Disabilities Act provisions, 24
  interpreters for, 183–185
Privileged communications between deaf persons and interpreters, 186–187
Probation officers, compliance with Section 504, provision of interpreter, 185
Program accessibility, HEW Section 504 regulation, 51–53
"Protection from harm" theory, mental health institutionalization, 131
Public accommodations, Americans with Disabilities Act provisions, 36–37, 210, 212–213
Public Broadcasting Service (PBS), 193–194
Public buildings. *See* Federally funded buildings
Public Law 94–142, 68–75
  children covered by, 69
  complaint procedures, 83
  definitions, 69
  due process hearing, 80–83
  Individualized Education Program (IEP), 70–74
  mainstreaming, 70
  procedural safeguards, 79–83
  purpose, 68
  reference publications (Appendix A), 233–234
  Section 504, Rehabilitation Act of 1973, and, 68
  Supreme Court cases involving, 74–75
Public school education, 67–84. *See also* Schools and educational institutions
Public service announcements, 27, 58
Public transportation, Americans with Disabilities Act provisions, 24
Public utility commissions, 204, 207–208

Q

"Qualified handicapped person," definition
  Section 501, Rehabilitation Act of 1973, 143
  Section 503, Rehabilitation Act of 1973, 143
  Section 504, Rehabilitation Act of 1973, 52–53, 143

R

Reading comprehension problems of deaf people, 5
Reagan administration, 217
Reasonable accommodation
    Americans with Disabilities Act, 17–18
    Title V, Rehabilitation Act of 1973, 145–146
Referral centers for deaf persons, 161–162
Registry of Interpreters for the Deaf (RID), 2–4, 174, 181
    Code of Ethics, 4
Rehabilitation Act of 1973, 47–64. *See also* Section 501, Rehabilitation Act of 1973; Section 502, Rehabilitation Act of 1973; Section 503, Rehabilitation Act of 1973; Section 504, Rehabilitation Act of 1973
    architectural barriers. *See* Architectural barriers; Section 502, Rehabilitation Act of 1973
    Title I funding, 162
    Title V sections, 47–48
    remedies, 141–165
    vocational rehabilitation services, 161–162
Rehabilitation counselors. *See* Vocational rehabilitation
Rehabilitation Services Administration (RSA), 161–162
Relay services. *See* Telecommunications device for the deaf
Remedies
    Americans with Disabilities Act provisions, 23, 37, 43
    Section 504, Rehabilitation Act of 1973, violations, 63
    Title V, Rehabilitation Act of 1973, 142–154
Revenue sharing funds. *See* Federal funding; Section 504, Rehabilitation Act of 1973
RID. *See* Registry of Interpreters for the Deaf
Right to attorney, 183
Rochester method of teaching, 76
Rouse v. Cameron, 131
Rowley, Amy, 74–75
RSA. *See* Rehabilitation Services Administration

S

St. Elizabeths Hospital (Washington, D.C.), 126, 132
St. Louis, Missouri, police department, 179
Schedule A appointment for federal employment, 151
    Executive Order 12125, 152
    legal challenges, 151–152
Schools and educational institutions, 67–84. *See also* Colleges and universities; Individualized Education Program; Public Law 94–142
    Americans with Disabilities Act provisions, 24, 35
    continuing education classes, 103
    Education for All Handicapped Children Act. *See* Public Law 94–142
    records, inspection, 101–103
    letters of request (Appendix B), 235
    Section 504, Rehabilitation Act of 1973, applicability, 67, 103–104

Schornstein, Ruth Ann, 91
Sears, Roebuck & Company, 194
Section 501, Rehabilitation Act of 1973
    accommodation. *See* Accommodation of handicapped persons
    applicability, 143
    complaint procedure, 154–158
    description, 47–48
    enforcement procedures, 154–158
    "essential functions," defined, 144
    federal court suit, 158
    informal precomplaint counseling, 154–156
    Notice of Final Interview letter, 155
    "qualified handicapped person," defined, 143
Section 502, Rehabilitation Act of 1973
    architectural barriers, 168–170
    description, 47–48
Section 503, Rehabilitation Act of 1973
    accommodation. *See* Accommodation of handicapped persons
    applicability, 143
    business necessity defense for employers, 148
    complaint procedure, 158–160
    description, 47–48
    enforcement procedures, 158–160
    "essential functions," defined, 144
    "qualified handicapped person," defined, 143
Section 504, Rehabilitation Act of 1973, 48–64
    accessible meetings, HHS regulation, 57–58
    accommodation. *See* Accommodation of handicapped persons
    administrative enforcement, 59
    applicability, 49–51, 143
    architectural barriers, HHS/ED regulation, 170–171
    colleges and universities, applicability, 87
    communication barriers, HEW regulation, 55–57
    complaint procedure, 50–51, 59–62, 83, 160
    description, 48
    different or special treatment, HEW regulation, 54–55
    education, 67
    Education Department regulations, 48–49, 87
    enforcement, 58–59
    equal opportunity, HEW regulation, 53–54
    "essential functions," defined, 144
    federal aid recipients, applicability, 49–51
    grievance procedures, 59–60
    "handicapped," defined, 51
    Health and Human Services Department regulations, 48–49
    health care services, 101–119
    hospitals, HHS regulation, 107–110
    interpreters, HEW regulation, 56
    investigation of complaint, 62–63
    judicial enforcement, 63
    Justice Department enforcement of regulations. *See* Justice, U.S. Department of
    medical examinations for employment, 148
    mental health services, HHS regulation, 136–137
    ORS regulation used to compel interpreters for deaf criminal defendants upon arrest, 179
    probation officer to provide interpreter to deaf defendant, 185

procedural safeguards, 79–83
program accessibility, 51–53
protections afforded by, 51–53
Public Law 94–142 and, 68
"qualified handicapped person," defined, 52–53, 143
regulations under, 48–49. *See also* Health and Human Services, U.S. Department of
remedies, 63
schools, applicability, 103–104
self-evaluation of compliance by federal aid recipients, 59
social services, 101–119
Supreme Court cases, 88–89, 160
Service animals, use in public accommodations, Americans with Disabilities Act provisions, 35
Shirey, Edward, 152
Shopping malls, TDD service, 210
Sign language, 2–5. *See also* American Sign Language
emergency medical treatment staff, 108, 112
instruction methods, 77–78
mental health service providers, 130, 133, 135
Miranda warnings, 176–178
police department to provide interpreter for, upon arrest of deaf person, 179–181
Simultaneous method of teaching, 76
Sixth Amendment rights, 182–183
Social Security Administration
interpreter services, 103–104, 239–244
TDD service, 103–104
Social services
agency responsibilities, 103–104
agency rules prohibiting discrimination, 102–103
interpreters, 101–103
Section 504, Rehabilitation Act of 1973, applicability, 101–119
state laws prohibiting discrimination, 104–105
Southeastern Community College v. Davis, 88–89, 90, 94–96
Soviet Union, neo-oralism, 76
Speech, use by deaf people, 8
Speechreading. *See* Lipreading
Sprint. *See* Telephone services
State civil and administrative proceedings, 185–186
State governments, 217–230
Americans with Disabilities Act provisions, 23–31
commissions or councils, 225–229
directory (Appendix E), 251–255
enabling legislation, Virginia as example (Appendix F), 256–260
contractors with, Americans with Disabilities Act coverage, 24
legislative process, 223–225
lobbying, 219–225
State laws. *See also specific states*
activists for legislative change, 135–136
architectural barriers, 171
employment discrimination, 160–161
legislative process. *See* State governments
mental health, 131–132, 134–135

model act to provide for interpreters for government and judicial proceedings (Appendix D), 245–250
nondiscrimination, 104–105
privileged communications between deaf persons and interpreters, 186–187
Statistics, deaf persons, 1, 6
employment, 141
institutionalized in mental health facilities, 121–122
Stewart, Larry, 141
Strathie v. Department of Transportation, 21
Supreme Court, U.S.
Alexander v. Choate, 97
Burlington, Town of v. Massachusetts Department of Education, 75
Hendrick Hudson School District v. Rowley, 74–75
Irving Independent School District v. Tatro, 75
Jackson v. Indiana, 124–126
Miranda v. Arizona, 176–178
O'Connor v. Donaldson, 128
Pennhurst v. Halderman, 133
Section 504, Rehabilitation Act of 1973, coverage, 160
Southeastern Community College v. Davis, 88–89, 94–96
Sussman, Allen, 141, 218

T

TAEA. *See* Telecommunications Accessibility Enhancement Act
TDCA. *See* Television Decoder Circuitry Act
TDD. *See* Telecommunications device for the deaf
Teachers of deaf students, 162
experience and educational level, 78–79
Teaching methods. *See* Individualized Education Program
Telecommunications Accessibility Enhancement Act (TAEA), 205
Telecommunications device for the deaf (TDD), 8–10, 203–215
Americans with Disabilities Act, accommodation, 18, 26, 29, 32–34, 36–39, 56
ANSI standard and, 169–170
ASCII, use of, 206
audiotext services, 214
Baudot code, use of, 206
convention centers, 210
directory of TDD numbers, 205, 213
emergency rooms, 110–111
emergency telephone services, 37
equipment funding and distribution, 205–206
HEW/HHS Section 504 regulation, 56. *See also specific public agency (e.g., Hospitals)*
accessible meetings, 57–58
hospitals, 101, 210
international symbol, 210, 215
libraries, 101
long-distance rates, 207–208
new technology, 214–215
operator services, 213
pay or public phones, 37, 203, 209–210, 213–214
police departments, 104, 187

portable, 209, 210
relay services, 37–43, 204–205, 208, 213
shopping malls, 210
Social Security Administration, 103–104
state commissions working with disabled to
   have, 230
state programs, 206
telephone directory listing, 8–10
Telecommunications for the Disabled Act, 211
Telephone services, 203–215. *See also* Telecommunications device for the deaf
amplifier switches, 10, 213
audiotext services, 214
customer assistance, 213–214
emergency services, 29
hearing aid compatibility, 211–213
Hearing Aid Compatibility Act of 1988 (HAC
   Act), 212
new developments, 214–215
operator services, 213
pay or public phones, 29, 203, 209–210, 213–
   214
rates, 203–204
   long-distance, 207–208
regulation by FCC, 203–204
state regulation, 203–204
Television, 191–199. *See also* Captioning
cable television, 195
emergency captioning, 191–193
"Line 21," 193–194
networks. *See specific network by name (e.g.,
   American Broadcasting Company)*
news programming, 193, 195
public service announcements, 27, 58
Television Decoder Circuitry Act (TDCA), 191,
   197–198
FCC enforcement, 197–198
Tennessee, interpreter privilege in, 186
Testing. *See also* Medical examinations
Americans with Disabilities Act, employment
   tests, 19–20
Civil Service examinations, 150
college and university admission tests, 88
Texas
   Camenisch v. University of Texas, 93–94
   commission for the deaf, 227
Text telephones. *See* Telecommunications device
   for the deaf
"Total communication," definition, 77

Training
   deaf persons for employment, 148–149
   health care providers, for, 117–119
   interpreters, for, 162
Transportation, U.S. Department of, 168
Treasury, U.S. Department of, 205. *See also* Office
   of Revenue Sharing
Trials. *See* Criminal proceedings; Legal system
TTY (Teletypewriter). *See* Telecommunications
   device for the deaf

U
Universities. *See* Colleges and universities; *for
   state universities, see specific state*
U.S. Constitution. *See* Constitutional rights
U.S. government. *See specific department
   or agency by name (e.g. Justice, U.S.
   Department of)*

V
Vernon, McCay, 122–123
Victims of crimes, interpreters for, 181
Videotaping of police communications, 182
Virginia, 104
   Council for the Deaf, 104
      enabling legislation (Appendix F), 256–260
   Department for the Deaf and Hard of Hearing,
      227
   Industrial Relations Committee, 227
   privileged communications between deaf
      persons and interpreters, 186–187
Visual warning systems. *See* Lights, flashing
Vocational rehabilitation
   counselors, 153–154
   deaf college students, 87–89
   services, 161–162

W
Warning systems. *See* Lights, flashing
Welfare agencies. *See also* Social services
   Americans with Disabilities Act provisions, 24
WGBH (TV), 193
Willowbrook State School (New York), 131
Wisconsin Bureau for the Hearing Impaired, 229
Written messages. *See* Notewriting
Wyatt v. Aderholt, 129
Wyatt v. Stickney, 129